designing with smart textiles

Fairchild Books
An imprint of Bloomsbury Publishing Plc

Imprint previously known as AVA Publishing

50 Bedford Square   1385 Broadway
London   New York
WC1B 3DP   NY 10018
UK   USA

www.bloomsbury.com

**FAIRCHILD BOOKS, BLOOMSBURY and the Diana logo
are trademarks of Bloomsbury Publishing Plc**

British Library Cataloguing-in-Publication Data
A catalogue record for this book is available from
the British Library.

ISBN: PB: 978-1-4725-6915-8
       ePDF: 978-1-4725-6916-5

Library of Congress Cataloging-in-Publication Data

Kettley, Sarah.
Designing with smart textiles / Sarah Kettley.
     pages cm
ISBN 978-1-4725-6915-8 (pbk.)
ISBN 978-1-4725-6916-5 (epdf)
1. Fashion design--Materials. 2. Smart materials.
3. Mixed media textiles. I. Title.
TT557.K38 2015
746'.04--dc23
                        2015007415

Cover design by Sutchinda Rangsi Thompson
Cover image © THEUNSEEN 2016
Photograph by Jonny Lee

Typeset by Roger Fawcett-Tang
Printed and bound in China

designing with smart textiles

Sarah Kettley

Fairchild Books
An imprint of Bloomsbury Publishing Plc

BLOOMSBURY
LONDON · OXFORD · NEW YORK · NEW DELHI · SYDNEY

How to use this book

This book will give you both a theoretical and a practical introduction to the design of "smart" textiles. You are encouraged to critique definitions used in this new field, and to explore intersecting design disciplines and team working, before being led through the basics of creating simple circuits using conductive yarns and fabrics. The book then maps out the potential for different textile specialties to contribute to the future development of the field, and through a series of case studies of contemporary practitioners, provides valuable insights into artistic and technological practice. It finishes by asking you to reflect on the presentation of your own work and skillsets, so you may contribute confidently to the evolving smart textiles community of practice. In the back of the book you will find lists of suppliers and links to resources.

The intended reader is the undergraduate textile design student interested in finding out more about smart textiles, but the book may also be useful to students from related disciplines such as interaction design, who have not worked with textile designers before.

Chapter 1 discusses the terminology being used and asks you to think about what "smart" truly means. It introduces the different scales of enabling technology and different scales of application. Two feature interviews highlight cutting-edge developments in e-fibers and in the application of smart textiles at the architectural scale.

Exercises: classifying terms, enabling technologies and systems; exploration of the relationships between skin, garments and architecture

Key Questions: discussion of the differences in functional garments and high-profile projects such as the Galaxy Dress

Chapter 2 contrasts the practice of studio textiles with approaches more often found in product design and human-computer interaction. A short case study and feature interview illustrate studio practice and interaction design. A section on industrial processes highlights the value of different approaches in taking the field forward, and the Cute Circuit case study brings these themes together.

Exercises: interaction design decisions checklist; redesign of an existing project for a different target user group

Key Questions: reflection on current practice and assumptions using design practice model; reflection on "openness" in practice; inquiry into target market understanding (using the automotive industry as an example)

Chapter 3 provides information on electronic components and the basic skills needed to create circuits using off-the-shelf yarns and fabrics. A series of skills-based exercises will build your understanding of basic principles and inspire confidence to create your own designs. These build in complexity until you learn when to use a microprocessor and how to start working with the Arduino platform. Some of the basic skills work in this chapter will be suitable for students coming from other disciplines who are new to textiles.

Exercises: a first sewn circuit; using a multimeter to test yarn resistance and continuity; stitched in-series and parallel circuits; textile pressure switch; textile tilt switch; using personas and scenarios in designing with sensors; prototype LED circuit with a LilyPad Arduino
Projects: three step-by-step projects giving you the opportunity to apply your new skills in making a high-visibility sports glove, a ball that responds to hugs, and a bag that alerts you when it is too heavy

Key Questions: troubleshooting a first sewn LED circuit; using the principle of continuity to check a circuit design; the meaning of sensed data; implications of output design decisions

Chapter 4 is a collection of case studies of designers working with textiles to create new enabling technologies, yarns, fabrics and applications. It starts with the work of Lauren Bowker and the materials exploration house THEUNSEEN (as featured on the cover), and will give you insights into creative material practices in print, knit, weave, embroidery and fabric manipulation. The final section includes textile practices driven by interaction design, and the design of individual components. The reading lists in this chapter are organized differently from those in the rest of the book; instead of a long list at the end, each case study features its own suggested readings. There are no exercises or key questions in this chapter; instead, each contributor has shared a "Tech Tip," valuable technical insight into their work that you can build on in your own textile practice. You should develop reflexive documentation of their experiments and creative work to take this further. Depending on the contributor, some of these Tech Tips can be used as exercises, an example being eCrafts Collective's card weaving tutorial. Many also include URLs for online tutorials.

Chapter 5 asks you to reflect on your evolving smart textiles practice through a series of encounters with creative tools for design management. This is particularly valuable for students who have already had time to develop their practice through internships in their final undergraduate year or who are embarking on a postgraduate course. It will also be useful for multidisciplinary teams who need to uncover tacit processes before proceeding on a large project. A reflexive case study is included of a student in her first year of doctoral study; she is interesting because she came through a multimedia textiles pathway, rather than from a process-specific practice such as knit or weave. Similar disciplinary issues are then discussed in the context of industry and manufacturing, and a further case study recounts one practitioner's experiences in taking on the innovation process herself. The final interview with a technical textile consultant challenges you to apply all you have learned within a radically changing industrial innovation landscape.

Exercises: framing projects and practice; differentiating your discipline

Key Questions: contextualize your design process

What are smart textiles?

The process of integrating textiles and technology isn't just surface deep; it actually begins at a molecular level.

Quinn 2010: 11

CHAPTER OVERVIEW

Chapter 1 introduces you to the terms and definitions used in the diverse field of "smart textiles." It discusses the differences between smart and technical fabrics and the different scales and sectors of application these materials lend themselves to. You will learn about key points in the recent history of smart textiles and be given an insight into new directions of research.

Smart textiles is a new field of design and engineering emerging in relation to technical textiles, wearable technology and smart materials. In its most basic definition, a smart textile is one that can exhibit repeatable behavior in response to a stimulus such as strain or temperature change. Such behavior can be integrated into the structure of a fabric or a fiber and may be classified as passive, reactive or interactive.

Figure 1.1 illustrates that not all technical textiles are smart; some definitions of smart textiles would call them all technical; furthermore, not all wearable technology uses smart textiles, and of course, not all smart textiles are used in wearable applications.

Smart textiles deliberately exploit the electromechanical properties of yarns and fabrics, meaning that the resistance and conductivity (as well as the "handle") of different materials are manipulated to create flows of energy; these in turn can drive changes in color, heat, movement, sound and other forms of output. Materials such as shape memory alloys (SMAs), electro-active polymers (EAPs), spacer fabrics, phase change materials, membranes or coatings and microcapsules can all be integrated with textile structures and surfaces as sensors or actuators. An example of reversible state change can be easily seen in chromic materials, which react reversibly to external stimuli. These tend to be named after the stimuli they react to:
Photochromic: external stimulus is light.
Thermochromic: external stimulus is heat.
Electrochromic: external stimulus is electricity.
Piezochromic: external stimulus is pressure.
Solvatechromic: external stimulus is liquid or gas.

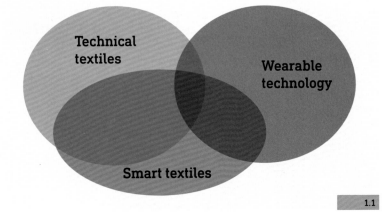

1.1

1.1
Smart textiles are related and overlap with other fields such as wearable technologies and technical textiles.

Definitions	
Smart textiles	Textiles with the ability to react to different physical stimuli; mechanical, electrical, thermal and chemical
SFIT	Smart Fabrics and Interactive Textiles (also defined as smart textiles)
Wearable technology	Any electronic device small enough to be worn on the body
Interactive textiles	Wearable technology that is integrated into a garment or controlled by an integrated panel or button
E-textiles	Textiles with electronic properties included in the textile fibers

Table 1.1
Definitions of different kinds of e-textiles according to a Danish White Paper (excerpt).

What are smart textiles?

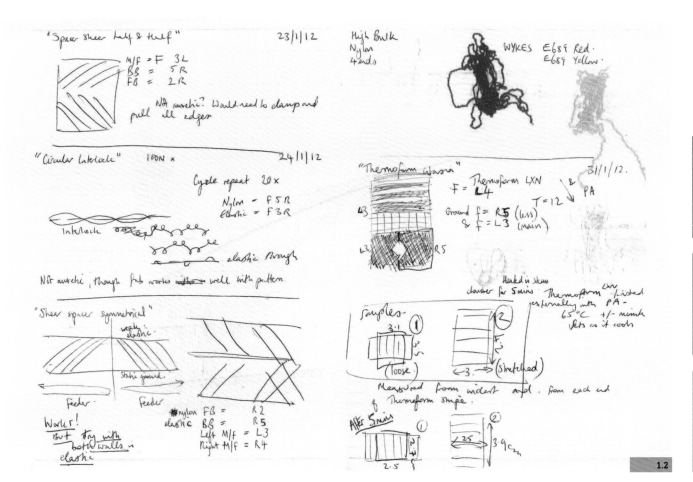

These textiles can be understood as enabling technologies for new forms of wearable systems, embedded computation in the built environment, and information and control systems at the archeological and geological scale. Textile knowledge is crucial and is increasingly being valued for its own holistic and "mixed methods" approach to design, which in many cases already blends scientific with artistic goals and ways of working. But the field also needs interdisciplinary teams to develop the textile as a product, such as service design, interaction design, and human–computer interaction. To achieve this, it needs a range of disciplines to create successful products, including science, technology, art and design.

Although smart textiles are enjoying increased attention now, these overlapping fields are not entirely new, and there have now been more than thirty years of academic publishing on smart textiles. Wearable technologies can be said to date back to the first eyeglasses, recorded in the thirteenth century, and metal fibers and yarns have been used by different cultures since around 2000 BC. Technical textiles have arguably existed since people have been wearing animal skins, later experimenting with stitch structure and the addition of oils to yarns to repel moisture; the development of man-made fibers around 1900 gave us the beginnings of today's technical textile industry.

1.2.
Textile knowledge is often already multidisciplinary; this notebook brings together different kinds of information and criteria for knit practice as the designer develops spacer elastic fabrics.
Martha Glazzard.

SMART OR TECHNICAL?

Technical textiles are engineered for defined end uses and are surprisingly ubiquitous, being used to support airport runways and prevent soil erosion ("geotech"), being found in the latest trainer technology or wicking running vest ("sporttech"), and helping reduce weight (and therefore fuel consumption) in haulage vehicles (as part of composite materials in "mobiltech"). In fact there are twelve classifications of technical textiles, based on the sectors they are applied in.

The term *flexible engineering materials* helps us think about textiles as a very broad classification of materials, processes and products. Technical textiles often include materials such as glass, carbon and plastics, for example, and recent research has produced fiber from amber (itself a natural polymer).

However, technical need not mean smart. Many of these textiles make clever use of structure without the state of the textile having to change in response to the environment. So while smart textiles are also engineered, they do more than technical textiles—they sense the environment and react to it.

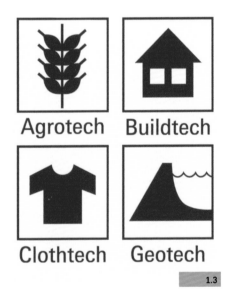

1.3

1.4

1.3
Four of the twelve commonly used technical textile application sectors:
(a) Agrotech, (b) Buildtech, (c) Clothtech, and (d) Geotech.
Techtextil, Messe Frankfurt Exhibition GmbH, Frankfurt am Main, Germany.

1.4
Textiles include a broad range of material; here amber has been processed to produce a polymer fiber.
Inga Lasenko.

Passive, reactive and interactive textiles

Generally speaking, smart textiles can be described as *passive smart*, *active smart*, or *very smart*. These terms are still being defined, and different researchers understand them in different ways. We show them in table 1.2 so you can reflect on what your own work is doing.

Some researchers also use the analogy of the body to describe these classifications: passive smart textiles might be thought of as "nerves," or as having simple reflex actions; active smart textiles have nerves and exhibit behavior—they have muscles; and very smart textiles are aware of themselves and their own actions in context—they learn and adapt.

1.5

1.5
Extreme conditions call for multi-purpose fabrics; here Kevlar is used for its strength, and is coated with gold to become conductive; NASA explored material processing techniques like these for applications such as tethers to be used in space. Lieva Van Langenhove.

Table 1.2
Range of definitions and terms used in smart textiles.

	Other terms used	Different meanings given		
Passive smart	Passive	Sensors or monitors only; react in a predetermined way	No user control	Provide the same function no matter what the environment is doing, e.g., antimicrobial; or light output independent of context
Active smart	Reactive; interactive	Include an actuator function, i.e., they do something as a result of sensed environment	Controlled by an integrated button or panel	
Very smart	Super smart; multireactive; ultra-smart	Have a range of behaviors so response to environment is dynamic	Self-adapting learning systems; they can sense themselves in addition to the external environment	Embedding entire systems into fabrics; inclusion of a processor

Passive smart textiles sense stimuli in the environment. These might include mechanical, thermal, chemical, electrical, or magnetic states. In one view, these textiles do not change in reaction to these states, but they may communicate information to a processor elsewhere. In another view, these textiles provide a consistent functionality without the need for computation or the use of conductive materials, and with no active user control. An example would be the knitted biomimetic fabric shown in figure 1.6 created for survival situations; technical textiles on the other hand are not "smart," but have enhanced performance for specific environmental conditions.

Active smart textiles may or may not require a microprocessor. In some cases an active smart textile needs only a switch operated by the user. In the switched-on state, the textile might then have a single aesthetic expression (e.g., light up and stay lit up), or it may cycle through a preprogrammed sequence of state changes (e.g., color changes).

However, if different stimuli require different responses, a simple program may be used to make dynamic decisions. For example, a number of textile switches can form part of a design, and a microprocessor can be used to understand which are open and which closed, therefore playing different sounds, or lighting different LEDs. A collar by the author shown in chapter 4 uses silver ink in a screen print to create three open switches around the neck, each part of a separate circuit connected to an Arduino processor. When the wearer rolls her head, skin contact closes a single switch at a time, playing the associated sound file through a small speaker in the collar. THEUNSEEN's piece, Air, reacts to multiple environmental stimuli through biologically and chemically treated inks and dyes applied to leather— see chapter 4 for a detailed case study.

1.7

1.6

1.6
Biomimetic textiles for survival clothing: the outer layer reacts to environmental conditions, while the inner layer responds to body temperature changes caused by exercise, creating a breathable system without the need to change clothes so often. Both layers use Nitinol shape-memory alloy wire.
Jacqueline Nanne.

1.7
A woven pouf with dynamic pattern change using thermochromic inks, conductive yarns and pigment dyes, developed to explore design processes for pattern change in fabrics.
Linnéa Nilsson, Mika Satomi, Anna Vallgårda, Linda Worbin.

Very smart, or *super smart, textiles* have the ability to react to multiple contextual information, and to be aware of their own status. In this way they differ again from some apparently complex active smart systems. Very smart textiles often make use of composite conductive fibers and can sense their own performance as well as external stimuli such as temperature, strain or air quality. These textiles do use processing and comprise, or are part of, a more complex system.

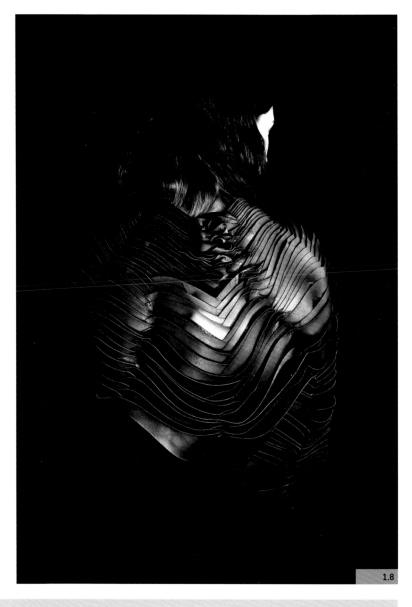

1.8

1.8
Air, a garment made of leather, treated with a special chemical compound, which allows it to change color in reaction to different environmental conditions. Lauren Bowker and THEUNSEEN.

Exercise One
Analyze smart textile projects

Collect images and descriptions of a range of projects. Create a classification system using some of the terms you have learned here, and group projects together that are passive, smart or very smart.

From smart garments
to smart fabrics

Professor Tilak Dias describes the progress made in
wearable technology as having three generations:
in the first, existing forms of hard technology
were housed in pockets created especially on the
garment; in the second, technology became part of
the fabric structure, woven, knitted or stitched into
it; and in the third, we are beginning to see smart
fibers with embedded microcomponents, which can
then be manipulated into fabrics.

1.9
Yarns are three-dimensional structures
made up of different fibers; the
"third generation" of e-textiles builds
electronic microcomponents into these
structures. Tilak Dias.

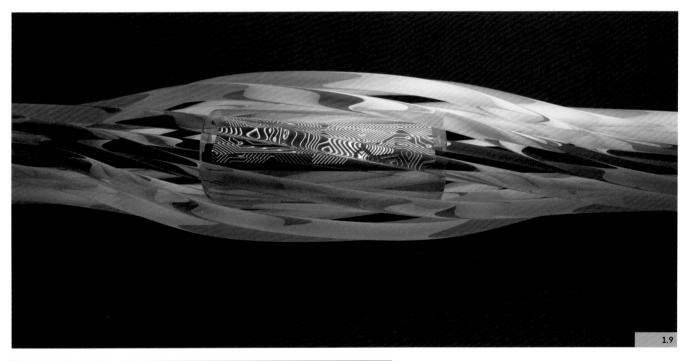

1.9

What are smart textiles?

The future—smart fiber?

Smart fibers are composites of different yarns and materials arranged so that their different (non)conductive and mechanical properties (such as twist or handle) can be exploited to create interesting or useful electronic and functional properties.

In figure 1.9, researchers at the Advanced Textile Research Group at Nottingham Trent University have devised a new process for encapsulating microcomponents in the twist of a fiber, creating an LED circuit in the length of the yarn. This means that fabric woven from the yarn does not need extra conductive threads or external resistors and LEDs stitched to the surface. Flexibility, washability and resistance to wear and tear are all improved (see the feature interview in this chapter for further details). Other engineering processes are also being explored to create smart fibers—the extrusion of polymers, which allows concentric layers to be built up, is a promising technique. Using this method, researchers in photonics at the Massachusetts Institute of Technology have produced fibers that can emit specific frequencies of light at controlled locations along their length. This has potential applications for health and well-being, as the light can be used to trigger the delivery of drugs in the body.

In the future we may even see soft and flexible fabric batteries made possible by smart fibers; this proof of concept by Maksim Skorobogatiy "looks and feels like artificial leather." Shown in figures 1.11 and 1.12 are two prototype fabrics developed by Skorobogatiy in collaboration with XS Labs that use photonic band gap (PBG) fibers to create function at the fiber level and exploit both active and ambient light properties for design.

1.11

1.10
Multifunctional fibers created using different materials arranged in concentric layers. Photo: Greg Hren.

1.11
Exploring textile techniques with new performance materials; silk double weave prototype with PBG (photonic band gap) fiber. XS Labs and the Karma Chameleon project.

1.12
This hand-woven illuminated malleable PBG-fiber fabric demonstrates both emissive and reflective light properties. XS Labs and the Karma Chameleon project.

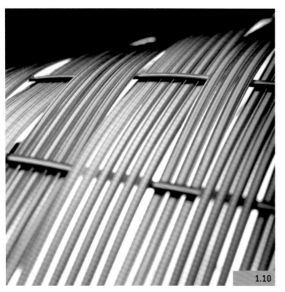

1.10

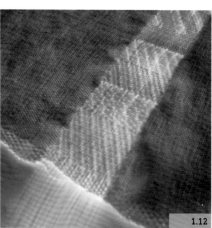

1.12

Feature interview: Tilak Dias

Professor Tilak Dias leads the Advanced Textile Research Group at Nottingham Trent University in the UK, developing textile-enabling technologies. https://www.facebook.com/NTUAdvancedTextiles

This interview coincided with a curated exhibition at the Bonington Gallery in Nottingham, which featured four examples of Professor Tilak Dias's research in smart and interactive textiles over the last decade. *Knitting Nottingham* (2014) included early proof-of-concept research for the Nike Flyknit shoe, textile heating elements and stretch sensors, and knitted ECG sensors.

Can you tell us about the work you did for the Nike Flyknit?

The knitted shoe is not in my opinion a smart material—it's a technology to create a complete seamless shoe upper. The reason this company came to us was, they found a lot of problems in their supply chain management; they were using fabrics from six to ten manufacturers, produced in different countries, and had to get them all shipped to where the shoe was made. This caused a lot of problems, and they wanted to try making a single-piece upper.

The different fabrics were used for their different moduluses in different areas of the shoe upper, so the real novelty was knitting all that in one step—if you look carefully at the structure you can see that we achieved that in a single piece of knitting.

We did this work around 2003/2004, but it took Nike about six to eight years before they could fully commercialize it, and they introduced it to the market during the last Olympics.

What were the implications for manufacture of this new technology?

Once we developed this proof of concept, Nike took it forward and they set up a small R&D lab, with two to three Stoll knitting machines. They employed some technicians who used to work in the UK and developed the manufacturing technology working very closely with Stoll in Germany. It's really taken off, but even in their current manufacturing they do have a certain amount of the original way of making uppers; it's replacing the existing Nike shoes but it hasn't replaced it 100 percent.

In the exhibition we can also see a trace from a heart monitor. Is this achieved with knitted sensors?

Yes. We used to call it a health vest because the idea was to measure the heart rate and also the breathing patterns. We developed a lot of technology around this, starting about 2002, and continued till about 2006/2007. It's out there in the market now, though I didn't commercialize it. This really gave us the knowledge of how to create these knitted electrodes and knitted stretch sensors— we did all the mathematical modeling, and developed a good understanding through that.

What did the mathematical modeling show?

This was the work of one of my PhD students, done in 2002. We broke it down and then we did the mathematical models. After that of course we had to verify these models; it was very difficult because it's very difficult to measure the currents flowing across these nodes, these links in the textile. But we came up with this crazy idea that maybe we can calculate all the currents flowing through it, because it's a network of resistors, and using network theory, we did that, we calculated all the currents. Then we converted them to heat, and we did thermal mapping and then correlated it. This was the only way we could really verify the modeling, and that was a very good match between the mathematical model and the practical measured values. That was the only way we could do it without destroying the structure. That then gave us all the knowledge we needed to develop the stretch sensors, as well as the electrodes.

Why is it better to measure ECG rather than heart rate?

Heart rate just tells you how fast your heart is—an ECG will give you much more information regarding the condition of your heart because it is looking at "QRS"—cardiologists have the experience to say if you have had a heart attack or have recovered from a heart attack. The QRS on the graph shows if the time interval is different—if you are suffering from some sort of a heart disease, they say that this goes further away and that demonstrates the movement of the heart muscles . . . then of course if you suffer from a heart disease, then also you might miss some beats, and in some you might miss part of that ECG trace, that's how it is determined.

And was the knitted ECG sensor reliable enough?

No, unfortunately! It's not reliable if we are moving, it is very reliable when we are stationary. So if we are resting it will give a good quality ECG. You can also have a seven-lead ECG by distributing all the electrodes at different positions around the garment; that way you can capture all the data. However, if you start moving around, it gets bad due to what is known as "motion artifacts." We believe that one of the reasons for these could be the movement of the electrodes on the skin due to the deformation of the knitted structure when you walk or run, for example. Also there could be some sort of a distortion coming through the stretching of the muscles as you move, because this electrical signal is first generated within the heart and then you are really measuring the electrical field around it. This is especially true with an electrode that is directly in contact with

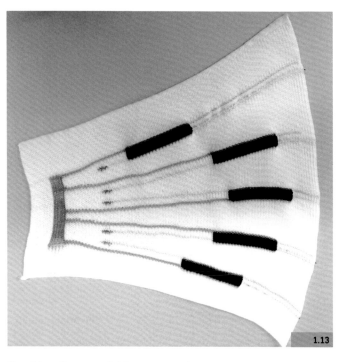

1.13
Carbon yarn knitted to create resistors for heated gloves. Tilak Dias.

the skin—there are fat layers, muscles, there's different types of skin layers in between, they are getting distorted when you move—so that has an effect on the signal. So we tried to minimize this by increasing the pressure—to do some clinical trials we wrapped compression bandages around the electrodes to prevent them moving, but still, we got these motion artifacts. Therefore that is an issue, whereas you can measure the heart rate because you are measuring the beats. Heart rate measurement is feasible in my opinion, but ECG when the patient is moving is not.

You also showed examples of the heated gloves in the exhibition. Are these available on the market now?

Yes, again this was a commercialized product—the company is called Exo Technologies. In fact, it was with these that I first moved into electronic textiles. They use a special yarn extruded with carbon micro/nano particles; they mix it with silicon before extruding it into a yarn. As a yarn it has a very high resistance, about 4,000 ohms per meter, and you can't really heat it with low-power batteries. But we developed an interesting method—by knitting it, we can reduce the overall resistance to about 10 ohms over a meter of yarn. That then made it possible for us to make these glove liners with heating elements on top of the fingers.

The advantage of this technology is that everything is made out of textile fibers . . . so it feels like textiles; the other conventional heated gloves on the market are all made with metal wires embroidered or sewn in, and the major problem is that if during use, if these conductive copper wires touch each other it can create a hot spot and burn your hand. That does not happen with the textile technology.

Is the kind of conductive fiber important here?

If you take a metal wire and heat it up, then the resistance keeps on coming down, due to the movement of the electrons in the atoms—as you heat it up all the molecules begin to move faster, it makes it easier for the electrons to jump

from one to another and the resistance comes down. But with this yarn called *Fabroc*, you can engineer the control temperature. In this particular case, the resistance goes up, so therefore you can program it, you can engineer it, so no matter how long you keep it switched on, it will never go beyond a predetermined temperature . . . it's a natural control temperature. This is where the mathematical modeling became really very helpful; in fact our starting point was to develop the mathematical models really, not to develop stretch sensors, but to develop these heating elements. It allows us to understand how many courses and how many wales there should be, and what influence that has when we knit this, and we realized that knowledge we could use for the sensor.

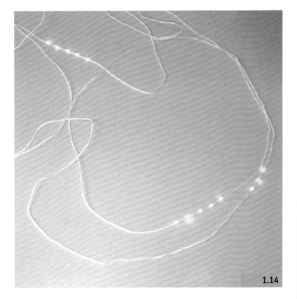

1.14

1.14
LED (light emissive diode) fiber proof of concept; the LEDs have been soldered to core conductive fibers and embedded in the yarn structure itself. Tilak Dias.

1.15
The LED fiber is woven to create a one-piece garment, demonstrating the lack of wires needed. Tilak Dias.

1.15

How did this help with developing the stretch sensor?

We found that for a stretch sensor you have to minimize the number of courses, in other words the rows, and you can increase the number of wales, so the optimum stretch sensor we found was just knitting one row of loops or course, and the number of wales is how many vertical loops there are. So as we increase the numbers, the sensitivity does increase, and rather than having a small stretch sensor you can have a longer one, by increasing the number of wales. But the way it works, it is completely outside the mathematical modeling really because we knitted with an elastomeric yarn, and as a result, after knitting, all the wales collapse—that's what happens in knitting—and that forces the loops of the conductive thread to compress against each other. Then when you stretch it they open up like a series of switches, which will be switched on and off depending on the structure, which has an impact on the resistance, and you model it that way. The advantage of that of course is it's very simple to produce and very reliable, and we found in our testing that the stretch sensor does of course change its electrical properties over time the more you use the fabric, but then once you wash it, it comes back.

The Advanced Textile Research Group at NTU is well known now for its work in yarn technologies. Can you tell us a little about this?

So, the basic concept is to integrate semiconductor devices into yarns: our dream is to build an electronic circuit on an element yarn and then encapsulate the devices with polymer micropods, and then to encase it in other fibers to create a yarn. You do have to power it, but we also have this RFID yarn, which doesn't need any power, within a single yarn. It just has a chip with a bipolar antenna integrated into the yarn. But this is our research program just now. One of my PhD students, Anura Ratnayaka, has developed techniques for soldering microcomponents to the element yarn, and we have these exciting proof-of-concept demonstrators, which have been shown around the world already. It is still early stages and we are working to make this method feasible to automate—just now, it is still all done by hand and is too slow. But some fashion and textile designers are collaborating with us to examine how we can design garments and products with such a yarn.

CONTEXTS OF USE

Technical textiles are recognized by industry across twelve established sectors (as seen in figure 1.3), but smart textiles have not yet been classified in this way. Strong markets are emerging in medicine, sports and entertainment, as well as the automotive industries, but if technical textiles can be seen as a model, smart textiles have a long way to go before they reach their full potential. Current trend reports vary wildly, but many suggest that our current obsession with tablets and smart watches might be short-lived if smart textiles can be successfully commercialized. We should also remember that textiles occur at vastly different scales—they can be found inside our bodies as well as on them, and are an integral part of the built environment around us.

The international research network Arcintex explicitly tries to join these scales and includes interaction designers as well as smart textile and architecture researchers to think about how they might work together in the future. Chapter 2 discusses the need for other emerging design disciplines such as interaction design and service design to collaborate with smart textile developers in order to consider user experiences of increasingly complex intelligent environments and services.

This is especially important, as smart textiles are only part of a much bigger story. Until recently, the idea of ubiquitous computing (meaning computing everywhere) was science fiction—smartphones, tablets and cloud computing have made this a reality. Now the vision is for an Internet of Things—a world in which every object is embedded with smart functionality.

What are smart textiles?

In the body

Traditional textile techniques and structures can deliver sophisticated implantable devices for medical benefits. Fibers coated with a biocompatible material (such as diamond, polymers and pure titanium oxide) are acceptable by the body and can be used to create stents in heart surgery and scaffolds for joint reconstruction. Material selection will depend on whether the device is to be permanent or whether it needs to dissolve in the body (such as polyglycolic acid), and will be subject to strict regulations through, for example, the MHRA (Medicines and Healthcare Products Regulatory Agency) in the UK, and the FDA (Food and Drug Administration) in the United States.

While some materials will be familiar, such as polyester, the search is always on for fibers with better properties. Ellis Development Ltd., a UK textile consultancy specializing in surgical implants, collaborated to develop products for nerve and cartilage repair, bone grafts and wound closure using a new biomaterial modeled on spider silk called Spidrex. This fiber is biocompatible and can be absorbed by the body over a period of months. It can be used as a platform to grow cells and ultimately create complex tissue structures.

While spider silk is itself biocompatible, and has been used for many years by different cultures to treat wounds, Spidrex is an example of biomimetics in design—it is the spinning process that was inspired by the way spiders and silkworms produce their silk, and the fibers used are modified moth silk. The process extrudes monofilaments from a concentrated solution of silk protein and creates fibers with well-aligned molecules, resulting in very strong and flexible materials.

1.16
Embroidery can be used to create both beautiful and functional applications; this shoulder implant for reconstructive surgery allows biological tissue to regrow. Peter Butcher and Julian Ellis.

1.16

Knitted structures can be as strong as ceramic or metal in these kinds of applications, while still being highly flexible, and they are useful where holes are needed with edges that will not fray. Companies such as BMS work with original equipment manufacturers to create custom textile structures based on their specific needs using textile engineering software.

Braiding allows a very flexible approach to the use of different materials in a single structure. Three or more strands are intertwined to create flat or hollow structures (as shown here), and properties such as softness, flexibility, porosity, degradation and expandability can be carefully controlled with the end use in mind. Typical applications include sheaths, tendon and ligament fixation, sutures and carriers for other devices.

Some smart materials like shape memory alloys (SMAs) have been used for decades in implants, such as in bone clamps, guidewires or orthodontic wires; these have more recently been joined by self-expanding cardiovascular stents, catheters

and orthopedic implants. The potential for precise medical applications of SMAs is huge: the biodegradable shape memory polymer transforms from its temporary shape to its parent shape in twenty seconds when heated to 40°C. Other materials such as magnetic SMAs are being investigated for their potential to create biomedical pumps, and porous SMAs may be used to improve elasticity. Persistent issues include corrosion resistance and the impact on MRI (magnetic resonance imaging) procedures. Very smart devices are still in their infancy with regard to approval, but concepts in development include intelligent stents and "smart" sutures that knot themselves.

Regulation issues are complex, and developers need to seek advice very early in the process. Due to a lack of experience with smart textiles, regulatory bodies might be seen to be "moving the goalposts" as they seek appropriate classification criteria and precedent product examples; it is becoming harder to identify whether these concepts are devices, materials or drugs.

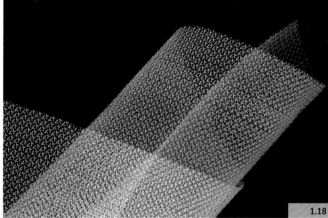

1.18

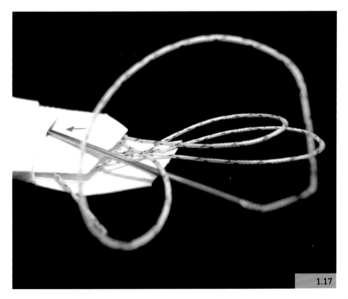

1.17

1.17
Spidrex surgical suture; biocompatible fibers produced using techniques inspired by spiders.
Oxford Biomaterials Ltd.

1.18
Different textile structures are useful in different surgical applications; this mesh is made of knitted monofilament.
Biomedical Structures.

On the body

Wearable technology covers a broad range of products, as the definitions of both *wearable* and *technology* are open to discussion. If technology is an extension or augmentation of human capability, then we can include all forms of clothing as well as the first corrective optical lenses discussed by Friar Roger Bacon in his *Opus Majus* (c. 1266). However, "wearable technology" has more recently come to mean the embedding of computational technology in clothing and jewelry. The mobile phone is sometimes considered a wearable technology, and the smartphone is certainly important in making new entrants to the commercial wearables market viable as a cheap data hub. Smart watches and *iGlass* are attracting a lot of attention and Apple, at the time of writing, is about to release its first smart watch. However, smart textiles offer acceptance by a wider market in combining the fashion and textile design processes, and "stylish" can become more fashion than technology oriented. Nike has demonstrated a successful design approach to awareness technologies that monitor the body's signals for personal goal setting and training: they did not introduce any new technology with the Nike Plus range of products, but recognized that the user experience with standard pedometers and heart monitors for running was something like using an Excel spreadsheet while having an ECG. The promotional video accompanying the products conveys a far more exciting and personalized experience.

Approaches to biosensing products with textiles range from the early proof-of-concept work such as the Wearable Motherboard (later the Smart Shirt) by the Georgia Institute of Technology, to artist projects such as Tara Carrigy's yoga wear with visual feedback, to commercialized products such as Exo Technologies' heated outdoor clothing and sportswear by Clothing+. Based in Finland, Clothing+ has succeeded because it has refined methods for attaching hardware to fabrics, using conductive fabrics to maintain stretch and to deal with strain issues when the product is being worn.

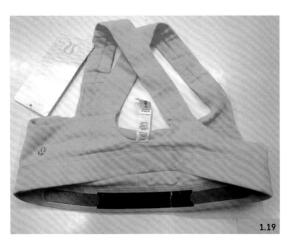

1.19
Clothing+ heart rate monitor; commercially viable processes for embedding electronics in garments.
Mikko Malmivaara.

1.20
The Nike Plus fuelband was developed to be stylish as well as technology-oriented.
Nike.

Fashion as a design context, of course, allows us to play with ideas of the everyday and the theatrical. This has been particularly useful while the hardware has remained bulky and inflexible, meaning scale can be a feature rather than a problem. Practical issues with power sources and fragility of components have been manageable in "loss leader" pieces for the catwalk, or showstoppers designed for one-off performances and the red carpet. The entertainment industry therefore provides wearables developers with a valuable platform for proof-of-concept designs with high levels of media interest. Cute Circuit has worked with the likes of Katy Perry, until in 2014 they became the first wearable technology house to send a complete wearables collection down the catwalk. See chapter 2 for a case study.

Designing for visibility is where the engineering and fashion worlds negotiate their underlying assumptions. Wearable technology was originally meant to be entirely hidden within existing garment forms, but textiles and fashion offer ways of manipulating which parts of a system are visible, when they are visible, and to whom. Much of this rests on how we understand our technology to be functional—whether consumers want textile keyboards as in the early Eleksen and Levi's examples, or whether illumination is a function in its own right, as in the AW2014 runway collections by Alexander Wang and Akris (in collaboration with Forster Rohner).

Wearable technology that is acceptable for everyday wear is becoming more feasible with advances in smart textiles. Lingerie firms are now showing interest in thermochromic, or color change, inks, applied to gold-coated threads for the luxury underwear market. Companies like Cute Circuit and Forster Rohner are instrumental in helping to change manufacturing of conductive yarns so that they are more compatible with everyday wearable technology applications, with less fraying (and therefore more reliable interconnects and fewer short circuits), and less wear and tear on machinery.

1.21
The first complete wearables collection to feature on a scheduled catwalk; New York Fashion Week AW2014 grand finale featuring dynamic LED garments. Cute Circuit.

1.22
In the Forster Rohner/ Akris collaboration, light is treated as part of the aesthetic expression. In these garments, the LEDs are not dynamic (they are either on or off). AW2014.

A major driver for the smart textiles sector is the functional apparel sector. Functional apparel refers to clothing designed specifically for extreme conditions, such as firefighting, polar exploration and space. Technical and smart textiles combine to create habitable environments for humans in the most inhospitable places. Testing is paramount as these garments must perform repeatedly and must meet international standards (see for example, the *Safe to Wear* report by Inditex) (2015), but again, classification can be difficult. Wear on components and power routes is minimized in the EVA (extravehicular activity) suit shown in figure 1.23 because lines of nonextension are followed on the body (i.e., placing critical components along these paths means they are not subject to strain caused by flexion of limbs or muscles). The "running man" made by Cyberquins Ltd. (figure 1.24) is a resident at the University of Minnesota in the lab of Associate Professor Lucy Dunne. He is used to test technical and smart textile applications in sports.

1.23
EVA (extra-vehicular activity) biosuit developed to minimize mechanical strain on life support systems embedded into the elastic under layer of a space suit. Professor Dava Newman, MIT: Inventor, Science and Engineering.

1.24
"Running man" is a moving mannequin used to observe performance garments in action.
Cyberquins Ltd., at the University of Minnesota, Lucy Dunne.

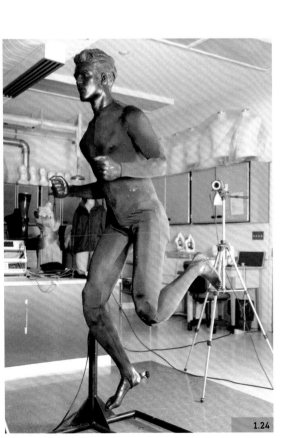

KEY QUESTION

What are the differences between everyday smart textile products, functional garments, and projects such as Cute Circuit's Galaxy Dress?

In the built environment

Smart textiles are also being used to manage environmental conditions, and any application of technical textiles has the potential to become smart where monitoring would be helpful. The vision of a highly connected world is leading us quickly from a world of fixed desktops to the worlds of physical computing; the "Internet of Things" is a current phrase used to explain how everyday items will not only be embedded with sensors and actuators, but will be connected to a vast network just as our smartphones, tablets and computers are now. The role for smart textiles in this future is still being written, and this offers a huge amount of scope for different disciplines to contribute. Important advances in smart textiles that will help this happen include embroidered antennae for wireless communication, woven batteries and energy-harvesting materials. See chapter 4 for more on creative approaches to electronic textile components.

Applications range from domestic and office interiors to load-bearing structures and adaptive architecture that responds to climatic conditions. The strength and addressability of textile structures are the main benefits here. Jenny Sabin is an architect who is interested in our bodies as well as textile structures. She researches textile structures such as knit, shown in figure 1.25, translated into construction materials through a range of processes, including casting and additive manufacture, to create load-bearing textile structures in different materials. More accessible processes can result in wondrous concepts: the work *Branching Morphogenesis* shown in figure 1.25 is made entirely of cable ties (over 75,000 of them) and represents the force network exerted by interacting vascular cells in our lungs. Philip Beesley constructs immersive, interactive environments, which he has described as "suspended geotextiles," and electroactive polymers are being exploited under tension to create structures that can dramatically change shape. Phase change materials such as Nitinol can be combined with textiles to create moving structures, but they often lack the force needed to move heavier loads. Figure 1.26 is a proof of concept for a building skin that controls temperature and shade, tested using the shape change material with felts.

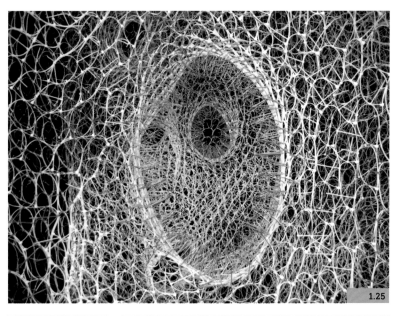

1.25

1.25
Branching Morphogenesis, LabStudio, 2008; a human scale environment built using plastic cable ties.
Jenny E. Sabin, Andrew Lucia, Peter Lloyd Jones; originally on view at the Design and Computation Gallery, SIGGRAPH 2008, and subsequently at Ars Electronica, Linz, Austria, 2009–2010.

1.26
Hylozoic ground; proof of concept adaptive architecture using shape change materials. PBAI.

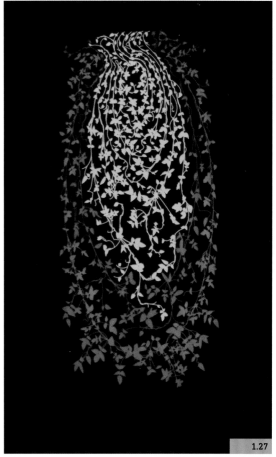

1.27
Digital Dawn; a window blind in which electronic sensors monitor changing light levels and trigger changes in the image. Rachel Wingfield (LoopPH).

1.28
EAP (electro-active polymer) workshop at Borås University. EAPs can be built into flexible frames to constrain the direction of movement; here they are treated as modules to create a moving surface. Delia Dumitrescu, Anna Persson and Riika Talman.

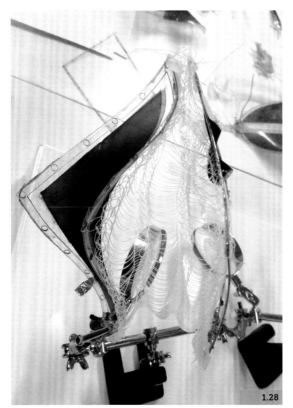

Textiles as skin: chemical, bacterial, nano

We can treat "textiles as skin" metaphorically or very literally. If we take a metaphorical approach, smart textiles can be said to have nerves (sensing capacity), neurological function (computer processing) and muscles (actuation). If we take a more literal approach to textiles as skin, we need to bear in mind the various functions our skin fulfills. David Bryson lists a number of these, including protection against friction, drying, ultraviolet light and bacterial infection; production of vitamin D; function as a variegated and extended sensory organ; excretion of water and salts; regulation of body temperature; and the storage, for example, of glycogen and lipids.

As we keep on covering it up, it is all too easy to forget what skin is capable of.

Bryson, in McCann 2009: 101

Some researchers, like Clemens Winkler and Stephen Barrass, investigate the way skin is both afferent (sensing external states and carrying information to the central nervous system) and efferent (sending information to the body and sensing internal states). These works are concerned with the tribo-electric effect, meaning a buildup of charge in a material due to contact or rubbing. Winkler's *Tensed Up* series explores whether the charge in the atmosphere can be made visible through fine fibers and plays with the charge human skin carries.

Barrass's research encompasses sonification (the way we interpret sound as information) as well as interaction with textile interfaces. He has developed a number of fun, publicly engaging projects using smart textiles based on this principle. *Scruffy Scally Wag*, developed with artist Elliat Rich, is a prototype "taxtile" or actively tactile textile. *Scruffy*'s nylon fur can "sense" when it is rubbed, and he wags his three little appendages in response. The changing relative charge of the nylon is conveyed through a network of conductive fibers to a microprocessor, which measures the change and directs the tail motors to run. Working with a range of materials and voltages means you will become aware of this effect—for example, using polyurethane foam to mock up wearable devices can cause problems because the foam is very positively charged—and any additional handling, such as repetitive cutting and forming, builds that voltage until it is discharged, often damaging or disrupting other components. On the other hand, precautions taken in public buildings might cause your project the opposite problem: when *Scruffy* was first demonstrated at the WearNow symposium in Canberra in 2007, he did not work because the carpet in the museum auditorium had been designed to ground the static.

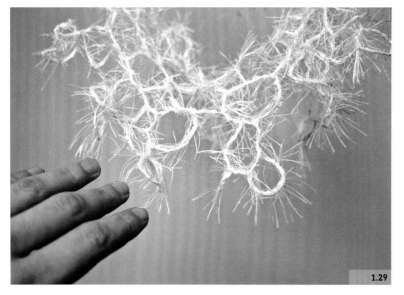

1.29

1.29
Tensed Up is a project that exploits the static properties of certain materials. Clemens Winkler.

What are smart textiles?

While undertaking research in Paris, Stephen noticed the Parisian fashion for wearing scarves in a particular way. He was also amused by the ubiquitous "air kiss," and bringing these together with his "taxtiles," he created *L'Escarpe a' Bisous*—a simple system for making visible the static electricity between two people in close proximity. The scarf is at once afferent and efferent. Stephen is aware that he is not a textile designer; instead he uses existing fabrics as the substrates for his projects based on electromechanical properties we would not normally notice, or on cultural meanings we are familiar with. His work is successful because it invites interaction with apparently affective feedback.

Though much of the work in this category is concerned with mimicking living membranes, it is important to remember that cells, all living things and we ourselves are part of an ecological system, in which parts must die to give way to new growth. Carole Collet's work as part of the Nobel Textiles project involved working with Sir John Sulston, part of the team awarded the Nobel Prize for discoveries regarding programmed suicidal behavior of cells. Collet's Suicidal Textiles collection referenced this through the use of both nonbiodegradable and biodegradable fibers in the construction of her *Suicidal Poufs*, so that the shape and skin of the pouf change over time. The final shapes are revealed after slow degradation of the biodegradable fibers, and the whole process mimics the process of programmed cell death (PCD).

1.30
L'Escarpe a' Bisous: interaction. Stephen Barrass.

1.31
L'Escarpe a' Bisous: taxtile sensor and vibromotor. Stephen Barrass.

1.32
The Suicidal Pouf, part of the Nobel textiles project, uses nonbiodegradable and biodegradable fibers to emphasize lifecycle processes. Carole Collet 2008.

At this new intersection of synthetic biology and textile design, speculative designs propose working at the molecular level. Collet's *BioLace* project discusses the potential for the cellular programming of plant forms to produce the sustainable textiles of the future as scientists demonstrate the possibility of binding gold nanoparticles to DNA. This means the very building blocks of life could be rendered highly conductive. As Collet says, "Living technology is about to remap the material and technological landscape available to designers." The *BioLace* project comprises a series of fictitious photos and animations, which act as design "probes" or provocations to future design and synthetic biology to act in a certain direction for a safe ecological manufacturing system of the future.

Like Collet, Studio XO and others build speculative projects to question the future of science, technology and design, demonstrating the ways in which intimate physiological data might be captured, translated and rendered in fibrous structures and ecological systems. They make use of the spectacular potential of fashion in works like the *Bubelle* Dress, and of existing (sub)cultural practices like tattoos to position future technologies. The *Skinsucka* project shown in figure 1.35 explores scenarios involving swarms of self-energizing biological microbots, which clean the skin and dress the body through the creation of new fibrous webs.

What happens to textile skills such as embroidery, when working with tissue engineering?

Amy Congdon 2015

1.33
BioLace, a design probe exploring potential sustainable textile production. Carole Collet 2012.

1.34
Sonja Bäumel's project Textured Self translates bacterial patterns into textile skins. Commissioned by the Textielmuseum Tilburg in The Netherlands.

1.35

Sonja Bäumel's *Textured Self* piece works from the body out, translating the bacterial life on the surface of her own body on one day into a hand-knitted and crocheted silhouette, showing the amount, color and structure found on her skin. Bäumel is fascinated with the skin as a membrane, a permeable interface between us and the world. Meanwhile, Suzanne Lee really is growing bacteria to produce flexible, skinlike materials that she manipulates like fabric to suggest a "biodesigned future." The microorganisms she has explored include fungi, algae, cellulose, chitin and protein fibers, and she creates the environments for them to ferment and grow using such everyday objects as baths as part of her ongoing *BioCouture* project.

Amy Congdon's approach is to grow skin cells on textile scaffolds, inspired by the textile structures being used as reconstructive medical implants. Her work, undertaken during a residency at SymbioticA, University of Western Australia, proposes a craft service through the bespoke design and build of personalized biologically and chemically functional textiles. Meanwhile, projects at Brighton University in the UK aim to construct chemically functional textiles that would respond to external stimuli such as temperature or pollution, protecting the wearer by absorbing or catalyzing contaminants in the immediate environment. The image here is a hand-crocheted scaffold cross-section of silk suture threads seeded with GFP+ hBMSc cells and stained using a standard histology dye called Haematoxylin that colors nuclei purple but also took extremely well to the thread.

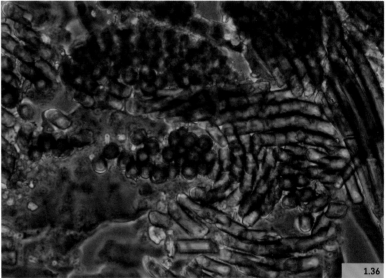

1.36

1.35
Skinsucka, 2011; a design probe exploring future scenarios in which we are dressed by web-producing swarms of robots. Clive van Heerden, Jack Mama, Nancy Tilbury, Bart Hess, Harm Rensink, Peter Gal.

1.36
Hand crocheted scaffold cross section (shown at 20x magnification), cultivated with dyed hBMSc (human bone-marrow) cells. Amy Congdon.

Exercise Two
Textiles as skin:
thinking about functionality

Explore the relationships between skin, garments and architecture. What functions do they share, and how do they communicate with each other?

Feature interview: Mette Ramsgaard Thomsen

Mette Ramsgaard Thomsen is based at CITA, an innovative research environment at the Royal Danish Academy of Architecture. Her work focuses on behavioral architectures and develops bespoke composite textiles to explore new paradigms of design, in which sensing and actuation are often collapsed together into one fabric. Here she introduces three projects: *Listener*, a site-specific curtain, and a ten-meter tower.

Can you comment on skin as a metaphor in your work?

Actually, we think quite a bit about that—one of the workshops we did was called Performing Skins . . . I mean, we talk about building skins in architecture, and the idea of the membrane. The idea here for us is that the skin has multiple performances—it collapses not only sensing and actuation, but also structure and construction. In the same way, the interesting thing about knit is that it's not a laminate, you're not just sticking things on top of each other; every movement in the textile is capable of bringing a new performance . . . so to bring these things together into one membrane, with skin as a metaphor, is very interesting.

How are these ideas explored in the *Listener* project?

So, it's this idea that because it is the same thing that senses that actuates, it means that you have a direct and very intuitive relationship to the materials. You interact with the material, and it also acts. In an architectural context, we live very directly—it's not like a computer with interface and buttons—we engage with space directly, and so the demand for these kinds of interfaces is to be part of a very direct relationship between self and space. I think the interesting thing is to figure out how to create these interfaces, and to ask what the requirements are for them.

We imagined *Listener* as being a sort of blanket, as relating to the side of the bed; it listens to you, and you listen to it—it has its own breath. We were very interested in Sophie Calle's project on sleep, where she shared her bed with lots of different people as an arts installation—we're interested in this idea of interaction as not being the conscious act of choice, but something more rhythmical and related to living.

How is *Listener* constructed?

The materials need to compose different properties; we are trying to understand how a single material can be created so that you get multiple performances. In *Listener* that's done by integrating three fibers with different properties: a conductive silver-coated fiber, which is used as the sensor—when you put your hand over it, it acts as a capacity sensor—so you are changing a charge in the magnetic field around the textile; then there are two other materials, an elastomer, which is able to expand and contract like a lycra, and then there is a network of Dyneema, a high-performance polyethylene, which allows the structure to not just be one big balloon, but to be a network that holds the material in space.

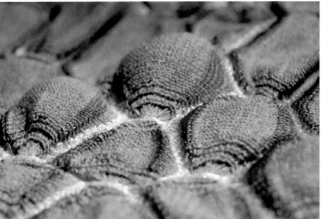

What have been the main research outcomes of this project?

Listener is really a lot of projects in one. One of these is about thinking about how you live with interactivity; another is about how you technically solve this; and then there's the question of material specification that arises through the project. But there's also the interface building—a very large part of the project has been to create our own bespoke interfaces that go directly from the architectural CAD environment, which is the way we draw, to the knitting machine; we go underneath the software that the CAD CAM machines run, and we write directly to the machine code, so we're driving the machine from the design environment . . . these machines are running in BASIC, which is a very old code language. I realized we could sort of go underneath the software—this means the project is also about how you make bespoke nonrepeatable textiles. Most textile logics are really based on patterns that are repeating, but in our projects everything is about the bespoke and the variants of how you actually do this.

1.38

1.37
Listener knitted actuation; a textile membrane that combines pneumatic cells with soft switches to continually react to its environment.
Mette Ramsgaard Thomsen.

1.38
Listener detail, showing the fine tubes embedded in the textile structure, feeding air to the pneumatic cells.
Mette Ramsgaard Thomsen.

1.37

Listener **reacts to human presence—is this the case in the site-specific curtain as well?**

No, in this case, one of the things we have been looking at is how to use sense information not for actuation, but for design . . . to be fed back into the design cycle, and then lead to the creation of bespoke textiles. We don't use a 3D scan, which is sort of finite, but we use a sensing strata, and then we use that to develop the design criteria, through which we can then knit or create bespoke materials for a particular use. It's really interesting because it places smartness in specification rather than in actuation. It still necessitates sensing, but the sensing is taking place somehow as part of the design cycle and not as part of the final object . . . we make a prototype curtain, which is sewn, with all the electronics and the sensors and so on, and we hang

it up to take a reading of the space over a particular time period; then we use the data, which is signal processed, as input to the design cycle. The outcome is a particular knitted surface that will be used as a curtain—so if you imagine a space was lighter at one end and darker at the other, then we would make a curtain that was less translucent, or more translucent, to even out the space.

What are you trying to achieve in using knit to construct a tower?

We are again using our interface between the design environment and the knitting machine to create knitted surfaces that are bespoke in terms of how they are structurally bearing. The project is really looking at how we can use active bending and membrane action in constructing a tower, a little bit like modern tents that have carbon tubes in them, and they have

this relationship between the tensile membrane and the compressive force of the carbon tube . . . working with knit is both very interesting and very complex because of stretchability and lightness of the material. We're working with ideas of resilience, of a soft tower that moves with impact from the environment but can also stand; we are creating bespoke knitted pockets for the fiberglass tubes, so that it can then become structural. We have learned a lot from *Listener* because it takes the whole interfacing and design process with it—it's not smart in the same way that the curtain is, because it doesn't use any sensor bands in it, but it is still smart in the way that we can try and understand how we can create bespoke textiles that are performing exactly for the context that they're in.

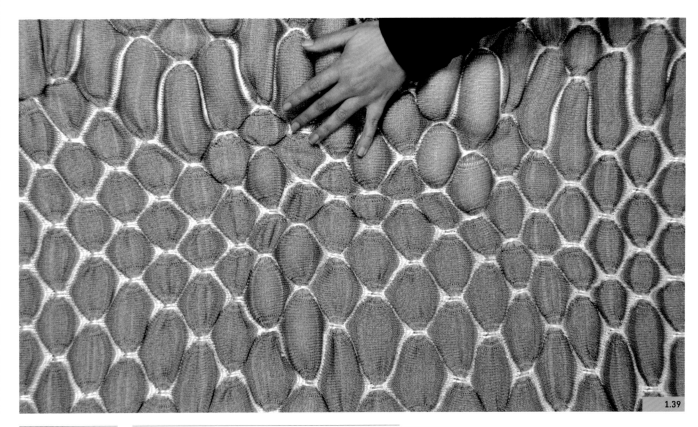

1.39

Chapter summary

This first chapter discussed the difference between smart and technical textiles, and their relationship with wearables, or wearable computing. It should be clear that these terms are contested and that in fact, "smart textiles" is a useful, if inaccurate, name for this field, and it does not correctly describe all the approaches you will come across within it. The chapter covered the many possible contexts such materials may be found in and pointed to a future where the yarn itself becomes "smart."

Suggested reading

Collet, C. (2012), "BioLace: An Exploration of the Potential of Synthetic Biology and Living Technology for Future Textiles," *Studies in Material Thinking*, 7 (Paper 02).

Amy Congdon. (2015), http://www.amycongdon.com/biological-atelier-aw-2082/ (accessed 15 October 2015).

Ellis, J. (1996), *Textile Surgical Implants*, Patent application number: EP 0744162 A2, http://www.google.com/patents/EP0744162A2?cl=en (accessed 15 October 2015).

Georgia Tech Wearable Motherboard: The Intelligent Garment for the 21st Century. Available online: http://www.smartshirt.gatech.edu/ (accessed 15 October 2015).

Gupta, D. (2011), "Functional Clothing—Definition and Classification," *Indian Journal of Fibre & Textile Research*, 36: 321–6.

House of Commons Science and Technology Committee (2012), *Regulation of Medical Implants in the EU and UK: Fifth Report of Session 2012–13*. Available online: http://www.publications.parliament.uk/pa/cm201213/cmselect/cmsctech/163/163.pdf. Accessed 15 October 2015.

Inditex, *Safe to Wear*. Available online: http://www.inditex.com/documents/10279/130571/STW.pdf/72fa5c5d-db0e-4aca-b3a4-2cae3f9818e7 (accessed 19 February 2016).

Inteltex (2010), *Intelligent Multi-Reactive Textiles*. Available online: inteltex.eu (accessed 15 October 2015).

Kirstein, T., ed. (2013), *Multidisciplinary Know-How for Smart-Textile Developers* (Woodhead Publishing Series in Textiles), Cambridge, UK: Woodhead Publishing Ltd.

Medicines and Healthcare Products Regulatory Agency (MHRA), "Legislation." Available online: https://www.gov.uk/government/collections/regulatory-guidance-for-medical-devices and https://www.gov.uk/guidance/decide-if-your-product-is-a-medicine-or-a-medical-device (accessed 15 October 2015).

Quinn, B. (2010), *Textile Futures*, Oxford: Berg.

Studio XO, http://www.e-fibre.co.uk/studio-xo/ (accessed 15 October 2015).

SymbioticA, http://www.symbiotica.uwa.edu.au/ (accessed 15 October 2015).

Mette Ramsgaard Thomsen: http//cita.karch.dk/Menu/People/Mette+Ramsgard+Thomsen

1.39
Interacting with Listener; the knitted surface also responds to touch as part of its environment. Mette Ramsgaard Thomsen.

The smart textile product: design processes

The term *textile designer* no longer has a simple definition—the role comprises a myriad of descriptions, including: engineer, inventor, scientist, designer and creative.

Gale and Kaur 2002:37

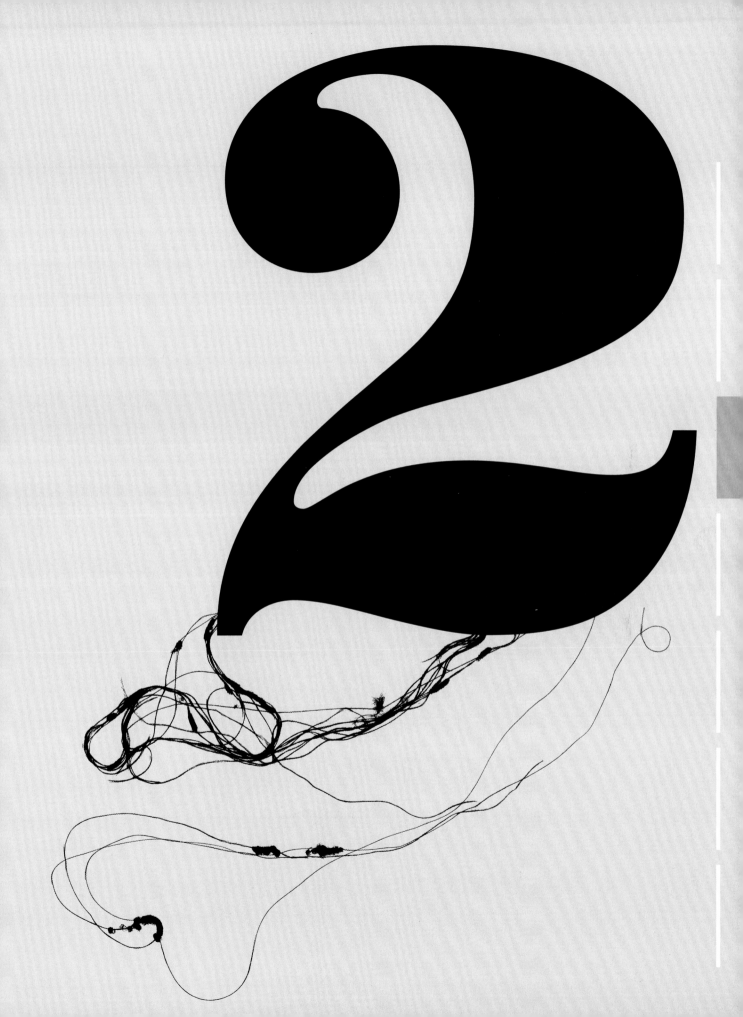

CHAPTER OVERVIEW

Because smart textiles inevitably include the potential for changes in aesthetic appearance and offer extra functionality, such as heat or light, working with them can introduce some challenges in terms of the design process. This chapter discusses studio textile practice, user-centered design, and interaction design as different models of the design process, and it will give you tools to think about how your own practice is situated in a broader creative landscape. You will also learn about the opportunities offered by state-of-the-art materials research and the constraints still holding smart textiles back from mainstream markets.

The following discussions of design disciplines are a broad introduction—if you are a textile designer you may find the overview of studio practice simplistic, but you may find the introductions to interaction design and user-centered design useful, and vice versa. The history and taxonomy of craft practices in particular has been massively condensed and will not do justice to nuances of complex and ongoing cultural histories—for further reading on these subjects, please see the suggested readings at the end of the chapter. Studio practice, user-centered design and interaction design each have their own section, followed by industrial processes.

Textiles is already a diverse creative field, with individuals working across a spectrum of approaches, from the very technical (e.g., chemical engineering, finishing), through trend-led or brief-led design, to craftsmanship with specific materials, to conceptual practices. The ways in which electronics are integrated into these different ways of working will then be quite different and will depend on goals and criteria for successful design outcomes (as defined by the client or the practitioner), attitudes about risk and the unknown in the process, the role of the end-user, attitudes about authorship and self-expression, the role of material, and relationships with other design disciplines. You can think of these as the elements that combine to describe a model of the design practice.

Dimension	Design practice: (e.g., Studio, Chemical Engineering, Industrial, Art, Service Design)
Goals	
Criteria for successful outcome (and who decides)	
Attitude toward risk and the unknown	
Role of the end-user	
Role of material	
Relationships with other disciplines	
Attitudes toward authorship and self-expression	

Table 2.1
Dimensions of design practice; different creative fields have different attitudes to dimensions like these.

KEY QUESTION

How do you design? What are your goals and attitudes about risk? Use table 2.1 to examine your own motivations and assumptions about the design process.

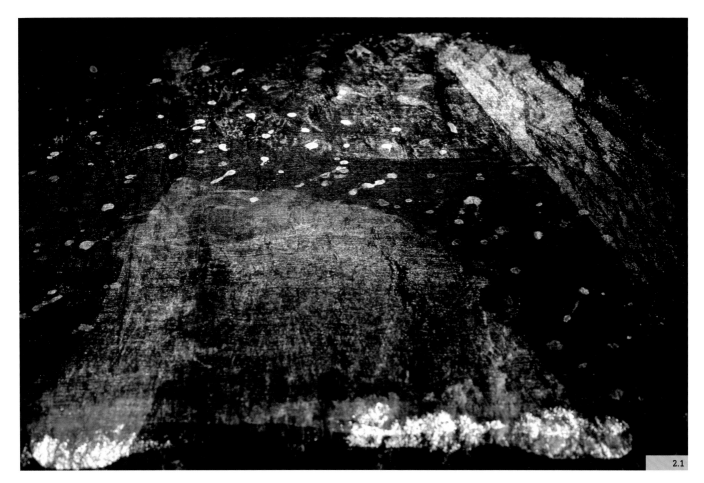

2.1
Kinor Jiang, silver
plating; Dr. Jiang's
creative practice involves
experimental metalized
and etched metallic
textiles.

As an example of the difference between a textile designer and a textile artist, consider Kinor Jiang's description of Junichi Arai (of Nuno) as a creator and not a designer. This is based on his exploratory, "processual" approach to fiber, color, texture and finish, and playfulness with the machinery and technology at hand, often resulting in novel production techniques as well as beautiful fabrics.

In contrast, designing a smart textile for the automotive industry requires the developer to think carefully about the situation in which the textile will be used, and what useful functionality it will deliver, and the ultimate goal is a functional product. Textile designers are increasingly working alongside creatives from other design disciplines to think about how the properties of the textile work with functionality and user experience as well as the integrated technology. This chapter discusses studio textile practice, user-centered design, and interaction design in terms of the design practice model previously described. You can also use these dimensions to think critically about the descriptions given here in relation to practices you see around you, and as new practices continue to emerge; the feature interview with Anna Persson reveals how she is working to define interactive textile design at the intersection of these disciplines. How teams work with each other across disciplines is discussed more fully in chapter 5.

STUDIO TEXTILE PRACTICE

The word *studio* carries a set of particular meanings when used to refer to creative practices. This has come about since the 1950s and 1960s primarily in Europe and the United States, and it applies to most of the subgenres of craft as defined by materials or processes, such as textiles, ceramics or metalsmithing. Where these practices had been trades, there was a diversification in the goals and markets of craft in response to the industrialization of manufacturing, increasing globalization, and changing perceptions of worth. Serious academic research in craft was hampered by the notion that objects should speak for themselves and that the ineffable, mysterious beauty of such objects (for the viewer) and of the process of making (for the creative practitioner) could only be damaged by analytical inquiry. At the same time, craft was seeking equal status with fine art and was increasingly exhibited in vitrines in the "white cube" gallery environment. The persona of the maker was that of a modernist hero or heroine— singular, individual, driven to express an inner essence through her work—and this lone genius's natural habitat was her studio.

The term *studio* is used here to create a point of difference from user-centered design disciplines, and to illustrate the powerful aesthetic force that excellent individual practice can bring to multidisciplinary teams. As makers engage more with electronics as materials, we can begin to see similar levels of commitment, engagement and skill in developing beautiful smart textiles—examples of these can readily be seen in the next chapter.

The ongoing situation is complex, with studio design and making practices operating alongside other forms of practice. Gale and Kaur (2002) discuss, for example, designer-makers, craftspeople, and designers as distinct ways of working, while Jorunn Veiteberg (2005) describes contemporary craft practices as postmodern, and even post-postmodern. For the sake of simplicity here, we concentrate on designer-maker and textile designer practices (though you may be interested in reflecting on your own work in relation to these definitions, and you can find tools to do this in chapter 5).

2.2

2.2
The Forest; printed artist textiles. Annie Trevillian.

2.3

Annie Trevillian, an Australian printer, talks about her process as happening between hand-drawn, scanned and manipulated images, painting and screen printing. In this way she can keep the process open and exploratory, producing unexpected and exciting developments that lead in turn to new directions. Trevillian's work demonstrates a very personal approach, as she uses it to document, understand and celebrate her life; she even suggests that her organization of motifs reflects a desire to order her mind.

Sara Brennan's woven tapestry explores a sense of space by continually revisiting the line of the horizon through enlarged drawings and its translation from a mark on paper to a mark in textile. Brennan uses terms such as *discipline, restraint* and *obsession* when discussing her practice, both in terms of the formal palette of colors and yarns she uses, and in terms of the commitment needed to complete a piece of work in this medium. **Marian Bijlenga** seeks to create new forms through the manipulation of fabric and horsehair. She works with the empty space between the dots, lines and contours of her textile "drawings," composing rhythm and movement in the creation of "spatial drawings." **Deborah Simon** is an artist from Brooklyn for whom textiles are just one of many media. For her, the "plush" nature of textiles allows her work to create unnerving associations with both taxidermy and childhood. She amplifies the disconnect she finds between the labeling, codifying and collecting of nature with the lived existence of plants and animals.

If we were to complete the design practice model for studio textiles, we might see something like table 2.2. In addition, most textile designers will attest to the nonlinear nature of their process, even when a client brief is involved. In this case, a designer will often be working either in-house or as a freelancer, focusing on, for example, surface pattern developments within given color ways (defined by trend predictions), scale and perhaps even motifs. Market levels (high, middle or low) can be characterized to some extent by the level of creative freedom of the designer within a system or team. At the higher market levels, authorship tends to be important in studio practice in the same way that art and fine craft champion the individual. Often, the work of a single textile designer will be recognizable, concerned with one or two particular aesthetic aspects such as texture or pattern.

2.3
Color dots, France, summer.
Horsehair, fabric
25 x 25 cm
Marian Bijlenga,
Landsmeer, 2009.

Among all cultural heritages, there is nothing more abundant than [textile] fabric.

Jun'ichi Arai 1968, cited by Gallery Gen

Dimension	Design practice: studio textiles
Goals	A series of samples and stand-alone pieces of fabric (e.g., wall hangings) that are innovative in their use of formal textile qualities such as handle, drape, manipulation, structure, surface texture and color
Criteria for successful outcome (and who decides)	Fine craft quality, excellent finish, novel visual and material language, gallery-quality work (the maker decides, followed by the fine craft world of curators, collectors and critics)
Attitude toward risk and the unknown	The process is defined by the unknown—it is explorative in nature but builds on a wealth of personal experiential knowledge with the same or similar materials and processes—what the object might be, or who the ultimate owner or user might be, may not be a priority
Role of the end-user	There may well be no function, and therefore no user beyond collectors, museums and galleries; where there is a use function, it will either be archetypal (scarves, hangings), or avant-garde (sculptural, narrative, political)
Role of material	Is of utmost importance, either for the embodied relational exploration of expressive possibilities or for its cultural meanings
Relationships with other disciplines	Are generally not acknowledged—if there is any sourcing out of aspects of the work, it tends to be seen as a trade relationship
Attitudes toward authorship and self-expression	As in art, authorship is crucial and is evidenced in the evolving personal style of the designer; this creates value in the products of the studio

Table 2.2
Possible design practice model for studio textile practice

Judging the success of this kind of process requires the artist to be reflective and able to constructively critique his or her own work. When building this form of practice, it is important to look at other work and to constantly discuss your work with peers and tutors to develop a critical vocabulary. In this way you will be able to develop the criteria that are important to you as the creator of the work; it may be that you want to devise the most effective method to produce a particular texture, or you may be more interested in the range of expressive opportunities a single material or even machine can offer you. This type of work can be challenging to other disciplines involved in smart textile development, as it is often characterized by extreme openness. That is, it may not be clear at the start of the process what the intended outcome should be. There will be periods of time when the designer will not be able to say for sure what he is doing, or how long it will take to reach a satisfactory outcome. In addition, it is rare that a textile artist will be thinking of a specific user or scenario in which the textile will be used, beyond other creative clients like interiors and fashion design, which can determine fabric handle or the scale of a pattern. The outcome of this process is at once the product of a creative discipline and the material for many others. At the opposite end of the scale is user-centered design, very common in product design and development; this is discussed more fully after the following case study, which describes research in a studio practice environment.

2.4

2.4 Zoku Zoku, Nuno
Zoku Zoku ("thrills and chills") is one of a series of books by Nuno, all with onomatopoeic names. Other Nuno textiles evoke different Japanese onomatopoeia—boro boro (raggedy), fuwa fuwa (fluffy), kira kira (shiny), shimi jimi (poignant), suké suké (sheer) and zawa zawa (rustling).

KEY QUESTION

In what ways is your own creative process "open"? Look back at completed projects and try to identify what you felt you had to make clear decisions on, and what could be left undecided. Using diaries, a blog or sketchbooks, obsessively document the process of your next project so you can understand where such openness occurs in your work.

Case study: Sara Keith

Sara Keith is an interesting case study here because she works across disciplines, creating collections of art textiles, but also textile jewelry and accessories. She has a background in costume design for the BBC, the Royal Ballet and the Royal Opera, and of her industry experience, Keith says that designing for opera and ballet gave her the most creative freedom. Keith completed her undergraduate studies degree in embroidered and woven textile design at the Glasgow School of Art, and she later undertook a PhD at Duncan of Jordanstone College of Art and Design at the University of Dundee. Her research there was concerned with the relationships of metal and textile: *Silver as dye: the organic idiom of shibori and electrodeposition.*

Keith has a diverse palette of processes, materials and inspiration to work with. When traveling, she collects traditional and indigenous processes, but her work is also consistently informed by the natural landscape of her home in Scotland. In using *shibori*, Japanese techniques of shape resist dyeing, Keith clamps, wraps, folds, binds and stitches material to create selectively dyed fabrics. Her distressed metallic textiles are made using a combination of *shibori* and electrolysis, coating the fabric (organza, silk or velvet) with a fine layer of silver, copper or gold. These can then be worked as metals to create different finishes (shown in figure 2.5 is burnishing); this collision of the organic and the mechanistic is of key interest in Keith's research, allowing cross-fertilization of concepts, textures and forms.

There is also an interesting note here on the nature of PhD research. Until recently it was very difficult to do postgraduate research by practice, but this has become more acceptable since ceramicist Katie Bunnell published her research using (at the time) novel multimedia formats. Sara Keith's website shows her doctoral exposition and the artist's books she prepared as research deliverables alongside the textile outputs; these books share the careful material sensitivity of the whole body of work and even incorporate textile binding techniques in their construction. For further reading on practice-based doctoral research programs, see Elkins (2014).

2.5
Silver-stitched strips;
silver deposited on fabric
using electrolysis, hand
stitched and burnished.
Sara Keith.

2.5

USER-CENTERED DESIGN (UCD)

Designing with users at the center of the process has become crucial to industrial and product design. The goal of this kind of process is to produce an object that is functional and useful; desirability is important for market share and owner attachment but is very often not the main objective. In order to achieve this, UCD works to identify users and their needs very early in the design process.

When designing a smart textile product in this way, designers ask questions such as: Who is it for? What will it do? What will the user want to do with it? What situations will it be used in? This model of the design process is still flexible, however, and the user may well be involved at different stages of the design. Historically, user testing was done with prototypes toward the end of the design cycle, which had the drawback of making it expensive to act on unexpected insights. More recently, users have been championed as the experts in their own lives, with more or less input throughout the design process. Now it is common to see such methodologies as participatory design and codesign in which the role of the designer as expert is challenged. In smart textile applications, which are often situated close to the body, user acceptance and comfort are crucial. The first experiments done with wearable computing involved medical applications in which inflexible motherboards were strapped to the body

for months at a time. However, few patients will wear an uncomfortable bio-sensing garment long enough for it to give meaningful data, and most do not want to wear a device that marks them out as having a medical condition. Understanding your market and the aspirations and needs of your users are important steps in successful product development.

The automotive industry is a large and immediate market for smart fabrics, and it uses a wide range of user testing techniques to minimize risk and ensure market demand. Methods such as Kansei Engineering support the design of cars that appeal to our sense of smell (scented polymers) and hearing (the sound of an expensive door closing) as well as sight.

In the design of smart sportswear, fit and comfort are essential. Clothing+ has developed a successful business working with existing conductive materials to fabricate clothing that can measure the body's performance through, for example, heart rate, blood pressure, oxygen levels and hydration levels. The M-Body EMG pants shown in figure 2.8 are turned inside out to make the sensors visible. The pants measure muscle activity, and with the help of an app, an athlete can tell exactly how much weight she is placing on either leg and if she is leaning forward or backward.

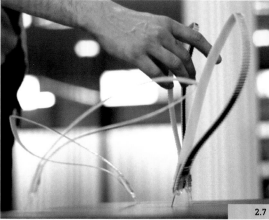

2.7

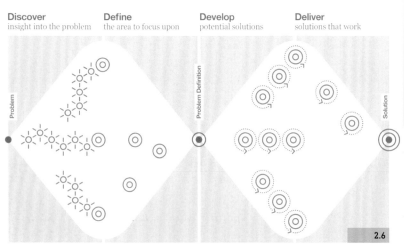

Discover insight into the problem   **Define** the area to focus upon   **Develop** potential solutions   **Deliver** solutions that work

Problem

Problem Definition

Solution

2.6

2.6
The Double Diamond process model from the UK Design Council consists of four main phases: discover, define, develop and deliver. The Design Council 2014.

2.7
BeTouched! An explorative Kansei design project; the strips of paper each have capacitance sensors on their front and back, and are attached to servo motors in the platform. The Kansei notion of "acting intuition" is the main focus of the work.
Pierre Levy.

One of the difficulties in realizing combined smart textile products and services is the need to bring together stakeholders from all the relevant domains. At TU/e, Eindhoven University of Technology, in the project Smart Textile Services (part of the European CRISP research program), a team of three therapists specializing in treating elderly people with Alzheimer's disease, an eldercare manager, a textile developer, an embedded systems designer and a design researcher are collaborating to develop a smart textile garment to support rehabilitation exercises. *Vigour* has sensor areas on the body that can be used to measure movement of the arms and lower back, and it demonstrates the possibilities of smart textile services for geriatric rehabilitation exercises. The design process was undertaken in the context of the stakeholders rather than in the university: meetings were held in the textile factories, and user tests were done on-site in the care facilities where the service will be implemented. You can see here user interviews with the design prototypes; specially designed feedback forms were used by the designers during observations to collect data on the performance of the garment and the responses of the elderly patients and their caregivers.

KEY QUESTION

Consider two different cars from the same range, for example, a Citroen C1 and a Citroen C5. Why does the manufacturer bring out a range of options for the consumer? What are the differences between these two models, and how does this suggest each car is likely to be used? Who buys these different models and why? How did the design team know anything about its market(s)? These are European cars—do these models exist in the United States? If not, why not? You should consider such factors as distances typically traveled, price of gas, status and cost.

2.8
M-Body EMG pants; laminated seams and techniques like laser cutting and ultra-sonic welding make for more comfortable, rub-free sports and medical garments. Clothing+.

2.9
Vigour user testing; doing rehabilitation exercises. Oscar Tomico.

2.10
Vigour knit detail; the long-sleeved top incorporates stretch sensors made of conductive yarn that can trigger sound or vibration output in response to movements.
Photo: Joe Hammond.

INTERACTION DESIGN

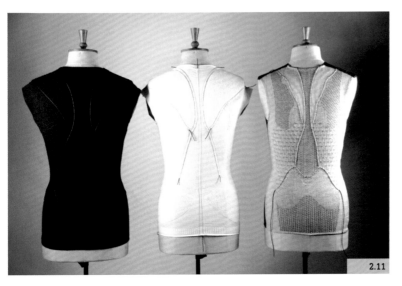

2.11

Aeolia stretch sensor project; three garments made using the same pattern block using embroidery, knit, and weave. Carbon-rubber stretch sensors are embedded in channels. Photo: Cat Northall and Tina Downes.

Interaction design deals with the planning and design of systems that include an input (such as a light switch, or the gestures used with interactive games), the processing to translate that input into a command (often but not always using a microcontroller), and an output (such as light, sound or movement). For the most part, interaction design has tended to focus on the user experience of the output, concentrating on creating atmosphere in an intelligent environment or an alarm bell in a safety system. Originally focused on the design of systems with a screen interface, a keyboard and mouse, interaction design has come to include other materials and is increasingly interested in tangible forms of knowledge and interaction. This means that the interface has become an interesting design opportunity for many researchers, and textiles offer exciting opportunities for tangible and colocated input and output. The three garment backs in figure 2.11 introduced an embroiderer, a knitter and a weaver to a commercially available stretch sensor to explore methods of incorporating it into their existing design practices; these interfaces are not defined by function first, but by creative textile practice and are seen as engaging in their own right. They can now be brought into a larger design program with users to develop functionality and refine the placement of the sensors specifically for different types of movement.

What do we do when we design an interactive textile? There are many more design decisions to be made when these fields meet, for example:

- What is the quality of the fabric?
- When is it encountered?
- How is it interacted with? (worn? handled? touched?)
- What should the surface be like?
- What is the input modality? (i.e., what triggers a change? temperature? humidity? touch?)
- What is the output modality? (e.g., sound, light, moving parts?)
- What kind of information is conveyed, and how ambiguous is it?
- When does the output happen? How often? How many times?
- Where does the output happen? In the same object or surface? On the other side of the world? Is it a cloud service accessible through any other device?
- Who has access to this output?
- How is the product powered? Is it mobile? portable?
- Are you designing for the near future, that is, are you assuming your product will enter the market as soon as it is feasible to manufacture? Or are you designing for five years' time, or twenty?

To become confident making decisions like these, you will need to practice interaction design skills as well as textile design skills, and as you become aware of the technologies involved, bear in mind the implications of your choices for manufacture. As an example, deciding to make your concept portable means you will need to consider the user experience of managing power, as well as the weight and bulk of a power supply. Interaction design skills involve sketching possible scenarios of use, and defining your user through the use of personas.

TexTales (Bedtime Stories) is an exciting project because it bridges the gap between academic research and commercial viability. Kristi Kuusk has developed QR codes hidden in the woven design on a bed cover for children; this can be read by recognition software on a tablet or smartphone. When a motif such as a woven flower on the fabric is scanned and recognized by the tablet computer held by the storyteller, the child can play with the textile to manipulate the digital visual. As a piece of interaction design, Kuusk has decided that output should be immediate (there is no time lag, and information is not stored anywhere for later access); it is experienced on the tablet computer, and not on the textile; input can be quite passive—achieved by moving the tablet around or pointing it at the woven pattern—or it can be more active, as in when the child moves the bedclothes to manipulate the character on the screen. Importantly, the whole interaction scenario involves more than one user— it is deliberately social.

2.12
Drawing for interaction design; a workshop run by user experience consultancy Adaptive Path highlighted the use of recognizable characters and practice in drawing hands interacting with objects.

2.12

2.13

2.13
Drawing for interaction design; it is important to include aspects of the interface to help make design decisions.

2.14

2.14
TexTales (Bedtime Stories); a visual recognition system on the tablet creates characters in response to hidden codes in the printed quilt cover. Kristi Kuusk.

2.15
TexTales (Bedtime Stories); images like these can both be part of user-centered research and communicate the interactive design concept. Kristi Kuusk.

2.15

Exercise Three
Doing primary research for interaction design with textiles

Find out as much as possible about the *Vigour* project and the users this was made for. Consider how this concept might be redesigned to benefit a different user group by trying out the following steps:

1. By interviewing people about movement, gather information about rehabilitation from injury, training for sports, or difficulties in working in extreme environments (e.g., in firefighting).
2. Take the main points from your interviews and use them to describe a fictional character that captures the common and particular experience of that user group. Give your character a name, age and gender.
3. Describe your character's goals and typical actions as he or she goes about the movement activity. You now have a persona you can design for.
4. Taking *Vigour* as a starting point, ask yourself how it fits your persona's lifestyle and how it supports your persona's activity. Identify where changes need to be made.
5. Use storyboards and sketching to focus on aspects like weight, grip or placement on the body.
6. Use the storyboards to consider the questions about information you have gathered .
7. Use sketches and annotations to think through any impact on the mental state of your persona—does it make them happy? Worried? Confident?
8. Does the story involve other people besides your persona?

Some useful books and links can be found in the Suggested Reading section on doing interaction design, personas and storyboards.

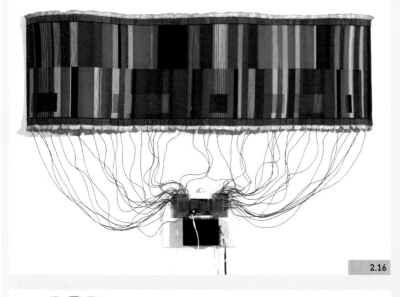

2.16

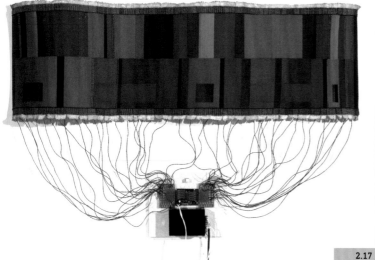

2.17

2.16
100 Electronic Art Years (on); current is flowing through the conductive yarns in the woven design, creating heat and changing the color of the thermochromic inks used. Maggie Orth.

2.17
100 Electronic Art Years (off); designing for state-change textiles means considering aesthetic expression when switched off as well as on. Maggie Orth.

Because smart textiles will often be dynamic and involve some kind of state change, perhaps of color or shape, it is useful to look beyond traditional textile practices for ways of working with temporal aspects in design. Related disciplines include filmmaking and animation, dance and movement and, of course, music. This area of work is gaining ground in design for architectural facades but is still new in textile design, and there is plenty of scope for you to develop your own framework for design. Doing this means listening to the language used by other disciplines and thinking about how it might help you make design decisions in your own work. Animation, for example, may lead you to think about frame rates as a way of exploring the timescale of color changes in a thermochromic weave (as in Maggie Orth's *100 Electronic Art Years*, figures 2.16 and 2.17), and the early days of media like this provide a wealth of low-tech ways of exploring the expression of frequency, rhythm, attack and movement. Other important researchers in this area include Linnéa Nilsson, Linda Worbin, Barbara Layne, Joanna Berzowska, Delia Dumitrescu, and Anna Persson, all of whom have tried to classify and make available methods of designing for formal changes in pattern and structure in smart textiles.

Finally, a very useful series of design tools are being constantly developed and refined by the Service Design community. In Service Design, the creative processes of design are taken out of the studio and placed in more corporate environments to facilitate new thinking and the codesign of new products, procedures and customer experiences. Because Service Design needs to include many different stakeholders, moments of interaction ("touchpoints"), and emotional experiences, its techniques are valuable as we try to envisage smart textiles as part of larger narratives of interaction. Ways of thinking about experience, such as *customer journeys*, can help us situate smart textiles as just one part of a user's day, for example, or understand how users might want to access information or communicate in different ways.

Customer journeys map the total customer experience across all the interactions between the customer and the business providing the service or product, and they include expectations, first contact, experience of purchase and satisfaction levels

after purchase. The concept of customer journeys capture both the experience the customer wants to receive and the experience the business would like to provide. *This Is Service Design Thinking* (Stickdorn and Sneider 2014) is an excellent introduction to the field (see Suggested Reading), and design consultancies such as Adaptive Path maintain great websites full of examples. Saxion University and Eindhoven University of Technology have been working together on a European research project to develop just this kind of methodology to support the creation of smart textile product service systems and the translation of societal issues into opportunities for smart textile innovation.

2.18
Migration (sketch); using a sequence of stills to explore animated pattern.

2.19
Journey map; stills combine to create a storyboard of experience of tangible and intangible aspects of a service. Kelly Fadem.

2.18

Emotional Journey Map for First Time BART Ride of San Francisco Tourist

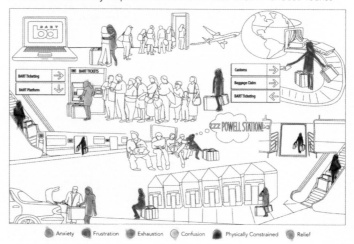

Anxiety   Frustration   Exhaustion   Confusion   Physically Constrained   Relief

2.19

Feature interview: Anna Persson

Dr. Anna Persson completed her PhD at the University of Borås in 2013. Her thesis was titled *Exploring Textile Materials for Interaction Design*, in which she investigated reversible and non-reversible changes in textile structures for communicative and expressive ends.

You came to textile design from another discipline, is that right? What kinds of tensions and opportunities have you encountered within this situation?

Yes that is right, I come from interaction design, and during my masters studies I came across interactive textiles in a collaborative project with the Swedish School of Textiles. From there on my interest in interactive material—especially textiles—grew strong. My background in interaction design has made me very aware of the different focus in these two disciplines—if textile design has a strong focus on material properties and construction, interaction design has more of a user perspective where the material is not always central. I would place textile interaction design just in the middle of these two disciplines, and one challenge is to agree on the terminology. What is it we design when designing smart textiles, what is relevant to focus on and discuss here? I think my non-textile background makes me ignore the do's and don'ts in textile design, which is very good when experimenting.

You have described fabric as being "open for further change" when used as material in another design process— can you talk a bit more about this? For example, how achievable is this when using the physical components of electronics? How would another designer select one smart material over another?

All together—the physical design of the textile, the connected electronic, the programming design and the user interaction—create a lot of design variables. An interactive textile is not really interactive before physical components of electronics are connected to it, and sometimes also programming design. Before it is connected, the textile has *the potential* of being interactive, to

perform, to sense and react in certain ways. This *potential* performance of a fabric of course also depends on the functions of electronic components connected to it. In this way, you could see the fabric as a raw material where a designer further could specify the textile performance by either (or both) the physical components of electronics connected to it and the programming design. Another perspective of a textile being "open for further change" would be that of the material itself (both the textile and the electronic components) in relation to the user interaction. Here the end-result of the textile expression depends on in what way, when, etc. the user interacts.

In this view, what would be the ideal relationship between the supplier (you) and customer (designer)?

At the Smart Textile Design Lab at the Swedish School of Textiles we created a material library with different interactive textiles where we have held workshops with both design students and design companies. What I've learned so far is that the designers trying the materials often want to take the textiles one step further before using them. I think a material library with some instructions is a good start for a collaboration, but I think also the materials need to be more specifically produced to meet the customers' specific aims. And again, what a raw material is, and where a product starts, is something that the collaborators must be aware of and agree on.

For details of Persson's knitted textile work, see the case study in chapter 4.

INDUSTRIAL PROCESSES

Industrial textile processes include the use of CAD interfaces for knitting and embroidery, the use of multihead embroidery machines, digital printing processes and power Jacquard looms in weave. Many of these processes are viable with conductive yarns, but they need some care and modification due to the interaction between the metal yarns and the machinery. For example, metal fibers can migrate and cause electrical problems within the machinery; repeated working with metals causes changes in fiber flexibility through work hardening; and machine parts can become blunted quickly from cutting metal yarns and fabrics. Integration of hardware components into fabrics and yarns has not yet been automated at an industrial scale, and the relationship between the technician and the machine is crucial in achieving results. Figures 2.20 and 2.21 show industrial circular knitting machines being used at the Swedish School of Textiles as part of the Smart Textiles research project in collaboration with industry.

Industrial textile production also includes finishing and coating processes, which can significantly alter the properties of a material, as well as nonwoven and composite materials production.

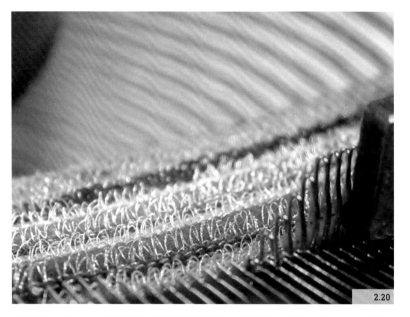

2.20

2.21

2.20
Camber Velnit machine; these industrial circular knitting machines are typically for warp knitted single jersey. Swedish School of Textiles, University of Borås.

2.21
Mayer & Cie Relanit machine; industrial single jersey machines for creating jacquard, plated, and striped jersey fabrics. Swedish School of Textiles, University of Borås.

Opportunities and challenges

There are two broad types of challenges facing the development of smart textiles: the first includes the development of enabling technologies, while the second involves new methodologies and ways of working across many different disciplines. While there has been a great deal of research in smart textiles and wearable technology, a number of technical barriers to commercialization remain; these include standardization of components and protocols, the robustness of connections between hardware and textiles, and the suitability of new types of yarn and fabric for existing manufacturing processes.

Different yarn structures suit different manufacturing processes: Shieldex's coated conductive thread is excellent for hand sewing or use in domestic machines at normal speeds, but it causes issues with tension when used in industrial processes at high speed. A ply yarn, on the other hand, is better for commercial-scale processes. These types of issues are now recognized by yarn developers; the London-based company Cute Circuit was one of the first design consultancies creating wearables as fashion to collaborate with manufacturers to minimize issues in their production processes with conductive yarns. As a result, Cute Circuit can offer a ready-to-wear collection as well as custom-made smart garments, and companies like Bekaert market their co-design and "thinking-with" approach as much as the range and quality of the yarn they produce. The literature includes promises regarding drapeability and comfort in contact with the skin, as well as electroconductivity, signal and data transfer capability. Yarns are available ranging from 70 to 1.4 ohms per meter, and with a range of average breaking loads. This means that yarns specific to end use can be selected (or custom specifications developed), depending on the level of wear and tear anticipated. However, you still need to be prepared for metal yarns to behave differently from the normal yarns you are used to. Because of the filament lengths and the tension held in the metal, you may find you have issues with kinking, twisting and fraying, for example. Figure 2.22 shows a knitted skirt project in which the conductive yarn frayed after a few wears; this was partly helped by using iron-on interfacing to fix the fraying ends and prevent the conductive yarn from coming into contact with itself and causing short circuits. Stretch fabrics like knit need extra consideration when integrating conductive yarns, and you may find using conductive Lycra a better solution for your own projects. Interfacing is very useful as an insulator for textile circuits, and it can also stiffen areas and support more fragile components through the selection of different weights.

2.22
Twirkle T-shirt; industrial processes had to be developed and refined to make these products commercially viable. Cute Circuit.

Standardization is one of the biggest challenges for smart textiles and wearable technology systems, as it needs to account for the multidisciplinary nature of smart textiles as textile, electronic, and potential product. Centexbel in Belgium offers a range of activities and services to the textile industry, including testing, certification and consultancy: workgroup 31 on Smart Textiles is dedicated to identifying and responding to standardization issues concerning smart textiles.

Although somewhat urgent, standardization is difficult even at the level of agreeing on terminology—the word *intelligent*, for example, caused controversy; in addition, classifying textiles as materials or products is debatable, and even what material or structure constitutes a textile can be ambiguous, as demonstrated by the regulations brought in by FINA, the international swimming federation, in 2010 after Speedo's LZR swimsuits helped athletes break thirteen world records in a single year (FINA defined acceptable fabrics as being breathable). Existing testing methods also need to be revised to make sure they are suitable, and new measuring tools and specifications need to

be defined. Individual sectors and application areas are then subject to regulation: medical products are particularly difficult, as the US Food and Drug Administration (FDA) requires innovators to identify an existing class of products that their new product will fit within. European consultancies advise on an interdisciplinary approach to standardization, and Centexbel works with telecommunications and electrotechnical committees to achieve this. In the United States, an initial standardization meeting was held in Atlanta in 2012, attended by delegates from seven relevant federal government committees including Textiles, Nanotechnology, Homeland Security Applications and Protective Clothing, all interested in developing "intelligence" in their clothing. At the time of this writing, a quick check seemed to suggest that there is not yet a technical subcommittee dedicated to smart textiles within ASTM International (the American Society for Testing and Materials). Elena Corchero of the UK startup Lost Values found that it took around twelve months and many revisions of her original design to achieve CE (European conformity) accreditation for her children's Loopin product, whose felt ears form a soft switch and light up its eyes.

2.23

2.23
Fraying fibers; non-stretch conductive yarns with a stretch fabric created stress and excess fraying in this garment, saved temporarily by patching with iron-on interfacing.

2.24
Loopin toys developed to teach children about simple textile circuits needed to comply with European legislation for product safety. Elena Corchero, Lost Values.

2.24

This new combination of materials and functionality is hard to find precedents for (the first step in FDA approval for medical applications) and to achieve conformity with health and safety legislation for (CE marking in Europe), but the multidisciplinary nature of the field also provides a wealth of new opportunities. Ramyah Gowrishankar (a textile designer) and Jussi Mikkonen (electronics design and programming) have been exploring creative solutions together. Their ideas include the use of electronic components on flexible thin film substrates, which can then be stitched through to create a connection on fabric. Gowrishankar digitizes textile circuit designs using embroidery CAD packages, placing components precisely (and tacking them in place with a tiny dot of fabric adhesive) and allowing the multihead embroidery machine to accurately stitch the component into place and create the electrical contact. Figures 2.25 and 2.26 are from a Textile Thinking for Electronics workshop held at Aalto University in 2013; they show the embroidery in action and some of the finished mitten projects with on/off textile switches.

Other exciting opportunities exist in additive manufacturing, which can be inspired by textile structures or the skin, and in printed electronics on fabric substrates. Different materials can be printed in three dimensions now, and researchers are developing ways materials can be mixed as printing takes place to control flexibility and strength in defined areas of a finished product. Freedom of Creation is famous for its printed chainmail work, and similar groundbreaking work is going on now in folding structures. If the durability issues with printed circuitry can be resolved, this could pave the way to many new soft products. Currently, screen-printed circuits promise some flexibility on solid rather than woven substrates. The flexible fabric watch in figure 2.27 was developed at Southampton University's Nanofabrication Centre using thick film printing techniques to achieve the electroluminescent display.

There is a choice to be made between using existing standard electronic components and developing textile versions to deliver comparable electronic functionality. Both require innovation in the design of connections. This is especially true when taking into account the connections between soft, pliable textiles and brittle electronic hardware; how to achieve this is the focus of a great deal of current research, such as the STELLA and PASTA projects (see Suggested Reading), and is crucial for commercial products to meet emerging standards and user expectations. Approaches include

2.25

2.25
Multihead embroidery with placed custom-designed electronic components—these were designed into the embroidery CAD file.
Jussi Mikkonen and Ramyah Gowrishankar.

2.26
Embroidered switches on mitten designs using the placed flexible electronic components.
Jussi Mikkonen and Ramyah Gowrishankar.

2.26

"packaging" design, which means using silicons and plastics to house the electronics, innovation in flexible electronics to bring them closer to flexible substrates, conductive epoxy adhesives to support joins, and "stapling" or stitching through conductive thin film. We also find some common fastenings combined with conductive fabrics, such as hook-and-loop (or Velcro-style) line connects, USB connectors, and buckles. It is possible to use hook-and-loop connectors so that some components such as batteries can be removed before washing. Researchers such as Clint Zeagler are studying how smart fabrics and fibers stand up to washing cycles, which components of the whole system we might expect to be able to wash, and at what domestic cycles and temperatures. The key issue is a potential change in resistivity that might occur in different materials due to the fragility of conductive yarn structures and the relative inflexibility of printed conductive traces. At the one-off creative project level, Australian jeweler Cinnamon Lee collects images of jewelry fastenings and connections for inspiration; Leah Buechley has developed the Lilypad Arduino microprocessor and components that can be sewn to fabric; and international creative team Kobakant has developed an impressive database of exploratory textile electronics. You can try many of these out in chapter 3 (for example, in the Sensors section), and you will find further relevant technical tips throughout the case studies in chapter 4.

There are different approaches to the issue of power for smart textiles. In small projects you will be able to sew a coin cell battery holder to your fabric, but for enduring projects and commercial applications, rechargeable and long-lasting power solutions will be needed. Many projects have looked at harvesting energy from movement—for example, through piezoelectric material in shoes—but the amount of power generated is typically inadequate. Inductive charging is a promising approach, and it also allows designers to remove some connecting traces (wire or fiber). Others have explored solar radiation, as in Elena Corchero's parasol with hand-pierced decorative solar panels (figure 2.28), and at the industrial scale, in the Dephotex project (figure 2.29), which is developing novel fibers with photovoltaic properties.

For further discussion on the challenges involved in commercialization and innovation, see chapter 5 and the interview with technical textile consultant Mike Starbuck.

2.29
Photovoltaic textiles; new approaches in materials science are focusing on making hardware more flexible. Dephotex project.

2.27
Functional electronic screen printing. Electroluminescent smart fabric watch. Marc de Vos.

2.28
Hand-pierced solar cells in embroidered fan. This is a good example of another approach to combining hard and soft components, and to the expressive potential of hardware as part of a design. Elena Corchero.

Smart yarn production

Fibers are what make up a yarn; fibers are traditionally a single material, but yarns are often composed of different fibers to achieve various qualities such as tenacity, handle and functions. You have already seen examples of smart yarns in chapter 1, section iii; in this section you will learn about other techniques for producing smart yarns, and even smart fibers.

Standard yarn production techniques include spinning of natural fibers to create twisted yarns with particular "tenacity" characteristics, while man-made materials such as thermoplastic polymers are often processed as continuous fibers using techniques such as melt spinning or solution spinning. In melt spinning, the extruded polymer material forms filaments as it passes through an airflow, and these are caught up and spun into a yarn, which is heat treated as it is stretched to create the required fineness and mechanical tenacity. To create functional (conductive or performance) yarns, other materials such as metals and ceramic fibers are introduced in different ways. Performance yarns can include a number of different staple fibers to become both antistatic and heat resistant, useful in firefighting garments, for example. Yarns for conductivity are created in three main ways: they can be metal wrapped, metal filled or twisted as staple fibers or filaments.

Metal-wrapped or coated yarns may be made by depositing very fine layers of conductive material such as gold, silver or copper on the fiber surface; this layer can provide very good surface conductivity, but it is easily damaged when the yarn is processed into a fabric, and it wears easily once in use, affecting the functionality. Metal-filled yarns include a filament or filaments of conductive fiber, surrounded by twisted or braided nonconductive fibers, which insulate the yarn along its length. Twist structures introduce the metal fibers to a nonconductive staple fiber that gives the yarn its strength and flexibility.

Now research teams are beginning to explore the potential of multimaterial and multifunctional fibers, that is, fibers that could function like devices in themselves. A team at the Massachusetts Institute of Technology (MIT) led by Yoel Fink has developed techniques based on hot glassworking, drawing a "preform" composed of semiconductor, conductor and insulator materials arranged in a specific architecture that preserves the optical, thermal and acoustic properties of the embedded materials. The functionalities made possible include: omnidirectional reflectors, photonic fibers, quantum communication, biocompatible photonic crystals, all-optical devices and photonic bandgap materials.

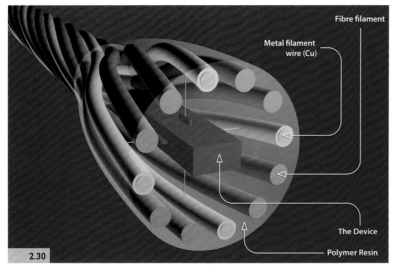

Fibre filament

Metal filament wire (Cu)

The Device

Polymer Resin

2.30

2.30
eFiber construction with micro components; the structure of a twist yarn provides opportunities to embed electronics if mechanical and electrical joining techniques can be developed. The fiber filament is shown in brown, the metal filament is shown in turquoise and gold, the device is in the center and the polymer resin is shaded gray.
Advanced Textile Research Group, Nottingham Trent University.
Tilak Dias.

These fibers will be able to detect light and convert it into electrical pulses that can convert sound into electrical signals and potentially store energy as capacitors. Drawing the fibers makes use of the different melting points of the embedded materials to preserve the structure of the thread composition, and it can be achieved at relatively low temperatures. The group has shown that functional fiber diodes can be created in this way; diodes act as one-way valves for electrical currents, allowing electrons to flow in only one direction, and they are among the basic building blocks in electrical circuits.

The Karma Kameleon project has begun this type of work with photonic bandgap fibers, which can ultimately be used as sensor devices as well as light displays. These fibers both reflect light and carry light along their length. They can be bundled together with a tube connector to ensure a good fit with the light source, and then the separate fibers can be worked into a fabric structure. In these wall hangings, the color of individual fibers can be controlled as each is addressable individually when the light source is programmed; this opens up creative possibilities for dynamic surface design in the changing relationship between guided color, reflected color, and the structure of the fabric (in this case a double weave created on a computer-controlled Jacquard loom). Images can be seen of this fabric in chapter 1, and you can find an interview with Joanna Berzowska about her work in chapter 4.

The nano-scale of smart fiber development means different materials can be deposited on thread structures to achieve a range of potential functionalities; for example, treated thread can be used as a flexible supercapacitor—or energy storage device—to drive other devices. Researchers are also working on making this stretchable in the future. In China, researchers have created nano-scale solar-powered fibers and demonstrated their potential in running an iPod from a sleeve containing the fibers. Structures like these can be designed for use in medical textiles and devices, such as those used to detect proteins and biomolecules in the blood, or to sense when the movement of fluids in the body is compromised through the use of acoustics.

Composite textiles

Composite textiles that incorporate different materials for their individual characteristics can be highly complex. Typical application sectors are aerospace and the automotive industry, where composites may make up the body of an aircraft or line the hood of a car. Composites are also important in the manufacture of webbing and strapping where strength, elasticity and tear or shear resistance need to be regulated.

Modeling the behavior of these complex structures is key to understanding how they will perform in situ. This means using computer programs and visualization techniques to predict drape and the internal rearrangement of layers and fibers. At the University of Nottingham, an open source software platform has been developed and made freely available, while in Stuttgart, architectural material researchers are interested in how external forces propagate through textile structures as they find their own form. The images show a glass fiber composite being manipulated and tracked with light to capture form data.

Different layers in a composite will have different reaction times, expanding and contracting in response to external stimuli such as heat or moisture, and this difference can be engineered to give movement. These kinds of structures give us breathable fabrics and adaptive architecture, opening and closing vents or pores to control heat, airflow and sound levels.

Many composites make use of ceramic, glass and aramid fibers for strength, and most composites have been developed for acoustic or thermal characteristics, or for weight reduction (and therefore lower fuel consumption) in haulage and transport systems. However, more are being developed that are capable of monitoring their own state using conductive fibers; this is sometimes called structural health monitoring (SHM). Structures used include braided ropes and broad woven bands of conductive fiber on either face of spacer fabrics. Applications include ropes used in winch ropes and lifting slings, parachute lines, mooring lines and elevator ropes, where there are clear safety implications. There are also applications where pressure indicates comfort, for example, in hospital bed and mattress design.

Finally, coatings and membranes offer another approach to creating multifunctional textiles, and these are a central part of the standard textile industry. Phase change materials (PCM) can be microencapsulated in a polymer compound and applied to the surface or laminated as a sheet to the surface of woven, knitted and nonwoven fabrics. Alternatively, the microencapsulated PCM can be incorporated into a bonded fiber web, creating a nonwoven composite fabric with special heat transfer properties—in other words, the thermal comfort of garments can be controlled. This means that PCM composites are useful in extreme conditions, and they can be found in protective firefighting equipment such as gloves, and in skiwear for protection against extremely low temperatures.

2.31
Glass fiber composite fabric. Part of a form-finding research project at 3D Spacer Textile Composites; extruded fibers and composite yarns mean a wide range of materials can become textiles. Nico Reinhardt and Achim Menges.

Nonwoven fabrics

Generally speaking, nonwoven structures are suitable for surface printing (rather than constructed) electronic circuits, but the interaction between the ink (especially its viscosity) and the qualities of the substrate (for example, smoothness) need to be taken into account. Tyvek, a well-known brand of polyethylene nonwoven often used in the construction industry, has a highly calendared surface that takes conductive ink very well. However, all nonwovens appear to crease at least to some extent after washing, and the printed circuit does not survive. Some researchers have successfully laminated circuits on nonwovens and used a meltblown elastomer to create a water-resistant barrier, protecting the ink even when the substrate broke and cracked. The meltblown structure is also microporous, and so it maintains the breathability of the fabric. Printing electronics onto paper substrates is currently more achievable, and PEL, a UK company, claims to be able to print chemically reactive and biologically active materials as well as conductive inks. Printing on a paper substrate means reel-to-reel processes can be used, and a single print can be kilometers long if required. PEL keeps track of the feasibility of printing the components necessary for a complete circuit with the aim of creating a complete "toolbox." Applications are typically graphics that can hide and reveal information or embed simple animation.

As printing technology advances, there are opportunities for creative development in printing on nonflat surfaces. Fergal Coulter's research includes exploratory development of processes for printing with materials, including carbon, on inflatable substrates. Proof-of-concept noncontact printing systems in industry show what is possible for printing onto safety equipment such as helmets.

In the textile studio, you will be able to explore other nonwoven structures using embellishers and Cornelli embroidery machines. These can be fun approaches to creating capacitive sensors and soft switches, but you should bear in mind that the structures are not robust and will shed fibers. This will create issues with short circuits and inconsistent readings, but you may be able to devise solutions for this.

2.33

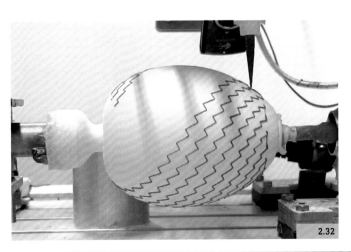

2.32

2.32
3D printing on inflated forms; the printed pattern will take on a different form once the substrate is deflated, meaning switch and sensor systems could be developed for forms that change shape in reaction to environmental conditions.
Fergal Coulter.

2.33
Exploration of nonwoven embellishing processes: Cornelli machine.

Case study:
Cute Circuit

Cute Circuit is a fashion brand and a pioneer in the field of wearable technology. Founded over a decade ago, Cute Circuit sparked the fashion and technology revolution through the introduction of groundbreaking designs and concepts that merge the worlds of fashion, design and telecommunication. http://cutecircuit.com/

Cute Circuit introduced internet-connected clothing and touch (haptic) telecommunication with products such as the HugShirt in 2002 (awarded by *Time* magazine as one of the Best Inventions of the Year in 2006). The Galaxy Dress introduced in 2008 (part of the permanent collection of the Museum of Science and Industry in Chicago) remains today the world's largest wearable luminous display. Social media–connected clothing such as the world's first haute couture Twitter Dress was introduced in 2012. Cute Circuit became the first fashion label to put wearable technology on the red carpet when Katy Perry wore a Cute Circuit evening gown to the MET Gala in 2010, a dress so stunning that it was featured on the cover of *Women's Wear Daily* and all the major newspapers worldwide the day after. The same year Cute Circuit introduced the first line of technologically advanced ready-to-wear in an exclusive collection for Selfridges in London. The latest collection presented on the schedule at New York Fashion Week introduces haute couture and ready-to-wear fashions that can be controlled via a smartphone app (Q by Cute Circuit) that allows wearers to change the color and functionality of their garments at the touch of a button.

All Cute Circuit garments are designed by Francesca Rosella and Ryan Genz. Rosella was a designer at an Italian haute couture house, when in 1998 she proposed to make an evening dress embroidered with electroluminescent thread that would light up in reaction to the wearer's movement. Nobody else wanted to experiment with something so new, but Rosella was really convinced that one day these kinds of interactive fashions would become the new normal. Finally Rosella resigned her position with these commercial ventures and received a research scholarship to join the Interaction Design Institute Ivrea (IDII) in northern Italy, the only interaction design research center in the world at the time. It was founded by Telecom Italia and Olivetti and drew faculty from such places as Stanford University and the Royal College of Art. At IDII she met Genz, who came from a design, arts and anthropology background and believed that interactions should not only be on

screen, using computers, but out in the real world through physical interfaces. Many people think that Genz is an engineer, seeing Cute Circuit's designs as very advanced pieces of wearable technology. Genz is actually a designer, but when Cute Circuit started, he became so frustrated with the hired engineers' attempts to design hard, square circuits that he decided to learn to design the circuits for the Cute Circuit garments himself. Since he has been doing this for more than ten years, as the saying goes, "practice makes perfect," and now Cute Circuit holds patents and patents pending for wearable technologies and innovative microtechnology designs.

2.34
Sketch for a dress worn by Katy Perry at the MET Gala. Francesca Rosella, Cute Circuit.

2.35
Galaxy Dress, the world's largest luminous wearable display, using more than 20,000 hand embroidered full color pixels. Four layers of chiffon diffuse the light. Cute Circuit.

Rosella and Genz started Cute Circuit as a fashion brand with the intention from day one to integrate smart materials and microtechnologies into clothing from a fashion perspective, designing with beautiful garments and emotional connection in mind. Ten years ago, the idea of "wearable technology" was still embryonic. Attempts in the field were called "wearable computing," and the only examples of it were literally wearable keyboards and goggles, strapped to the body, and designed with the intention of replicating a desktop computer, complete with wires and huge battery backpacks. Rosella and Genz saw an opportunity there to disrupt the "wearing-a-computer" metaphor and bring new magical powers to clothing instead, for the purpose of connecting humans with each other rather than connecting humans to their desktop machines. Many of the materials used in Cute Circuit garments today did not exist when the brand first started, so they had to invent some of them. Today there are conductive ribbons and fibers, micro-LEDs and processors, smartphones and tablets. All of these technological advances were not available ten years ago, so out of frustration with their inability to find anything remotely fashionable to make a garment as they wished it to be, they had to convince manufacturers that creating a special component or ribbon just for Cute Circuit was going to be a good future investment.

The first garment they designed was the HugShirt in 2002, the world's first haptic telecommunication device. The HugShirt is a T-shirt that allows the wearer to touch a loved one on the other side of the world through sensors embedded in the fabric, transmitting the hugs via a mobile phone app and re-creating the physical feeling of a hug through actuators on the other side of the world. The HugShirt was recognized as one of the Best Inventions of the Year by *Time* magazine in 2006, and it contributed to giving wearable technology a fashionable and human aspect that had been lacking until then. The new version of the HugShirt was launched during the Fall/Winter 2014/15 Fashion Week. The HugShirt was designed as a response to the challenge of creating something desirable, a product so emotionally engaging that it truly satisfies the need of a user. During this challenge, Rosella and Genz interviewed hundreds of people and asked them what they truly desired and the answer was "a hug"—the feeling of closeness and well-being that can only be conveyed through touch between friends and loved ones. Through further research they found out that a human needs at least fifty touches per day in order to avoid depression, and that if children are not hugged by their parents while growing up they might become socially awkward as adults. The response to the product was amazing; each

person who tried it could see behind the simplicity of the hug as a gesture and could truly understand the feeling of human connectedness that this kind of interface creates, its deeper meaning, and its potential applications in fields such as rehabilitation and patient care. The HugShirt has become one of the most copied projects in the world; at least one student in any major university has tried replicating it.

Over the years, Cute Circuit has designed many groundbreaking and iconic garments such as the world's largest wearable luminous display, the Galaxy Dress (a dress embroidered with 24,000 micro-LEDs that continuously changes color), the MDress (a wearable mobile phone dress), Katy Perry's MET Gala evening gown, and the world's first haute couture Twitter Dress for Nicole Scherzinger.

2.36
HugShirt 5; the system uses textile sensors and Bluetooth Java to communicate the strength of the hug, skin warmth, and heart rate of the sender, much like an SMS message. Cute Circuit.

2.36

Cute Circuit's Fall/Winter 14/15 Collection, presented on February 12, 2014, was the first-ever completely interactive fashion collection presented on the schedule at New York Fashion Week. The show featured fashions that include advanced wearable technology, seamlessly integrated in beautiful ready to wear. The Bluetooth low-energy–enabled dresses and accessories allowed the models to control what their dresses would look like on the runway, via the dedicated Q by Cute Circuit app, in real time. This was a genuine first in fashion's history. With the Q smartphone app, the wearer can change the color of her iMiniSkirt at any time because the garments are made of Magic Fabric, a special fabric covered in thousands of micro-LEDs, designed and developed by Cute Circuit. Magic Fabric is perfectly smooth and comfortable like other fashion fabrics, but also seems magical, as it can change color, play video (at 25 frames per second), and connect to the internet and social media to display tweets in real time. The new Q software will also allow users to experience how digital fashion integrates into daily life by downloading new patterns to their garments in real time.

Cute Circuit's current product line includes three separate collections: Cute Circuit Haute Couture for the red carpet, Cute Circuit Special Projects for stage performance and special events, and Cute Circuit Ready to Wear. The manufacturing methods Cute Circuit uses in creating these garments are clean and carefully chosen, respecting the environment and the wearers because a beautiful product should be beautiful inside and out. The technology used in the garments is 100 percent RoHS compliant; this means that no hazardous substances are present in the products and that they are free from lead and mercury and are safe to wear. The textiles used are also Oeko Tex certified; this means that they have been tested for safety and manufactured without harmful materials. This integration of fashion and technology in an ethical and clean way is not an easy or quick thing to do, and everything begins with a challenge. One of the first collections included the Twirkle dress and T-shirts that light up and change color in reaction to the wearer's movement. For this T-shirt series Cute Circuit developed a now-patented construction method that allows for garments with embedded microelectronics to be washed in a washing machine. After two years of wash tests and experimentation the collection was ready for the market and continues to be sold today.

2.39

2.37

2.38

2.37
Mini skirts from the Fall/Winter 14/15 Collection, New York Fashion Week. The patterns on the skirts can be controlled from a smartphone app, and custom designed fabric-mounted flat LEDs allow the garments to remain flexible and comfortable. Cute Circuit.

2.38
Garment care instructions; different approaches to embedding electronics mean companies will need to provide detailed care instructions. Cute Circuit.

2.39
Twirkle Top; these can be machine washed without removing the electronics. Cute Circuit.

Chapter summary

This chapter introduced some of the other design approaches taken to developing smart textiles in context, including user-centered design and interaction design. It contrasted the studio textiles approach with industrial practice and discussed smart yarn production techniques and composite and nonwoven structures for smart textile innovation. The case study demonstrated how studio practice can have relevance to industrial innovation, and how craft knowledge remains extremely valuable.

Suggested reading

Anna Persson: http://smarttextiles.se/en/textile-interaction-design-explores-new-expressions/

Edwards, C., ed. (2015), *Encyclopaedia of Design*, London: Bloomsbury Academic.

Elkins, J. (2014), *Artists with PhDs: On the New Doctoral Degree in Studio Art*, Washington, DC: New Academia Publishing.

Gale, C. and J. Kaur (2002), *The Textile Book*, Oxford: Berg.

Kettley, S. (2011), "Technical Textiles," in A. Briggs-Goode and K. Townsend (eds.), *Textile Design: Principles, Advances and Applications*, Cambridge, UK: Woodhead Publishing Ltd.

Kirstein, T., ed. (2013), *Multidisciplinary Know-How for Smart-Textile Developers* (Woodhead Publishing Series in Textiles), Cambridge, UK: Woodhead Publishing Ltd.

Moggridge, B. (2007), *Designing Interactions*, Cambridge, MA: MIT Press.

Nicholas, P. (2014), *Designing Material—Materialising Design, Cambridge*, ON: Riverside Architectural Press.

Orth, M., (2009), On the Short Life of Color-Change Textiles. Available online: http://www.maggieorth.com/art_100EAYears.html (accessed 5 February 2015).

Ramsgaard Thomsen, M. and K. Bech (2012), *Textile Logic for a Soft Space*, The Royal Danish Academy of Fine Arts. Available online: http://issuu.com/cita_copenhagen/docs/textile_logic_for_a_soft_space_-_sm (accessed 5 December 2014).

Sara Keith: http://www.sarakeith.com/Home.html

Stickdorn, M. and J. Sneider (2014), *This Is Service Design Thinking*, Amsterdam: BIS Publishers.

Usability.gov (2014), "Personas." Available online: http://www.usability.gov/how-to-and-tools/methods/personas.html (accessed 7 April 2015).

Veiteberg, J. (2005), *Craft in Transition*, trans. Douglas Ferguson, Bergen, Norway: Bergen National Academy of the Arts.

Doctoral programs in smart textiles may be found through:

http://www.findaphd.com/

http://www.jobs.ac.uk/

Design with smart textiles

Our possibly utopian hope is that e-textile design can, over time, become a means through which hobbyists, craftspeople . . . and children can become technologically fluent—and can express themselves creatively.

Buechley and Eisenberg 2008: 200

CHAPTER OVERVIEW

This chapter will introduce textile designers to basic electronics principles, off-the-shelf components useful for prototyping interaction concepts, and some introductory textile component construction. It includes tips for working with different types of conductive yarns by hand and introduces the microprocessor. If you are unsure of technical terms, a glossary can be found in in the appendix; any words in *italics* are explained briefly there.

Three projects with step-by-step instructions are included in the chapter. They are intended to keep some things simple, so that you can focus on making:

- A parallel circuit to indicate turning when cycling
- A parallel circuit that you can hug when you're a bit stressed
- A textile sensor that tells you when your bag is overloaded

Some of these objects are slightly ambiguous, while others are more recognizable as things that already exist in our lives. You will make most of them from scratch so that you get to think about how the structure of your future textile designs might need to be altered to support hardware and manage electronic connections and insulation.

Depending on how you learn best, you may need to practice some of the skills exercises before tackling these projects; Chapter 4 is full of inspiration for you to then develop your own smart textile practice informed by the different roles yarns and fabrics can play in a circuit.

In many ways this information is no longer hard to find as the maker and hacker communities share techniques and projects online. This chapter will be useful in its focus on the textiles at the center of the process, and it leads into more integrated approaches in chapter 4. Here you can get started using off-the-shelf fabrics, yarns and haberdashery to create smart textile systems. There are exercises that will take you through some skills step by step; other projects are available online at: aninternetofsoftthings.com/categories/make/. These projects were developed for workshops by Sarah Walker and Martha Glazzard (who also designed the diagrams) as part of the research project *An Internet of Soft Things*.

Many familiar processes and fastenings can be used, combined with standard electronic components to build functional and expressive garments, soft products and interior concepts. You will learn where to source tools and materials, how to work with different conductive fabrics and yarns (and how to insulate them using textiles), the basics of circuit designing with textiles, when you should consider using a microprocessor, how to code a simple project, and where to find support for more complex ones. You will make your first soft textile switch to turn on a light, learn about using textiles for "sliders," and explore textile possibilities for creating sensors. We will discuss different kinds of output, such as sound and movement, before you build a more complex project that brings together your new skills in craft, circuitry and coding.

Figures 3.1 and 3.2 are two examples of courses and open source learning material, developed by two of the major leaders in the field, Leah Buechley, when she was at the Massachusetts Institute of Technology (MIT), and the design research collective Kobakant (Mika Satomi and Hannah Perner-Wilson).

EXAMPLE PROJECTS	SENSORS
WORKSHOPS	3D PRINTED SENSORS
ACTUATORS	CIRCULAR KNIT INFLATION SENSOR
CONNECTIONS	CIRCULAR KNIT STRETCH SENSORS
POWER	CONDUCTIVE POMPOM
SENSORS	CONSTRUCTED STRETCH SENSORS
TRACES	CROCHET BUTTON
CIRCUITS AND CODE	CROCHET CONDUCTIVE BEAD
WIRELESS	CROCHET FINGER SENSOR
CONDUCTIVE	CROCHET PRESSURE SENSOR
MATERIALS	CROCHET TILT POTENTIOMETER
NON-CONDUCTIVE	CROCHET/KNIT PRESSURE
MATERIALS	SENSORS
TOOLS	CROCHET/KNIT SQUEEZE SENSORS
	EMBROIDERED POTENTIOMETERS
	FABRIC BUTTON
	FABRIC POTENTIOMETER
	FABRIC STRETCH SENSORS
	FELTED CROCHET PRESSURE
	SENSOR

Sensors
CROCHET/KNIT SQUEEZE SENSORS

This squeeze sensor can be made by knitting or crocheting a ball including resistive yarn. The ball can then be stuffed with different materials to achieve different kinds of squishiness. The ball can also be hand or machine felted, giving the surface a more uniform appearance.

Crochet

This example was crochet from regular pink yarn and stuffed with a spool-knit tube of Nm3/10 conductive yarn. Either end of the spool knit conductive yarn protrudes out from the crochet ball at opposite ends.

How to crochet a ball >> http://www.instructables.com/id/How-to-crochet-a-ball-or-a-hackey-sack/?ALLSTEPS
How to felt a knitted piece in the washing machine >> http://www.instructables.com/id/How-to-felt-a-knitted-piece/
How to felt scraps with dish washing soap in the sink >> http://www.instructables.com/id/Felt-Balls-from-Scrap-Yarn/

3.1

Assignments and Final Project

COURSE HOME

SYLLABUS

READINGS, LECTURES & TUTORIALS

□ ASSIGNMENTS AND FINAL PROJECT

ASSIGNMENT 1: SOFT CIRCUIT

ASSIGNMENT 2: "HELLO WORLD" FABRIC PCBS, PART 1

ASSIGNMENT 3: "HELLO WORLD" FABRIC PCBS, PART 2

ASSIGNMENT 4: YARN

ASSIGNMENT 5: NONWOVEN

ASSIGNMENT 6: NETWORKED WEARABLE

ASSIGNMENT 7: FINAL PROJECT PROPOSAL

ASSIGNMENT 8: KNIT, WOVEN, EMBROIDERY, OR PRINT

ASSIGNMENT 9: FINAL PROJECT

RELATED RESOURCES

DOWNLOAD COURSE MATERIALS

ASSIGNMENTS	SUMMARY	DETAILS AND SAMPLE STUDENT WORK
1. Soft Circuit	Construct an interactive circuit out of soft materials.	Details and sample student work
2. "Hello World" Fabric PCBs, part 1	Install the appropropriate AVR microcontroller toolkit your laptop.	Details
3. "Hello World" Fabric PCBs, part 2	Work in teams to create an artifact that includes a fabric PCB.	Details and sample student work
4. Yarn	Make a yarn that consists of two or more different materials.	Details and sample student work
5. Nonwoven	Make a piece of flexible nonwoven fabric at least 12"x12" with some noteworthy characteristic.	Details and sample student work
6. Networked wearable	Work in teams, in collaboration with the *Communicating with Mobile Technology* class, to build a textile that talks to a mobile phone.	Details and sample student work
7. Final project proposal	Short (5 minute) presentation for the class, plus a brief online description.	Details and sample student work
8. Knit, weave, embroider or print	Knit, weave, embroider or print a novel textile.	Details and sample student work
9. Final project	Ten-minute presentation and complete written documentation about the final project.	Details and sample student work

3.2

3.1
How To Get What You Want; an excellent source of e-textile techniques and inspiration. Kobakant website.

3.2
New Textiles course overview. Courses change, so keep checking for up-to-date information. MITOpenCourseware.

SMART TEXTILE PRODUCTS, FABRICS AND YARNS

In this section you will sew your first fabric circuit. You will learn about the range of yarns and fabrics you can use as you become more confident in exploring and testing materials for your own projects. This section also includes some basic tips for working with conductive yarns and fabrics and a list of the basic tools you will find useful.

Conductive yarns come in different guises. A popular starting point until recently was Lamé Lifesaver's steel-spun yarn (ten yards for ten Canadian dollars), repackaged from Bekaert, and originally sold to the fencing community for, you guessed it, the repair of worn lamé fencing gear. Now it has become easier to purchase nonindustrial quantities of conductive yarns, and you can find a list of suppliers in the appendix.

Very useful comparisons of different yarns have been published by Mika Satomi and Hannah Perner-Wilson, and you should keep your own technical notebooks of how well different yarns behave when hand sewing, when used in a domestic machine, and when transferring to semi-industrial methods. Keep notes on metal content; these yarns are conductive because they have a metal fiber twist or coating. They may use copper, steel, silver or gold, for

example, and all have different behaviors in different textile processes. Check the ply and construction details, too—if the conductive fiber is held within an insulating braid, your construction techniques for connecting will need to change.

When selecting yarns, be aware that copper oxidizes quickly. This means it forms a layer on its surface, which not only discolors it, but degrades electrical connections. Silver is known for its hypoallergenic and antimicrobial properties, making it popular in medical and well-being products. All metal becomes work hardened in production, so the manufacture of very long lengths of fiber is a technical challenge. When you work with it, the metal becomes springier. In metalworking techniques, this would be relaxed again through annealing—heating and quenching—but this is obviously an issue for textiles (heating would burn the textile fibers), and where the differing tension between the materials has a cumulative effect, it can cause bunching and knotting.

Because of this mix of fibers in conductive yarns (metals will often be mixed with cotton or polyester), fraying is a common issue. The quality of your crafting will be determined by how well you finish your work and protect the yarns from wear (see the practical exercises later in this section). You need to avoid migrating metal fibers in your work—at best they will change the values in a circuit, giving unexpected behavior, but at worst they will create short circuits, stopping the circuit from working altogether and creating a potential fire hazard.

Table 1. Design of Conductive Yarns

	Verstraeten	Dhawan	Cottet	Post	Watson
Conductive Part (# of Strand)	Copper (1)	Copper (28)	Copper (1)	Steel (spun 20%)	Steel (4)
	d=148 μm	d=70 μm	d=40 μm	Not Known	d=35 μm
Non-conductive Part (# of Strand)	Steel (3)	-	Polyester	Polyester (80%)	Polyester (1)
	d=12 μm ×275		150.3 denier	4.5 denier	600 denier
Structure (Location of conductive material is described in darker colors)					
Twist Density (tpm)	Z100	Not Known	Not Known	Not Known	S350 & Z350
Resistance (Ω/m)	1.2	0.2441	15.7 – 17.2	~5,000	180

References
1. Verstraeten, S., J. Pavlinec, and P. Speleers, "Electrically Conductive Yarn Comprising Metal Fibers" U.S. Patent No. 6,957,525 (2005), assigned to N.V. Bekaert S.A.
2. Dhawan, A., T.K. Ghosh, and A.M. Seyam, "Fiber-based Electrical and Optical Devices and Systems" Textile Progress monograrph series, Manchester: The Textile Institute, 2004.
3. Cottet, D., et al., "Electrical characterization of textile transmission lines". IEEE Transactions on Advanced Packaging 26 (2), 2003: 182-190.
4. Post, R., et al., "E-broidery: Design and Fabrication of Textile-based Computing" IBM Systems Journal, 39 (3/4) 2000: 840-860.
5. Watson, D.L., "Electrically Conductive Yarn" U.S. Patent No. 5,927,060 (1999), assigned to N.V. Bekaert S.A.

3.3
Conductive yarn structures; different twist structures and metal content mean different mechanical and electrical properties. Textile World.

3.3

3.4
Two-ply and four-ply
conductive yarns; try
working with different
yarns—two-ply can be
easier to work with, but
four-ply often has a lower
resistance.

3.4

3.5

When selecting yarns for projects, you should consider their electromechanical properties—that is, both their handle and feel, and their electrical characteristics. Yarns are available with different levels of resistance depending on what you want to achieve with them. If you want to simply replace wires in a circuit with flexible threads, you need a yarn with very low resistance; if you want to create heat, you will need a higher level of resistance.

Be aware of "metallic" yarns that are actually plasticized, as they will not conduct at all. See How-to: Using a multimeter in the next section to test materials for *continuity*. You will also find elastic conductive yarns, although these are more rare. Check whether they change their *impedance* (*resistance* value) when stretched or whether they stay the same. If they change their impedance when stretched, they should be treated as a *variable resistor* in your circuit, and the values can be useful for measuring changes in length or pressure. If they deliver the same current when stretched, they can be useful as traces in products that come under a lot of strain, such as clothes. Check how well your yarns recover their original length and resistance value after stretching, too—this can have a big impact on the reliability of a system. If you are designing for a critical application where repeatability is very important, as in medical devices, these behaviors need to be managed through programming.

The color of conductive yarns is largely determined by their metal content, but it is possible to dye some of the fibers they are mixed with without affecting their electrical properties. An alternative approach is to treat the yarn as a metal and follow recipes for metal coloring as in Hughes and Rowe (1991). In this case you will need to be aware of the action of certain chemicals on the textile fibers. Lynn Tandler is a specialist in this technique, and you can find her work in chapter 4.

3.5
Dying conductive yarns:
the non-metal fibers of
a conductive yarn can
be dyed—here showing
polyester and cotton
mixes. Kobakant.

Basic Tool Kit

Sewing	Electronics	Other useful crafts	Set up and health and safety considerations
— Yarns (range of conductive and nonconductive)	— Starter kits from Oomlaut, Kitronik, etc.	— Jewelry tools, such as good round-nosed pliers, end cutters	— Steady work surface
— Fabrics (range of conductive and nonconductive)	— Soldering iron, holder and sponge (instructables author Jseay recommends the Hakko 888)	— Jewelry findings, such as head and eye pins, jump rings	— Good light
— Mesh fabrics (range of hole sizes)	— Solder	— Nonslip materials such as cut-up bath mats, silicon gels, and latex	— Water supply nearby
— Interfacings	— Multimeter	— Various tapes and glues	— First aid kit
— Needles	— Wire stripper	— Sandpapers and sticks for fine work	— Firebricks, wooden board or solid card for soldering
— Embroidery hoops (medium—large)	— Batteries—1.5 to 3 V	— Rotary tool with selection of attachments	— Helping hands
— Domestic sewing machine—with spools, selection of presser feet	— Battery holders and snap packs	— Heat gun	— Goggles
— Set square	— Selection of resistors	— Glue gun	— Mask
— Meter rule	— Selection of LEDs		— Ventilation
— Tape measure	— Alligator clip wires		— Smoke detector
— Pins	— Heat shrink tubing		— Fire extinguisher
— Unpicker	— Other components such as photoresistors, flex sensors, potentiometers and capacitors (often found in starter kits and "grab bags")		— Separated areas for storage of textiles, electronics and other craft materials
— Pattern cutting paper			
— Thin card			
— Embroidery scissors			
— Fabric shears			
— Fastenings—hooks and eyes, zips, snaps, Velcro, etc.			

Basic skills: Working with conductive yarns and fabrics

Threading a needle with conductive yarn
- Have different needle sizes on hand for working with different yarns and fixings (holes in snaps can be small, but threading conductive yarn can be tricky).
  - Needles are available for different purposes such as beading (very fine and long), general craft (heavier, larger eye), and upholstery (very large, sometimes curved).

- Use a needle threader.
  - If you do not have one, use a strong piece of cotton or a very fine wire doubled over to pull the conductive yarn through the eye of the needle. Use pliers to hold the wire to do this—it is easy to cut yourself.

- Cut the end of the yarn at an angle to minimize fraying.
  - You can also dampen it with wet fingers. DO NOT lick metal materials—heavy metal poisoning and stray fibers are not good for you.
  - Some people also use nail lacquer to fix the ends.

Tying knots and securing ends
This can be problematic and takes a bit of practice, but these skills are crucial to your functioning circuit and will make your projects more professionally finished. There are many ways of achieving a secure finish—try these and develop your own.

- Always leave 2 to 3 centimeters of yarn at the end of a sewn line.
  - This means you will have enough to work with when securing ends later. If you leave your ends too short, any fraying can be enough to undo all your good work before you finish. Just be careful not to tangle these ends in the work as you carry on.

- Use a slipknot to start (a knot with a loop, which disappears when you pull both ends).
  - With your needle threaded and a slipknot formed at the end of the longer length of yarn, bring the needle gently through the fabric from the back to the front, being careful not to destroy the knot. When you take the needle back down through the fabric, pass it through the loop in the slipknot. Gently tighten the knot around your yarn before continuing with your stitched line.

- Use iron-on interfacing fabric to secure all loose ends.
  - Interfacings are nonwoven fabrics used to stiffen, attach or protect areas of textile work. For this job, you will need the iron-on kind, with a fine coating of glue on one side. Test your interfacing with your iron on a low heat setting on scraps first—it is easy to melt the lighter-weight fabrics if your iron is too hot. A mini craft iron is very useful for small areas.

Other approaches to try: silicon skin; two-part epoxy glue; fabric puffy paints; brush-on electrical insulation; heat shrink tubing; textile techniques such as couching.

3.6a
Interfacing fabrics
are used in garment
construction to add
strength or stiffness.
They come in a range
of weights and can be
stitched or ironed to the
base fabric.

3.6b

3.6b
Heat shrink tubing is
made of thermoplastic
materials and can be
found in a range of sizes
and colors. It can be
used to protect wires
from abrasion, to prevent
contact with other metal
parts, or to hold parts
together.

3.6c

3.6c
Embroidered couching.
Leah Buechley.

Using conductive yarns in a domestic sewing machine

Because of the twist, tension and thickness of most conductive yarn, it tends not to work well in the needle of a domestic sewing machine. Fill your spool with it, and check tension and stitch length on scraps of fabric before starting work. Keep a log of the settings that work best for future reference.

Sewing jerseys and stretch fabrics

Use a zig-zag stitch that will stretch with the fabric if your yarn is nonelastic (a straight running stitch will break or will not allow the fabric to stretch). Be aware that this changes the length of your stitched conductive path and therefore the values in your circuit.

Use a conductive jersey fabric in place of a stitched line. Conductive jersey is quite expensive but is very versatile in this situation. Cut a thin strip and bond with fabric glue or tack in place with a (conductive or nonconductive) yarn. This is often used in commercial applications.

3.7
Conductive stretch jersey is very flexible and useful for connections in garments where there is repeated movement or stretch. It can be a good choice for longer fabric connections or for maintaining low resistance.

3.7

Exercise Four:
First sewn circuit

Let us get started and make something that works. This exercise introduces you to the design of a very simple circuit and allows you to practice your crafting skills. You will integrate a battery in a sewn circuit with a resistor to light up a single LED.

You will need:
- Embroidery hoop
- Woven fabric
  - A lightweight embroidery fabric; cotton or wool works well.
  - Make sure it is at least a centimeter larger than the hoop all the way around.
- Coin cell battery and holder (3 V)
- Sewable LED with resistor
- Conductive yarn
- Needle and threader
- Embroidery scissors
- Pencil for marking fabric

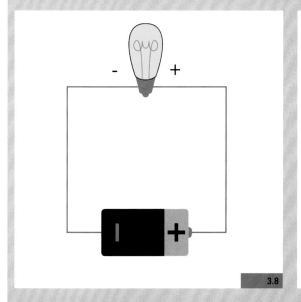

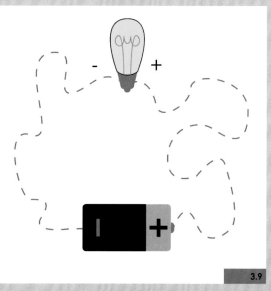

3.8
Circuit plan (orthogonal); diagrams are often simplified using straight lines. Martha Glazzard.

3.9
Circuit plan (decorative stitched). This is the same electrical circuit, but the meandering line breaks with schematic conventions. You can stitch any outline shape with your conductive thread to make this connection.
Martha Glazzard.

How-to:

1. Depending on which kind you have, the embroidery hoop has a screw or a tension clasp to take the two rings apart. Cut a piece of fabric a few centimeters larger than the hoop all the way around, and insert it between the rings. Gently pull the fabric around the outside of the hoop to get an even tension.

2. Use a pencil to mark on the fabric where you will place each component: the battery holder and a sewable LED (with resistor on board). Mark the positive and negative terminals of each component so that positive will be connected to positive and negative will be connected to negative.

3. A coin cell battery holder has four holes. Use conductive yarn to stich from the positive hole to the positive connection of the LED board. Tie off the thread here with a knot and snip the end to about 1 centimeter.

4. Using conductive yarn, stitch from the negative battery hole to the negative connector of the LED board, again tying off neatly.

5. Test the circuit by touching a coin cell battery to the holder (make sure it is the right way up).

6. Use normal cotton to stitch down the other two corners of the battery holder.

3.10

Other how-tos online

Open circuits: using pop studs and applique.
http://aninternetofsoftthings.com/categories/make/

3.10
An example of a finished basic circuit, as described by both circuit plans.

SOURCING CONDUCTIVE FABRICS

This section continues with an overview of the smart and conductive fabrics available to buy. You will find out about the different ways conductive fabrics are structured, how to select appropriate fabrics for different parts of your projects, how much of these fabrics you might need to achieve your design goals and how to get the best out of them. You will learn how to use a multimeter to test for continuity and resistance in different fabrics.

There is a tension in the textile designer's approach to using conductive fabric. You want to learn through playful experimentation—you need to make mistakes to learn—but you also want to be careful with expensive and hard-to-find materials. Materials for design can be thought of in terms of dots (powders, inks), lines (fibers, wires) and surfaces (two-dimensional planes like paper, fabric), and smart materials are available to varying extents in these forms as the relationship between material science and market demand shifts and changes. There is a problem here in that it can be hard to find samples of active smart fabrics, because by definition they include already designed circuitry, which cannot be supplied by the yard or meter. We cannot collect sample swatches of complex textile functionality without having to make them ourselves. Some researchers have started to address this problem by creating libraries, like the one at the Swedish School of Textiles in Borås, for visiting industry and academic research teams, or by exploring swatch book formats demonstrated at conferences (see Zeagler et al. [2013]).

So it is hard for designers who are used to handling fabrics to approach this area of design because their expectations need to be adjusted—there is a wide range of conductive fabrics out there, but it has a long way to go before it matches the nuances of handle, drape, texture and color available in the wider textile field. Having said that, some companies are now able to provide you with sample size squares (often large enough for complete projects) of a range of fabrics using different metals, textile yarns, structures and finishes. See Suggested Reading at the end of this chapter and Suppliers in the appendix.

3.11

3.11
Order a conductive textiles sample pack to feel the surface textures, weight, and handle of the different fabrics; you should receive data sheets with them too. Mindsets.

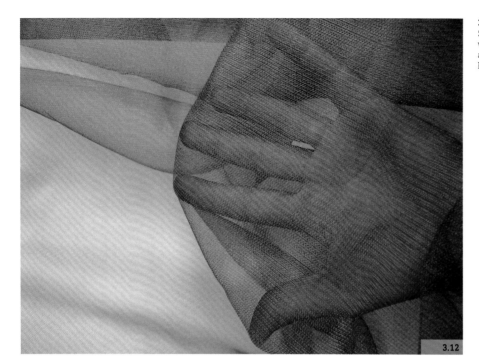

3.12
Stainless steel fabric,
with metal warp
and weft.
Plugandwear.

3.12

Conductive fabrics are often woven, but of course they may be knitted, laminated or impregnated with other materials to make them conductive. Bekaert produces a rib stitch knitted fabric made with *plated* spun steel yarns and polyester; LessEMF makes a surface-treated copper on polyester fabric; and figure 3.12 shows Plugandwear's woven stainless steel fabric with no other textile component (the steel is used as both warp and weft), while figure 3.13 shows its double-faced knit that is conductive on one face but not the other.

To give you an example of prices, and the kinds of technical information you can expect to find when looking for these, consider the double-faced knit fabric with a woven face by Plugandwear. This is an unusual fabric in that it combines structures, is 1.5 millimeters thick and is unstretchable but very flexible. It can be cut with scissors and used in standard sewing machines. The data sheet gives resistance in ohms both vertically (warp or wales) and horizontally (weft or courses). The resistance across is very low at 1.5 ohms per square meter, meaning current can be carried easily along the horizontal. It is sold by the linear meter (1.094 yards) at 43 Euros plus 22 percent VAT. See Suggested Reading for a link to step-by-step tutorials using this, such as making a shaped analog sensor.

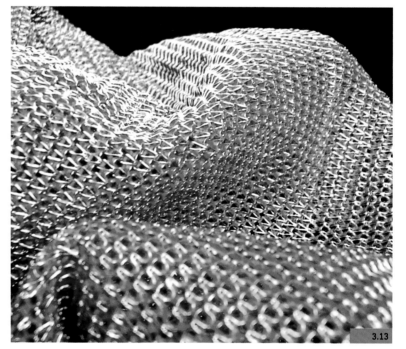

3.13

3.13
Double-faced conductive
knit fabric, with different
electrical characteristics
on the front and back.
Plugandwear.

Be aware of the fundamental difference between knitted and woven textiles—even manufacturers sometimes mix these terms up, but they refer to very different structures and properties. Woven fabrics are not stretchy, while knitted ones are—you could not pull a woven T-shirt over your head. In manufacturing terms they are also very different. A knit structure typically uses one long, single yarn worked in a series of interlocking stitches, while weaving requires a loom to be set up with a series of many *vertical* warp threads, through which the *weft* threads can be passed. Loom setup is time consuming, and once in place, the same warp threads will be used for multiple fabrics.

These differences mean that conductive fabrics will behave differently and will require some different techniques to get the most out of them. For example, it is quite easy to find conductive taffeta in a wide range of colors in high street fabric shops (it is unlikely that the assistant will be aware that the fabric is conductive—take your multimeter with you to test them). But this attractive and accessible textile is conductive in one direction and not the other. If you come across this and need to ensure continuity in all directions for your project, you can easily create a dual fabric—see exercise six in this chapter.

You would normally not expect to build a circuit on top of a conductive fabric because it would simultaneously connect all components, and the current would not be directed in a way that a circuit would be created. These kinds of fabric are useful instead for making switches and sensors, or they can be used instead of stitched lines to create connections in a circuit. See the following sections for exercises in making your own.

Having said this, Plugandwear has devised a quite unique approach to using its conductive double-faced knit as a perfboard. Perfboards are usually made of a resin or epoxy composite, and they are used to build circuits with components soldered onto them. In fact, their knit is more similar to a *stripboard* or solderless *breadboard* in that the horizontal courses of conductive yarn are a continuous connection, rather than a series of isolated holes waiting to be connected with solder— see the link in Suggested Reading for more details.

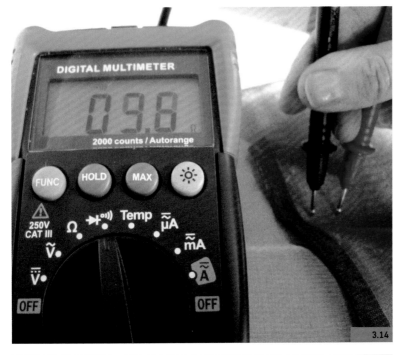

3.14
Multimeter readings showing continuity, meaning there is a flow of current through the material.

Design with smart textiles

Because this knit structure does not fray, you can cut the connecting conductive courses at the back of your electrical components, so the current flows through them and not around them to create a circuit. See the Plugandwear site for their own tutorial. If you are skeptical of this and the possibility of conductive rows touching each other (why would you want a flexible substrate otherwise?), there is a very useful tutorial by Jseay (see Suggested Reading). Because she is using fine bus wire to knit with, the floats can indeed be cut without fraying, and she also discusses how far apart the conductive courses should be, bearing in mind the size of components you want to attach, and the likely use of the finished piece. The two examples also differ in how they attach components. Jseay is soldering to her bus wire, while Plugandwear advocates stitching the leads of components in place with conductive yarn by hand.

Other textile materials can also be explored, such as foams and extruded silicones, while some makers are developing their own approaches to creating metal fabrics, such as Lynn Tandler, who sees her process as *forging* as much as weaving (see the chapter 4 for a short case study).

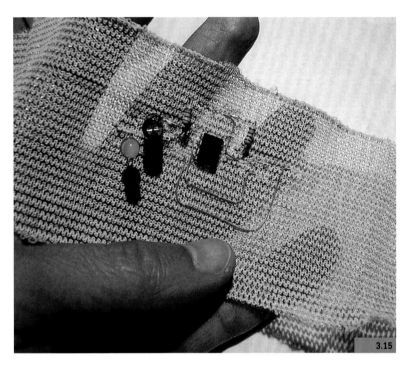

3.15

3.16

3.15
Fabric perfboard; designed for components to be attached to create a circuit. Plugandwear.

3.16
Knitted perfboard; the structure of this knit is such that it can be cut without fraying. Jseay: Jesse Seay.

KEY QUESTION

If you have stitched an LED to a conductive fabric, explain why your circuit will not work. How would you remedy this problem?

Using a multimeter

Limor "Ladyada" Fried publishes many tutorials online through "Adafruit," which can supply you with good soldering irons and other equipment, as well as tutorials (see Suggested Reading). This book aims to make the starting points easy to find for you, but there is a wealth of material online if you want to sift through it and find your level. Adafruit does include beginners' videos and instructions in everything from threading a needle and using an embroidery hoop to the more advanced skills like building your own computer with Raspberry Pi.

Using a multimeter to test continuity

Here you will learn how to use a beeping device to determine if that metallic-looking fabric is really metal or not—is it going to be good for your project? This is a multimeter; it does far more than give you a yes/no answer to the preceding question, but this is a great place to start. A multimeter is a very useful device, and like everything else, a good choice makes all the difference. Your main concerns are likely to be continuity (is it electrically connected?) and resistance (measured in ohms).

When buying one, these are likely to be the main things you want:
- Continuity testing with piezo buzzer
- Resistance test down to 10 ohms (or lower) and up to 1 megaohm (or higher)
- DC voltage test down to 100 mV (or lower) and up to 50 V
- AC voltage test down to 1 V and up to 400 V (or 200 V in the US/Canada/Japan)
- Diode testing

It is also useful to be able to replace the batteries easily, so look for one that uses AAs rather than coin cells. You will probably also appreciate a stand to keep it upright on your table as you work.

- Find a meter that has a symbol like soundwaves, like those shown in figure 3.17. This means it will be able to give you a small beep alert when you touch the two probes to electrically connected points.
- To find out if a fabric is conductive, turn the dial on the meter to this setting (you may need to select the mode by pressing a button if the setting has more than one function), and touch the two probes to the fabric in question.
- If nothing happens, check the probes against each other—they will create a circuit and a beep to show continuity. Try the fabric along both the warp and weft (vertical and horizontal yarns) in case it is conductive in only one direction.

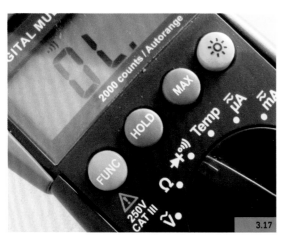

3.17
Continuity with a multimeter; the three lines that look like soundwaves mean the device has a continuity setting (not all do). When a current is flowing, the device will beep.

Design with smart textiles

Exercise Five:
Using a multimeter to test
continuity and resistance

Resistance means how much a material fights the flow of current, and it is measured in ohms. Your multimeter will tell you how resistant a yarn or fabric is between two points; this is useful when comparing materials. If you want to effectively replace a stiff wire with a flexible yarn, you need a material with very low resistance. If you want to protect an LED by creating resistance in the circuit, you need to know how resistant your yarn is; if you want to work with heat (the energy given off due to resistance), you will need a material with high impedance.

- Select your yarns and lay them on a surface so that you will measure the same length each time.
- Switch the multimeter on and select a high range in ohms.
- Hold the probes to the material 10 centimeters apart.
- If you get OL or 1 as a reading, select a lower range.
- If you get OL or 1 as a reading on the lowest range setting, your material may not be conductive at all—test it with the continuity setting, too.

In figures 3.18 and 3.19, Becky Stern is demonstrating the difference in resistance between similar lengths of two-ply and three-ply steel yarn. Both have low resistivity: the two-ply is sold by Adafruit as having 16 ohms per foot, and the three-ply as 10 ohms per foot.

3.18
Finding resistance of yarns—two-ply; the resistance is shown in ohms on the multimeter. The lower the value, the more conductive the yarn is. Adafruit.

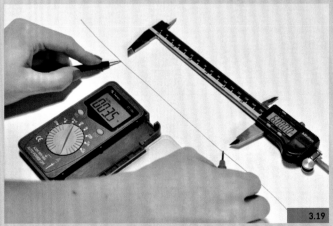

3.19
Finding resistance of yarns—three-ply; more metal fibers in the ply will mean a lower resistance value over the same length. Adafruit.

Normally the resistance setting on a multimeter would be used to find the value of a resistor (see the next section to learn about resistance as part of a circuit). Resistors are color coded with their values ranging from single ohms through kilohms to megohms. However, if you are not confident reading these, it is also useful to know how to use the multimeter to find their value.

- Resistance is not direction dependent—it does not matter which way you use the multimeter probes.
- Do not test resistors already in a circuit—you will not get a true reading.
- Select the highest range on the multimeter first—if it reads OL, or 1, then you need to select a different range. This will usually happen if you are on a range that is too low.

- Touch a probe to each lead of the resistor.
- If you were expecting a 1 kilohm reading and get 0.988, this is because no resistor will be perfect—they come with an indication of tolerance to plus or minus 5 percent; your resistor in this case measures 0.988 kilohm and can be used as a 1 kilohm.

See Suggested Reading at the end of this chapter for a list of links to excellent tutorials and explanations online.

Exercise Six
Creating reliable continuity with conductive taffeta

So you have found a local fabric shop with some conductive taffeta. Here is how to make sure you get reliable continuity across the whole fabric (this would be used in making a soft switch, for example—see later sections in this chapter for more details).

- Take two squares of taffeta the same size.
- Using the multimeter to test continuity, find out which direction the conductive fibers are running in.
- Place one piece of taffeta on top of the other so that the conductive fibers in one are running vertically, and in the other, running horizontally.
- Stitch the two pieces together to create contact between the conductive fibers.
- You can use nonconductive or conductive thread to do this—the number of stitch lines and how close they are to each other will also affect your results.
- You can measure resistance between two points to compare different samples if you try making a few.

You may want to finish the edges with petersham or another woven tape to stop fraying.

3.20

3.20
Taffeta with directional conductivity. Two faces have been stitched together orthogonally (at right angles) to make sure there is electrical contact in both directions.

KEY QUESTION

How might you use the continuity setting on a multimeter to check problems in a stitched circuit?

THE TEXTILE AS PART OF A SYSTEM

This section covers more about the system as a whole, including the relationship between voltage, resistance and current (Ohm's law), the basic principles of input and output (I/O), and working safely with power and textiles. You will practice making electrically sound connections between soft textiles and hard components, and you will extend your understanding of the circuit by making an in-series and a parallel version of the same design with multiple LEDs.

Conductive threads and fabrics will only form part of your larger system. You will need to work with hardware components, software programming and a range of other textiles and crafting materials to bring everything together and solve all of the fabrication and interaction problems involved in your creative concept.

You learned about interfacings and other ways to insulate exposed threads and knots at the start of this chapter. Now we will take a look at how designers are managing resistance in creative circuits.

The relationship between voltage, current and resistance (Ohm's law)

The analogy of water flowing through a pipe is well worn, but that is because it is intuitive in understanding how a circuit works.

Voltage (V) is defined as a difference in electrical potential. It is a force, something waiting to happen given the chance, and it can be imagined as water waiting to flow from a high tank through a pipe. A reading of 9 volts refers to a measurable difference between the high tank and a low tank, or between two points in your circuit.

Current (I) is the rate at which electrons flow through a given point, and it is measured in amperes (but we use I, not C). A higher voltage will push electrons through a "pipe" faster.

Resistance (R) is like a narrowing in the pipe getting in the way of the flow of the current. You can imagine it will either slow the current or result in a release of energy in another form (often heat) as the force increases inside the confines of the pipe.

The relationship between these is quite simple, and we use the equation $V = IR$ to work with it. This means, of course, if we know two of the values we can find the third by using simple algebra.

As an example, you have a 9-volt battery and want to limit the current to 30 milliamps (0.03 amp). To work out the value of the resistor you will need to limit the current to this amount, you rearrange the equation to become $R = V/I$. Here is your solution given $V = 9$ and $A = 0.03$:

$$R = 9/0.03$$
$$= 300 \text{ ohms}$$

Why do this? Because many components can only cope with so much current. Get into the habit of checking data sheets, and use your multimeter to check values. See the Other How-Tos online to work out the resistors you need in a textile circuit.

3.21
Ohm's law describes the relationship between voltage, resistance and current and is used to calculate circuit values.

Design with smart textiles

Instead of using off-the-shelf resistors stitched onto a fabric, some researchers are playing with the resistivity of conductive yarns and fabrics to make their own, more expressive resistors as a more integrated approach to the design of the whole textile system. Ramyah Gowrishankar has developed a range of repeatable embroidered motifs using specific yarns that she knows can be dropped into a stitched circuit design to introduce a predefined level of resistance (figure 3.22).

Jesse Seay did not use a resistor for her knitted perfboard circuit (figure 3.23) because she calculated that the resistance needed to protect the LEDs would be provided by the conductive yarn used to stitch it.

A team of fashion designers, e-textile specialists and electronic engineers at Hong Kong Polytechnic University has taken all this a step further and devised a complete design approach to making textile circuits look less technical and more "textile." Assuming that resistance across a two-dimensional fabric shape is dependent on length, team members calculate the total resistance of the conductive path simply by adding the resistance of all of the similar shapes of conductive fabric together. This total resistance can then be redistributed among new shapes that are more in keeping with the aesthetic goals of (in this case) the garment, as long as the total area of the conductive fabric remains the same. This frees up the design team to iterate the aesthetic expression of the visible circuit, making it a design feature integrated into the whole concept.

3.22

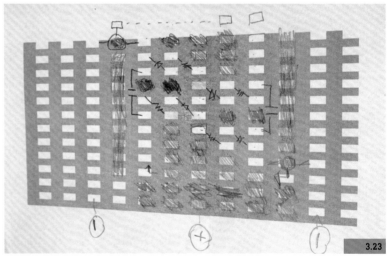
3.23

3.22
Motifs with specific resistance values can be developed through a systematic approach to yarn selection, area and stitch density in embroidery. Ramyah Gowrishankar.

3.23
Planning a circuit on fabric perfboard. Jesse Seay.

3.24
Calculating the conductive path value; the two garments have circuits with the same resistance values, but the layout is different and becomes part of the fashion design process. Li Li et al.

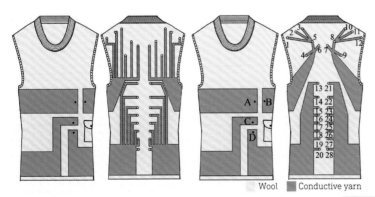

Wool   Conductive yarn

3.24

Basic principles of input and output (I/O)

In any system, there will be inputs, some kind of processing, and outputs. Inputs can refer to switches, sensors, triggers, thresholds and so on, which are recognized by a processor, which runs the appropriate output through actuators. This might be text on a screen ("Hello world!"), a motor to drive an interactive sculpture, playing back recorded sounds or, of course, blinking lights.

If you are an interaction designer or a user experience designer, it is likely that your design process begins with a definition of the desired output (the interactive sculpture should retreat quickly from an audience, just like a startled starfish). However, if you are working with textiles, the chances are you are just as interested in the experiential qualities of the input, and you might not consider output until later on.

This is something to bear in mind when working with other designers, as you will ask different questions and have different goals. The development of satisfactory input and output experiences takes time, and it is hard to do both well. Factor in the skills necessary to program the processor that manages all this, and you can see how you start to need teams (or plenty of time) for more complex projects.

You will be introduced in more detail to the kinds of available input and output devices later in this chapter.

Working safely

Putting electricity into textiles might seem like a recipe for disaster, and of course there are some basic rules that will keep you safe rather than sorry.

- It is the power that will kill you. Keep the power low in your projects.
  - Power is voltage (V) multiplied by current (I), and it is expressed in watts (W). While only a tiny amount of amperage is needed to interrupt your heart, the body itself protects us—our skin has a resistance of about 5,000 to 15,000 ohms, significantly slowing the current. High voltage on its own does not kill—the continuous flow of current does.
  - A static shock that feels like a sting may be between 20,000 and 30,000 volts, but the amperage, or current, is tiny and so not harmful.
- However, it does not take much to interfere with the electricity that regulates our muscles and nerves—stay safe and do not lick batteries.
- Do not recharge batteries while in a holder on fabric—risk of fire!
- Keep long hair out of hot or fast-moving components.
- Turn off all equipment after use. Take coin cell batteries out of holders when not in use—they drain quickly and will need to be replaced more often.
- Wear goggles and masks if working with dusts and vapors.
- Do not lick conductive threads to get them through a needle.
- Always clear up loose threads after working— they migrate everywhere, cause trouble in later projects, and can be hazardous to small children and animals.
- Be aware of the different materials even in textiles, and be careful with low melting point man-made fibers.

FIBER BURN CHART

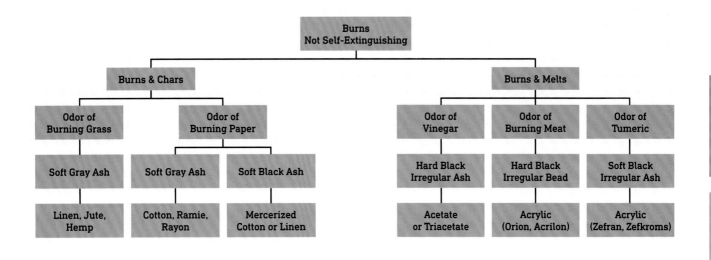

Burns Not Self-Extinguishing

- **Burns & Chars**
  - **Odor of Burning Grass**
    - Soft Gray Ash
      - Linen, Jute, Hemp
  - **Odor of Burning Paper**
    - Soft Gray Ash
      - Cotton, Ramie, Rayon
    - Soft Black Ash
      - Mercerized Cotton or Linen
- **Burns & Melts**
  - **Odor of Vinegar**
    - Hard Black Irregular Ash
      - Acetate or Triacetate
  - **Odor of Burning Meat**
    - Hard Black Irregular Bead
      - Acrylic (Orion, Acrilon)
  - **Odor of Tumeric**
    - Soft Black Irregular Ash
      - Acrylic (Zefran, Zefkroms)

Does Not Burn
- Glass, Asbestos, Metal

Burns Self-Extinguishing

- **Burns Briefly & Chars**
  - **Odor of Burning Hair or Feathers**
    - Black Soft Bead
      - Silk
    - Irregular Dark Ash
      - Wool, Cashmire, Mohair, Alpaca, Llama, Etc.
    - Open Lava-Like Ash
      - Weighted Silk
- **Burns Briefly & Melts**
  - **Odor of Celery**
    - Hard Gray Bead
      - Nylon
  - **Odor of Burning Asphalt**
    - Hard Tan Bead
      - Olefin
  - **Odor of Sharp Acrid Chemicals**
    - Hard Black Irregular Bead
      - Moda Acrylic
  - **Odor of Sweet Chemicals**
    - Hard Black Irregular Bead
      - Vinyon
    - Hard Black Round Bead
      - Polyester

3.25

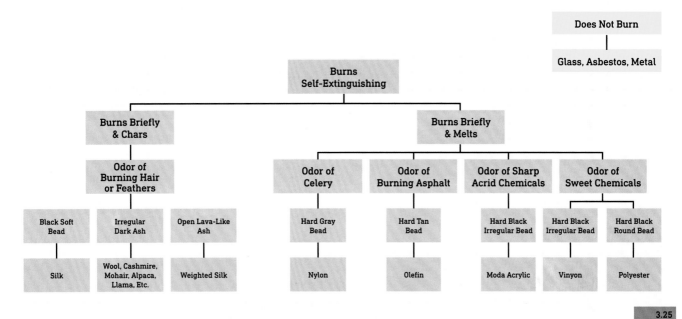

3.25
Fiber burn chart; fibers have different flammability characteristics, and may smolder, scorch or ignite quickly. Polymers will melt. Karen Gray; Copyright 2002–2012 Ditzy Prints

3.26
Soft Circuits Basic Kit. There are many starter kits on the market; Plugandwear's are unusual because they provide textile components like potentiometers and buttons. Plugandwear.

3.26

Exercise Seven:
Stitching in-series and
parallel circuits

You have already sewn your first series circuit with a single LED. If you re-create the same circuit design with another two LEDs in line, notice what happens to the brightness of the lights (make sure all the + and – signs are facing the same way). Why might this be? Now add a second battery to this circuit—what happens to the brightness of the LEDs? You have learned why a parallel circuit is useful; it can drive a larger number of outputs from a single power source. Following the diagrams shown, use crocodile clips to prototype a parallel circuit with three LEDs (it is quite fiddly). This helps you check how connections should work before you start sewing.

Now draw a parallel circuit on some fabric and using the embroidery hoop again, stitch your circuit with three LEDs, remembering to finish your line of conductive stitching each time it meets an LED (do not continue stitching across the back of the LED). Figure 3.29 shows a workshop participant creating a custom guitar strap with multiple LEDs using a parallel circuit.

3.27a & b
In-series and parallel circuit plans. In the in-series circuits, the voltage provided should equal the voltage drop across the components. In a parallel circuit there is a limit to how many LEDs you can add. Martha Glazzard.

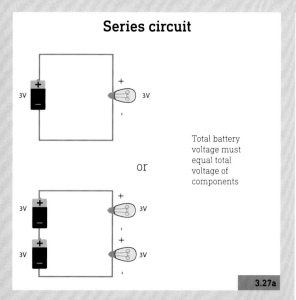

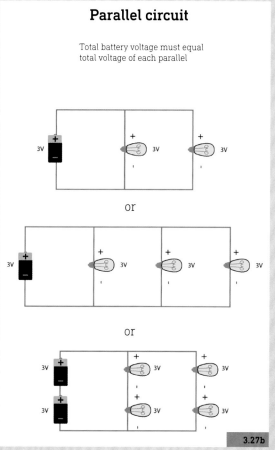

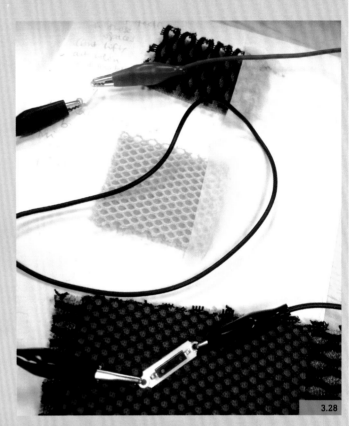

3.28

3.28
Using crocodile clips to
prototype a circuit; check
the connections needed
as part of your planning
process. This image
shows a magnetic switch
in the on state allowing
current to flow to an LED.

3.29
Making a guitar strap
with multiple LEDs in
parallel.

3.29

PROJECT ONE:
VisiGlove

Familiar form—stitched circuit—gestural touch switch—LED output—output as signal function

This project was developed by students on the Design and Technology (D&T) Subject Knowledge Enhancement (SKE) course at Nottingham Trent University. This course was designed with the aim of helping student teachers develop a deeper understanding of fundamental D&T concepts with particular emphasis on the Design and Make process that is inherent in the secondary D&T Curriculum. During the eight-week course, students work on a variety of modules, including a team Design and Make project that involves the design development of an electronic textiles (e-textile) product, on the theme of "Being Visible," sponsored by local company Kitronik, who supplied the sewable components. VisiGlove is reproduced here by kind permission of Kitronik and students Natasha Thorogood, Sian Toon and Joanne Deane. Extra images for VisiGlove and other related project tutorials can be seen online at:
kitronik.co.uk/baglight
kitronik.co.uk/visiglove
kitronik.co.uk/glosport
kitronik.co.uk/smartband

3.30
Project materials and tools.

3.30

Things you will need:
- A pair of gloves (cycling gloves of your preference but must not be fingerless)
- High-visibility/reflective fabric (150mm x 50mm)
- Base fabric—black cotton (200mm x 50mm)
- Velcro strips x 2 (30mm x 80mm)—preferably in the same color as base fabric
- Thin plastic—top layer (200mm x 50mm) (not essential if you don't need your gloves to be waterproof)
- Conductive thread—3 meters
- 20 sewable LEDs (kitronik www.kitronik.co.uk/c2714-electro-fashion-led-boar)
- Glue (all-purpose)
- White nonconductive thread
- Black nonconductive thread
- Sewing needle
- Iron and ironing board
- Fabric scissors
- Paper scissors
- Tailor's chalk
- 3V coin battery x 2
- Sewing machine
- Laser cutter
- Scalpel and cutting mat
- Nonconductive fabric (40mm x 120mm)
- 4 strips of conductive fabric (8mm x 35mm)
- 4 strips of Bondaweb (8mm x 35mm)

Step 1: Get ready

— Collect together all of the equipment and materials listed above.
— Print and cut out paper templates on A3 for actual size.
— Lay out the templates onto the different fabrics and cut out all necessary pieces. (It will be helpful to pin the paper templates onto the fabric and cut around or use tailor's chalk to draw around the templates.)

Step 2: Stitch on your Velcro

— Stitch the softer half of Velcro onto the base piece fabric of the arrow by machine or by hand (using the sewing machine will make the join stronger).
— Note: You may need to cut the Velcro down to size.

Step 3: Mark out the LEDs

— Use tailor's chalk to mark out the positioning of the LEDs using the paper template.
— Glue the LEDs in place, checking that they line up with the holes in the reflective layer arrow.
— Allow glue to dry for at least 20 minutes.

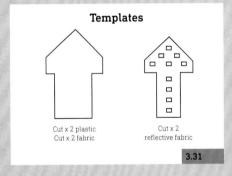

3.31
Templates.

3.32
Machine sewing the Velcro.

3.33a
Tailor's chalk.

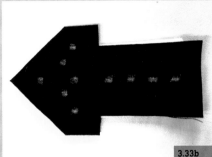

3.33b
LED template.

3.33c
Marking the LED positions.

3.33d
Tack LEDs in place.

Step 4: While the glue is drying, make your soft battery holders

— Iron the Bondaweb strips onto the nonconductive fabric, as shown, with the rough side down.

— Peel off the paper layer of the Bondaweb and iron on the conductive fabric strips.

— Sew, by hand, through one piece of nonconductive fabric with conductive thread (ensure it goes all the way through to the other side so it will touch the battery).

3.34a
Soft battery holder components.

3.34b
Bondaweb ironed onto felt.

3.34c
Conductive fabric ironed onto Bondaweb.

3.34d
Hand stitching through conductive fabric.

3.34e
Hand stitching through conductive fabric.

3.34f
Stitched contact for battery.

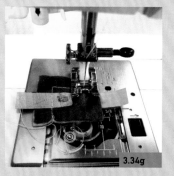

3.34g
Joining front and back.

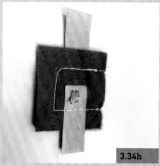

3.34h
Battery holder front.

Design with smart textiles

Step 4: cont.

— Stitch the two pieces of nonconductive fabric together on the sewing machine using nonconductive thread along the three sides of the square (see template).
— Sew battery holders inside both of your gloves using nonconductive thread. (Ours have been sewn into the inside/top of the glove so that they are on the back of the hand.)

Step 5: Sew on your LEDs

— Sew LEDs that have been glued onto the base piece of fabric using conductive thread in the pattern shown on the template.
— Connect all of the positives together and then all of the negatives together so that the circuit is joined in parallel.

— Place your two 3V batteries into the battery holder and check that your circuit works (that the LEDs light up).
— Note: MAKE SURE YOUR CONDUCTIVE THREAD DOES NOT TOUCH WHEN TWO THREADS CROSS OVER.

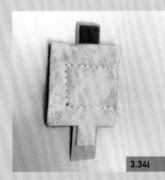
3.34i
Battery holder back.

3.34j
Attaching battery holder to glove.

3.35
Sewing LEDs to glove according to the stitch template.

Step 6: Glue on reflective arrow

— Use a small amount of glue on the reverse side of the reflective arrow to stick it down over the top of the LEDs.
— On the reverse side of the arrow, stitch through with conductive thread to attach two small squares of conductive fabric.

Step 7: the glove

— Sew the other side of the Velcro onto the glove using nonconductive thread.
— Sew two small squares of conductive fabric onto the Velcro with conductive thread (to match up with the pieces on the LED arrow).

— Note: The right square should be attached to the bottom LED through the positive connection and the left square through the negative connection of the bottom LED (ensure that these squares of conductive fabric are not touching).
— Stitch the two fingertip pieces of conductive fabric onto the outside of the glove using nonconductive thread.

3.36
Other half of Velcro attached to glove.

3.37a
Attaching the fingertip electrodes.

3.37b
Glove with fingertip electrodes in place.

Step 8: Connect the fingertip switch

— Sew with conductive thread from the positive side of the battery holder through to the square of conductive fabric on the rough side of the Velcro (the small square of conductive fabric on the outside of the glove).

— Then connect the negative side of the battery holder up to the tip of the thumb (connect this to the conductive fabric on the tip).
— Stitch from the negative side of the arrow up to the index finger tip (connect to the conductive fabric on the fingertip).

— Note: It is advisable to sew along the seam of the inside of the glove so that the stitches are not visible from the outside and will not interfere with using the glove.

3.38
The finished glove.

3.39
The visiglove in action.

OTHER MATERIALS: ELECTRONICS, HABERDASHERY AND OTHER FABRICS

You can use a wide range of other crafting materials with or instead of e-textiles. Anything that can be built up to make patterns with strong tonal contrast can be used to make QR codes, for example, see the dress by Thorunn Arnadottir in figure 3.40 (and try your own illustrative version using *Aestheticodes* in chapter 4).

Similarly, bring your skills from other areas. Jewelry making provides a wealth of excellent tools and techniques that can be adapted in working with small components. Check out round-nosed, flat-nosed and D-shaped pliers, end cutters for wire, eye and head pins, jump rings, chains and fastenings. The equivalent of *haberdashery* in jewelry is *findings*. Just be aware that the solder used with precious metals is different from that used with electronic components, and they do not mix. Try Cooksons for a wide range of findings and quality tools including Dremel rotary tools (for small-scale cutting, sanding, polishing and drilling), and look out for clever ways of holding things like sandpaper—the sprung sticks with looped strips in figure 3.41 are very accurate to use. Needle and riffler files are great for finishing, deburring and opening up small spaces for electronics to fit into; and jeweler's piercing saws will allow you to cut *non-orthogonal PCB* boards and decorative solar panels with some practice.

Haberdashery departments and hardware shops offer endless creative possibilities. You can use standard metal zips, hooks and eyes and snap fastenings as parts of your stitched circuits. Just make sure they have not been coated with a plastic—although if they have, you can just sand it back to reveal the bare metal.

3.40
QR U?. Quick recognition (QR) codes depend on the code color being dark, and on good contrast. Codes can still work with up to a third of the data missing. Scanning a QR code with a smartphone enables online content. Thorunn Arnadottir 2011.

Design with smart textiles

Other conductive materials are also available, such as Velcros and tapes, paints, inks and glues. Quantum tunneling composite (QTC) foams such as *Velostat* are conductive, but they are also useful for making squishy analog sensors. Heat shrink tubing can be used creatively, too. This is a thermoplastic sleeve you cut to cover exposed wires and solder joins; when heated it shrinks by up to a third of its original diameter. Use a heat gun to do this, but make sure children know it is not a hairdryer—a heat gun is significantly hotter. When introducing batteries into your work, bear in mind not only the voltage you need (and whether you need rechargeable), but also the form factor—do they sit flat, or are they raised up above the surface of the fabric? Do you need to create a pouch for them, or is there a holder you can use? Coin cells are a very good choice as they are quite flat, and many of the holders can be easily sewn or modified.

3.41
Sandtaper sticks are used in jewelry making. The tapered end allows the maker to finish small or hard-to-reach surfaces, and the spring-loaded design means the sandpaper can be easily replaced.

3.42
Snap studs (nonconductive). These black snap studs are coated and therefore not conductive; use the silver uncoated snaps for an electrical connection.

SWITCHES AND SLIDERS

In this section we will talk about the difference between a switch and a slider. Both are input devices, but they represent the difference between digital and analog. If you were to open up a light switch you would find inside a simple mechanism that only has two states: open (off) and closed (on), or in binary terms, 0 or 1. Earlier, you made a circuit with a binary switch—your LED was either on, or it was off—there was no in-between state, and only one action was needed to switch from one state to the other.

An analog system allows you to work with in-between states by capturing a range of different values within given parameters. If you were to open up a slider it may look something like figure 3.44.

Other related terms include variable resistor and potentiometer. These are closely related; while a variable resistor may take many forms (including textile), a potentiometer ("pot") is normally used to split out some of the voltage in a circuit to other components, or as a guide to the activity of the circuit, through a third output pin (it is a *voltage divider*). Pots can be analog (you turn a knob or slide a lever by hand) or digitally controlled. They are similar to variable resistors in that the pot mechanism consists of a contact moving along a length of resistive material to control the resistance between two points. One major implication of working with in-between states in this way is that you will generally need a processor to make sense of the values that are being produced and to exploit the differences between them to make other things happen. This will be covered in more depth in the microprocessor sections of this chapter.

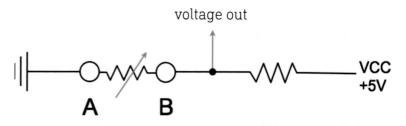

3.44

3.43
Schematic of a simple switch; A and B are not joined so the switch in this diagram is off.
Leah Buechley.

3.44
Schematic of a variable resistor. The zig-zag line with an arrow through it between A and B is the symbol for a variable resistor (such as a stretchy piece of conductive fabric).
Leah Buechley.

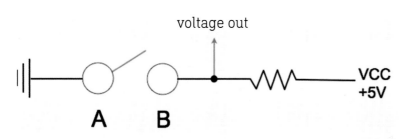

3.43

There are many ways to construct switches, including reed switches, tilt switches and magnetic switches, and trying to make one yourself from first principles, like the version in figure 3.45 by Robin Petterd, is a great way to learn about them. It is also a great way to think about the potential of all electronic components for expression in your work—Robin's switch triggered sounds of the sea.

Textiles are great for making switches, and you should also explore Kobakant's open source tutorial pages ("How To Get What You Want") to build up your skills. Even simple binary switches can challenge you to think about the human experience of using them—the behavior and actions or gestures needed, how easy or difficult those will be to achieve, and the material quality of the interaction. Lara Grant's Push Reset collection of experimental felt interfaces incorporate conductive and resistive fabrics, yarns and threads, some of which produce sound.

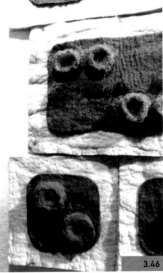

3.45
Tilt switch with water; salt water is far more conductive than ordinary drinking water. In this pendant, water is used to connect the two electrodes as part of a visible tilt switch. Robin Petterd.

3.46
Textile variable resistors, available for tactile exploration in the gallery. Lara Grant.

Exercise Eight:
Make a textile pressure switch

To make a pressure switch, you need to separate two layers of conductive fabric with a piece of wadding or felt with a hole cut in it (meshes can also be used; experiment with different sizes). When pressed, the conductive layers need to meet as shown in figure 3.47b. The stitched trace leading to the negative electrode of the battery should be connected to one layer and the trace leading to the positive electrode should be connected to the other so that the circuit is incomplete until the conductive fabric layers touch. Think about what your switch looks like—cut out fabric motifs and hide the switch behind them.

3.48

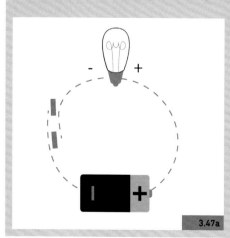

3.47a

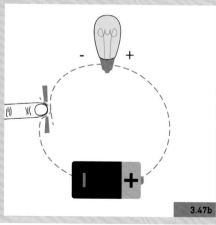

3.47b

3.47a
Pressure switch construction off (the conductive fabric layers are held apart). Martha Glazzard.

3.47b
Pressure switch construction on (the pressure of a finger forces the two conductive layers together). Martha Glazzard.

3.48
Pressure switch with applique design; the foam holding the conductive surfaces apart has been decorated with another piece of floral fabric. Sarah Walker.

Exercise Nine:
Make a textile tilt switch

A simple tilt switch can be made by having multiple traces leading from one electrode of the battery. The end of each trace should have a conductive patch, here made with cut-out conductive fabric shapes, to make contact easy. A trace leading from the other electrode should then be made to swing between the contacts. Thread a metal bead onto the end of a conductive yarn, or try making a pom-pom with some conductive thread in it; insulate the length of the conductive thread with wooden beads.

3.49a

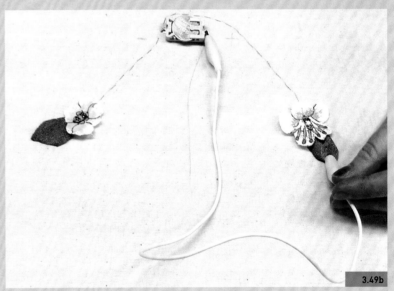

3.49b

3.49a & b
Tilt switch, testing with crocodile clips. The battery and each LED are connected in turn. Sarah Walker.

3.50a-d
Tilt switch schematic showing connection with each open switch in turn. Martha Glazzard.

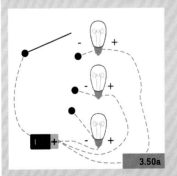

3.50a

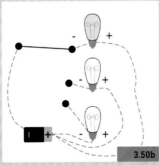

3.50b

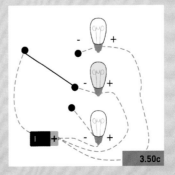

3.50c

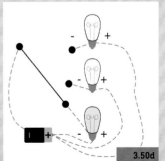

3.50d

INPUT (SENSORS)

This section introduces different kinds of sensors, including off-the-shelf electronics, textile components, and crafted experimental textile sensors. In addition, we will look at some fundamental questions to ask as you design a system with sensor inputs, consider other input data options and think about future input techniques.

Off-the-shelf electronics

Flex sensors are useful if you want to capture certain movements, and they can be found in lots of interactive glove designs along the fingers. They give a change in resistance when bent. Care should be taken to mount the fragile base securely so that only the functional part of the sensor gets bent. Sparkfun has a nice tutorial on using these, which includes Arduino code (see Suggested Reading).

Photoresistors are light-dependent resistors. They will give a change in resistance value when the light around them changes, so you can have your textiles automatically light up as the sun goes down.

Proximity, direction and GPS are noncontact forms of sensing, and there are different means of doing this depending on what materials you want to sense— for example, magnetic (reed switch), inductive, capacitive or photoelectric (transmitter/receiver).

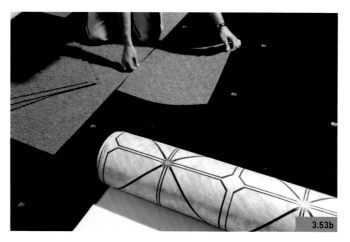

3.51
Flex sensor; as the sensor is flexed its resistance increases.

3.52
The resistance of a photoresistor (light sensor) goes down as the light gets brighter.

3.53a&b
SensFloor fitting. Each square meter of 3mm textile underlay has a grid of 32 proximity sensors integrated into it, and sends data to a base unit through radio communication. © Future-Shape GmbH.

SensFloor is a large-area proximity sensing technology based on a measurement algorithm developed by Future-Shape. All conductive materials can be used as sensor areas to detect an approach from a distance of several centimeters; the challenge in large area sensing is to filter out irrelevant electromagnetic noise. Sensor areas can be metallic surfaces, conductive textiles, woven or stitched wires or conductively coated glass or foils.

Textile components

Sensors with a textile form already exist in industry, even if they are not widely available commercially. Quantum tunneling composite (QTC) is a fascinating conductive compound that foams and other open structures can be soaked in to create capacitive sensing. The structures are good for sensing organic molecular compounds in the air—effectively "smelling" out chemicals.

PeraTech.

Textile knowledge is essential for translating concepts into working reality. Tessa Acti contributed her embroidery knowledge to a research project in the UK to develop working fabric antennae for search and rescue applications, systematically exploring stitch density, length, fiber content and twist structure of yarns to create prototypes that could then be tested for improved functionality (see chapter 4 case study).

Temperature and humidity can also be measured; humidity can be sensed by amplifying the current flowing between two metal areas and setting a threshold value above which moisture content in the air is understood to be high (the higher the humidity, the more conductive the air).

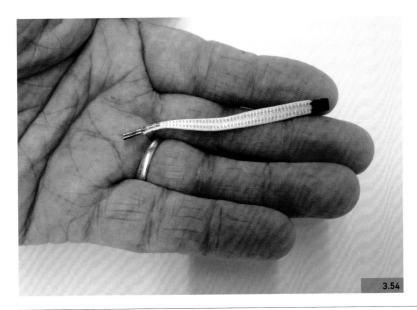

3.54
QTC "nose sensor." The material expands and changes its resistance in the presence of certain molecules, and can be incorporated into textiles to monitor the presence of dangerous chemicals.

Crafted textile sensors

Kobakant has taken the concept of open source software and applied it to learning in e-textiles. Figure 3.55 shows a wide range of pom-pom, tilt, stroke and touch sensors made entirely from textiles, and their website, "How To Get What You Want," provides instructions for making them all. Try out crochet, French knitting, and many other crafty textile techniques, and see the projects here for a couple of introductory exercises.

Design questions when gathering data about people become ethically and politically loaded. When you are making design decisions, you will need to bear in mind the trade-offs between (perceived) usefulness and privacy. *Big data* refers to the streaming of information about many individuals to *cloud* storage for the purpose of remote behavioral pattern recognition. Some apps on your mobile phone are designed to harvest user information from other apps in the background, and most of us are unaware of this happening. App developers themselves cannot take into account every permission setting available to them (there are a great many), and many of us do not understand what we are agreeing to when we give our permission.

Have a look at this quote from a large research project:

Textile-based sensors offer an unobtrusive method of continually monitoring physiological parameters during daily activities. Chemical analysis of body fluids, noninvasively, is a novel and exciting area of personalized wearable healthcare systems. BIOTEX was an EU-funded project that aimed to develop textile sensors to measure physiological parameters and the chemical composition of body fluids, with a particular interest in sweat. A wearable sensing system has been developed that integrates a textile-based fluid handling system for sample collection and transport with a number of sensors including sodium, conductivity, and pH sensors. Sensors for sweat rate, ECG, respiration, and blood oxygenation were also developed. For the first time, it has been possible to monitor a number of physiological parameters together with sweat composition in real time. This has been carried out via a network of wearable sensors distributed around the body of a subject user. This has huge implications for the field of sports and human performance and opens a whole new field of research in the clinical setting.

Coyle et al. 2010

3.55
A variety of textile sensors including stroke, press and tilt switches, using different textile techniques. Kobakant.

3.55

Diffus

The Diffus sensor dress makes information about the environment more visible, such as levels of carbon dioxide, pollution and gas.

3.57

KEY QUESTION

When you start designing for sensing on the body, ask these questions of your system:
— **What is being sensed exactly?**
— **Who is aware of the collection of data?**
— **How accurate is it?**
— **What does it actually mean?**

3.58

3.56

3.56
Biosensors—monitoring and diagnostic. Biological responses such as enzymes, blood sugars and acids are converted into electrical signals for medical and healthcare applications. This ECG (electro-cardiograph) sensor is not textile based and demonstrates the potential for other soft, flexible materials to play a role in the same application areas as textile systems. IMEC copyright.

3.57
Climate Dress senses pollution, gas and CO2. The dress was part of a research project between diffuse design studio Forster-Rohner, the Alexandra Institute and the Danish School of Design. It allowed partners to develop new industrial techniques for embedding soft circuitry into computerized embroidery production. Diffus.

3.58
Climate Dress detail with the LilyPad Arduino processor. This allows the LED response to be dynamic, not merely on or off. Light patterns range from slow to hectic depending on the levels of pollution sensed.

Other data streams, and the future of input devices

Sensing technology developments include input directly from the brain and flexible skin "tattoos," and we saw in earlier chapters that some of the issues with noise when sensing chemical changes and small movements of the body are being resolved with photonic fiber technology. Necomimi products measure brain activity through a sensor on the forehead and one earlobe, and respond to three mental states: attention, relaxed and "in the zone." Collaborations with name textile designers such as Nobuki Hizumi extend the market.

Temporary gold circuit tattoos on the skin are being created to measure a range of biological functions such as blood flow, skin conductivity and even cognitive function within five years. It is possible to measure temperature very accurately, and it can be used as an indicator of physiological health due to minute changes in metabolism when we concentrate, feel happy, or feel tired. One of the possibilities for this is the early warning of infection, something that textile sensors are already providing in performance sportswear.

The England rugby team has been using a smart textiles kit for some time now, and trainers and physiotherapists have found that through familiarity with the biometric data each player constantly produces through his garments, they can predict when a player is about to come down with a cold or infection, even before the player himself is aware of it. Decisions about starting lineups are now informed on a regular basis by these insights. In the meantime, Foxtel brought the Alert Shirt to the market in time for the 2014 Six Nations rugby tournament, allowing viewers to feel how their favorite player is feeling. Haptic feedback motors transfer match data through a phone app to a shirt so you can feel the nerves, elation and exhaustion of your team.

Speckled Computing is a European research project closely related to the "smart dust" developed at Berkeley, California, in the 1990s. This group has designed a computer (including sensors, processing, memory, power, output and wireless communication) that measures only 5 cubic millimeters. These "Specks" have low power and little memory, but clever programming based on swarm behavior means that hundreds of Specks can work together, passing information across the network and transmitting real-time data about the environment they are in. While the physical shape of an individual Speck makes it a design challenge to integrate into comfortable clothing, this is a very powerful platform for building distributed textile concepts. Multiple Specks on one body can be used to replace expensive camera motion tracking systems in the animation industry, or they can be distributed across social networks and crowds to explore social psychology aspects of fashion and cultural expression.

3.59a & b
Alert Shirt with smartphone app. Small vibrator motors in a pack situated over the chest area translate physiological data into haptic feedback. Foxtel.

Exercise Ten:
Using personas and scenarios
in designing with sensors

First create a persona—a character who will help you think about how users might experience a product.

1. Interview three people about the Diffus Dress. Make sure they are of a similar age, background and gender. Find out what jobs they do, where they shop, what streets they walk down in your city, and what concerns them about the environment. Audio-record the interviews.
2. Listen to the recordings and bring together the answers for each question. You can choose to select the most common answer or combine aspects of answers.
3. Draw a fictitious character that includes aspects of your three respondents—the character will have the same gender, age, etc.
4. Describe the character's habits, aspirations, concerns and lifestyle, using your interview data to create a convincing hybrid of all your respondents. Write the description on the sheet beside the drawing. Name your persona.

You can use this persona in different ways. It can inform your design process—what would he or she like in terms of functionality or aesthetic expression in the wearable you are working on? Or you can create a scenario for the character to walk through and use this to think about how their experience of the product is affected by context and use.

To create a scenario:
1. Visualize a context, such as a busy crossing in a major city. What is happening there? What senses are being engaged? Is it noisy, deserted, or full of traffic? Is there information on advertising screens, on road signs, in shop windows? Are other people walking dogs, or on their mobile phones?
2. Now think about your persona: what is he or she trying to accomplish today? What are they doing in the context you have described?
3. Now add the wearable technology or smart textile. If it is the Diffus Dress, when do the LEDs light up? Does the character know what it means? What does she do about it? How does she feel about it? What about observers?

Persona and scenario techniques will give you more accurate insights the more research you put into their creation. You can also use scenarios as walk-throughs for yourself and your colleagues—thinking about how you would react in that situation with that technology. This is called heuristic research.

OUTPUT (ACTUATION)

The different modes of output are all specialized fields in their own right. Consider this quote from Lara Grant:

Sarah will be playing a felted origami "fortune teller" device. As she opens and closes the different segments, she will change the resistance across the felt. This will alter the playback speed of the sample. Lara will be playing the sewing machine. . . . Two switches are created by wiring the needle and sewing through conductive fabric, each of the two switches triggering different sounds. These switches are connected to an Arduino Diecimila talking to Max/MSP on a computer, via the serial object. The knobs and buttons on the machine control the music loop played, the speed, and the frequency. Matt will process these sounds using a Monome, an open source controller, and the software Max/MSP to build textures and rhythms into the music. Peter will be spinning electronic beats to keep the models stepping, syncing to computers and sewing machines, and incorporating sounds synthesized from scratch and sampled from lo-fi electronics, into an electronic, synthetic fairy tale soundtrack. Using custom software he wrote from his phone, he'll be commanding the ensemble wirelessly from his hand.

Diana Eng, Makezine 2010

If anything makes collaboration necessary with smart textiles, it is achieving meaningful output using sound. Lara Grant's quote demonstrates the kinds of different technical and creative skills needed when transforming streams of sensor data into sound or musical output. Max/MSP is a popular software platform used by sound designers and new media artists. Max/MSP has expanded rapidly to allow artists to work with visual outputs including animation, three-dimensional effects and video. Kobakant provides an excellent introduction to the basics of working with sound as part of its Chipmanband workshop documentation (see Suggested Reading), including the physics and mechanics as well as cultural concepts. A more accessible software platform for the beginning smart textiles designer is Processing. Designed by Casey Reas and Ben Fry, it has a very similar feel to the Arduino programming environment, and like Arduino, it has a very active community who are happy to share not only advice, but also chunks of code. You will practice your first Arduino exercises in the next section. Processing has been used to generate output from textile sensors, to drive actuators in textile projects and wearables, and also to generate patterns for use in textile surface design. Casey Reas uses it to create visual artworks.

3.60
Knit stitch structures showing arrangements of different material yarns. These will affect the behavior of the final fabrics in tandem with motor controlled movement. With kind permission of Delia Dumitrescu.

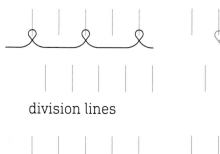

division lines

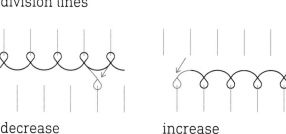

decrease   increase

3.60

Of course there are many modes of output besides sound, just as there are many modes of input. We will take a quick look at movement with motors, shape memory alloys and electroactive polymers; at regulating heat and driving color change in thermochromic inks and dyes; and, of course, at quantified output in the form of raw data and data visualization.

Delia Dumitrescu creates knitted textile structures for interiors that use motors to control multiple sections of a jersey fabric. She prototypes the form, scale and movement with card models before manipulating the placement of different yarns to create foldable structures. Soft pemotex yarn and fine polyester monofilament yarn are knitted together to form the overall shape. Knitting the yarns when soft allows accurate stitch transfer without breaking the loops. After knitting, the textile is heat pressed at 100 degrees Celsius to stiffen and shrink the fabric by about 40 percent; from being soft, the textile becomes stiff and similar in appearance to a nonwoven textile.

Driving motors requires more power than an Arduino can deliver—in fact, LilyPads and Arduinos can only supply enough power for LEDs and small speakers. Fans, motors or heating elements need to run from a separate power supply, which can be achieved through a relay, or a switch, which the Arduino closes to allow the other power supply to take over. Future solutions may include more use of solar cells, human-generated power, or the integration of mechanical power (as in the wound-up wristwatch). This is one of the reasons so many projects we see, particularly by beginners, use LEDs. You can learn how to drive a motor from an Arduino in the next section.

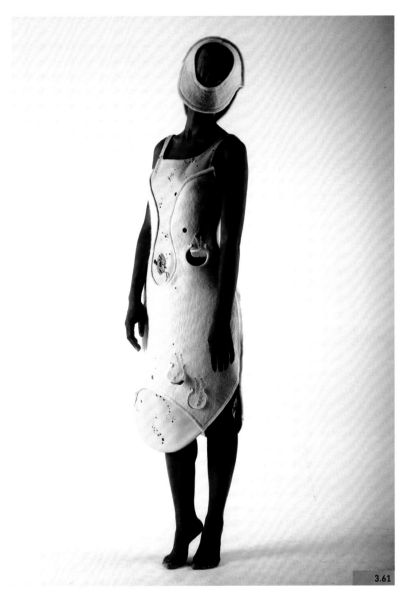

3.61

Shape memory alloys (SMAs) were very popular for a time. These alloys can be "trained" with heat to return to an original form. In figure 3.61 you can see work by fashion designer Di Mainstone in collaboration with XS Labs, using SMAs to control openings and movement in felted garments. Many designers have found that SMAs work well in one direction but that they do not have the strength to work against heavy fabrics, so movement is good in one direction but not in the other.

3.61
Enleon is part of the Skorpions collection, and is a sculptural garment that uses Nitinol shape memory alloy to slowly move. It is not "smart" in that it is pre-programmed and does not respond to external stimuli. Di Mainstone, Joanna Berzowska.

EAPs, or electroactive polymers, can also give you movement. They are lighter and faster and have a bigger range of movement than SMAs (up to 300 percent), requiring only a small amount of power. EAPs react to voltage, while SMAs react to heat. Other movement actuators include pneumatic systems (as in Mette Ramsgaard Thomsen's knit structures) and piezo or ceramic materials.

Called Hidden, this coat created in 2007 by High Tea with Mrs. Woo (figure 3.63) is constructed using cotton, silk, polyester, conductive thread and nylon ripstop, nichrome, copper PVC, hook-up wire, and nickel-metal hydride rechargeable batteries. The coat incorporates heated elements activated when the hands are placed in the pockets and the decorative cuffs come into contact with the pocket lining.

Design methods for working with color change and dynamic patterns are emerging from researchers like Hannah Landin, Linda Worbin, Barbara Jansen and Linnéa Nilsson. They have developed ways of working between paper and print with thermochromic inks heated by resistance in stitched conductive traces. In figure 3.64 you can see the metal grommets arranged down the edge of the fabric that the stitched conductive thread runs to—these can be connected to a current to create heat.

You can also use metal ink as a heating element, and inks can be screen printed to give a good, even coating—a tutorial is listed from ETH Zurich in Suggested Reading.

Thermochromic inks react at different temperature ranges: cold (clear to color at 15°C/59°F); touch-activated thermochromic (color to clear at 31°C/88°F); touch-activated liquid crystal ink (color change within the visible spectrum when rubbed—color sequence is black » red » green » blue between 25–30°C/77–86°F); and high temperature (color to clear at 47°C/117°F). You may need to use a binder if buying slurry, and this gives you further opportunities for mixing color.

3.63

3.62
Electroactive polymer fabrication. EAPs change shape when a voltage is applied; in Kretzer's ShapeShift project, layers of EAP thicken and flatten out in response to voltage, pulling against the flexible frames holding them, and creating large movements. From workshop images. Manuel Kretzer.

3.63
Hidden Coat. A circuit is completed when the conductive embroidery on the cuff touches a contact inside the pocket, where resistance creates warmth. High Tea with Mrs. Woo.

3.62

In addition to these output modalities, many applications require raw data or filtered quantified data as outputs—values that may indicate high performance, visualized as graphs, statistics and so on. Text output is so familiar it is easy to forget about, but it can also be very poetic, as in Camille Utterback's work, Text Rain (1999). Finally, you can make use of online datasets to either drive interaction, as in Natalie Jeremijenko's Live Wire (1995), or as output in response to textile sensors, as in Hazel White's Hamefarers' Kist (2010). In this project, Hazel linked up RFID tags in knitted cushions to Flickr datasets to connect elderly relatives to their families in other parts of the world.

KEY QUESTION

Just as with input, when designing with output, you need to bear in mind a bunch of questions that have technical, social, experiential and political implications. These can be explored through the interaction design and service design processes discussed in chapter 2.

— Where does the output happen?
— When does it happen?
— How legible or recognizable is it?
— Who sees it?

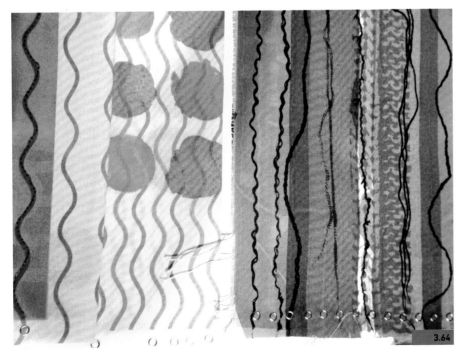

3.64
Linda Worbin thermochromic print workshop. Conductive stitched lines can be seen, over printed with different heat reactive inks.

Ambiguous form—stitched circuit—magnetic switch—LED output—affective output

HUG was a project commissioned by the City of Edinburgh Council for its Traveling Gallery exhibition Access All Areas in 2007. The concept was for the object to seem to return the affection of a human hug, through the use of soft switches, recorded sound and vibration. The feedback of visitors to the exhibition was extremely positive—it seems like the very simple interaction has something powerfully affective at its heart.

More than this, HUG demonstrates how many design decisions there are to make in a reactive textile project. Each step below gives you instructions to create a HUG with LED output, but also asks you to consider the alternatives open to you as a designer. This image shows three different versions of the ball: the pink one was purchased from Marimekko; the purple one with fur was made for Access All Areas, and includes vibration feedback; and the patterned one is being developed for the Internet of Soft Things project with LED output. These are all about the size of a football.

For a 25cm diameter HUG you will need:
- Strong cotton twill (for the outer shell)
- Calico or similar (for the inner shell)
- Spacer fabric or foam
- Zippers: 1 x 28cm (11 inches) fine toothed and 1 x 80cm (31 inches) larger toothed
- LEDs: 8 sewable surface mounted with resistor (such as Lilypad range)
- Filling—polystyrene beads, memory foam, Kapok, etc.
- Magnetic switch and magnet
- 3V coin cell battery and holder
- Conductive yarn (3 or 4 ply is easier for hand sewing)
- Needle, needle threader, embroidery scissors
- Sewing machine
- Dressmaker's chalk
- Fabric shears
- Pins

3.65

3.65
Variations on the HUG ball.

Step 1: Form

To create a ball, copy the pattern pieces shown here. Use a strong cotton twill for the outer shell, and a calico for the inner shell.

Mark the pieces on your fabric with chalk. Using fabric shears, cut six pieces for the outer and inner shells, plus the circular bases. As a guide, the circle measures 15cm in diameter, including the seam allowance on both sides, and the long panel measures 31cm down the center, also including both seam allowances.

Design decisions:
— Explore other ways of creating the same form. Look at existing examples in toys and furniture. Try slicing the pattern up in different ways.
— Explore other three-dimensional forms. A pillow is far simpler than a ball to embed electronics into and does not suffer from structural problems as it is scaled up. Consider how changing the form will change the interaction of a body with it.

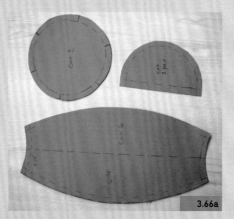

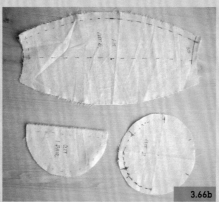

3.66a
Card pattern pieces.

3.66b
Pattern pieces cut in calico.

Step 2: Output

Following the pattern shown here, stitch a parallel circuit with 8 LEDs on one of the panels. The parallel circuit is like a ladder, with the LEDs forming the horizontal rungs. The yarn does NOT travel across the back of the LED board. Make sure all the LEDs are oriented the same way round—for example, with all the + to the right. This piece is marked "G" because my LEDs are green.

Design decisions:
— Change the layout of the LEDs and test your new circuit design with crocodile clips.
— Think about the number of LEDs being used. How many can the circuit take before the current doesn't flow? After completing the project, consider how you might create a HUG with LEDs on every face.

3.67
Parallel circuit with eight LEDs.

Step 3: Input

Cut a circle of the spacer fabric and, using the cotton twill base pieces, capture the magnet in the center by stitching through all the layers at regular intervals.

Make the inner ball: Sew the zipper to two of the faces. Leaving a 1cm seam allowance and, sewing right sides together, complete the inner ball. Turn right side out and test the zipper.

Complete the circuit: Following the layout shown, stitch the battery holder and magnetic switch to the inner ball top face. Making sure you join the + of the battery holder with the + sides of the LEDs, stitch a connection. The switch can be either way round (it does not have polarity). Remember to start and finish the stitched conductive yarn on either side of the switch—do not continue sewing behind it.

3.68

3.69

3.68
Inside top face with magnets stitched into spacer fabric.

3.69
Outside top face of inner ball showing circuit layout.

Insert the battery (+ side up). Test the magnetic switch by bringing the magnet close to it—your LEDs should light up. If they don't, see the troubleshooting tips below. Fill the inner ball.

Make up the outer ball: Insert the zipper first, and continue with right sides together.

Insert the inner ball, making sure the magnet in the top face aligns with the switch on the inner ball. Test for the interaction needed to activate the switch. You may need to add a foam ring between the layers if the LEDs light up too easily.

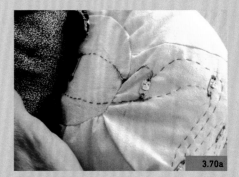

3.70a

3.70a
Magnets being held away from inner ball switch— LEDs off.

3.70b
Magnets brought close to inner ball switch— LEDs on.

3.70b

3.71a

3.71b

3.71a
Add a foam ring if magnet switch is on all the time.

3.71b
Insert the inner ball.

Design decisions:
— The magnetic switch could be replaced with, for example, a soft switch, or a tilt switch. Consider how choosing a different switch would affect the structure of the ball and the circuit.
— Try different fillings and test the change in interaction needed to activate the switch as a result.

TROUBLESHOOTING
If your LEDs won't light up at all, are intermittent, or if they stay on until the switch is activated, check for the following:
— All LEDs should be the same way round—all the + to the same side.
— Connect positive LED to positive battery holder electrode, and negative to negative.
— Yarn should be stitched through component holes a few times to create a good electrical connection.
— There should be no loose ends or stray fibers anywhere. Finish ends neatly and thoroughly.
— There should be no conductive yarn stitched behind components, or the current will bypass them through the yarn.
— Battery should be new, and the right way up (+ is marked on one face of the holder).
— The switch should be between the battery and the LEDs.
  If the LEDs seem dim, try them in a darker room!

Remember you can use crocodile clips and a multimeter to check individual parts of your circuit.

3.72

3.72
Interaction gesture— squeezing to activate the switch.

LEVELS OF COMPLEXITY: WHEN DO YOU NEED A MICROPROCESSOR?

When a simple on/off switch loses its thrill, it might be time to consider using a processor in your project. As we discussed in the first chapter, there are different definitions of "smart," but if you want to control how many times something happens, or specify a time it will happen, or set off a series of events to run on their own, then you will need to bring in some electronics and programming.

Decide for each project what your main aim really is, and think about what is really needed—do you need twenty flashing LEDs to explore human engagement? It may be that you do not even need a battery.

However, let us assume that you do want twenty LEDs, and that you want them to light up in a certain pattern when someone brushes past. You could rig up twenty separate circuits each with a textile sensor (on the wall?), so that a person brushing past them in turn will close each circuit and therefore switch on each light in turn; no processor would be needed for this. But if you wanted the same contact to trigger a pattern that, say, runs for five minutes and then stops, you need a processor.

3.73
Oomlaut Arduino kit; these kits include instruction booklets and come in a useful components box. Jonathan Sanderson.

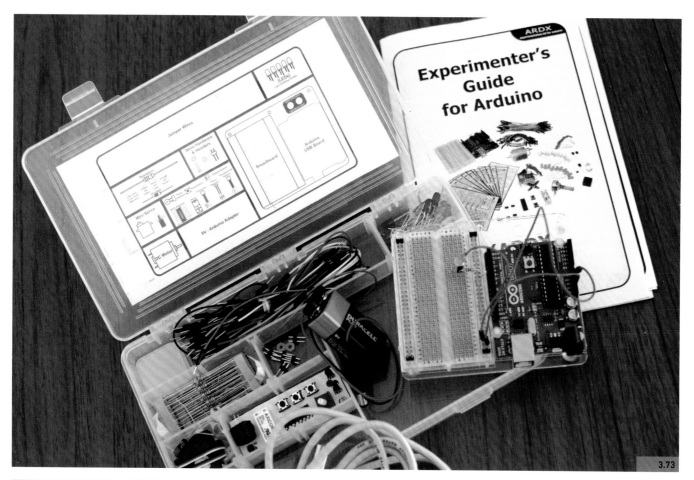

3.73

Design with smart textiles

These decisions come back to the interaction design process, or the user-centered design process, or the service design process—deciding what you need to achieve and how best to do it technically. If this does not match your normal design process—if, for example, you play with materials and craft something beautiful as an end in itself—then playing with light output for its own sake would be an equally useful way to work. You will need a processor. Finally, on and off only give us two states in a system. Sometimes we find in-between far more interesting: fading and brightening an output, or pressing harder to get a louder sound. To measure the differences in these analog behaviors, you need a processor.

There are kits available to help you get started, ranging from simple, fun products for children (such as the Loopin by Elena Corchero shown on page 57), to more flexible collections of parts and materials. Simple kits can be used to practice basic construction techniques for soft products, and these will typically include some conductive fabric (in the Loopin's case, the ears are a conductive felt). LilyPad and Arduino kits by the likes of Oomlaut have ranging benefits depending on your level of expertise. Oomlaut is particularly useful because components are well organized and they are accompanied by a tutorial booklet.

Having convinced you that this will be worthwhile, there are further levels of complexity open to the specialist, such as using a separate motor driver processor in a moving sculpture, having a MIDI sampler handle the playback of music in a sound installation, or letting a server handle internet connectivity in a networked project. When there are multiple processors involved, but they do not communicate much with each other, this is called parallel processing.

3.74
Kitronik kit. Kitronik supply materials for design and technology teachers in the UK. Kevin Spurr.

3.74

WORKING WITH MICROPROCESSORS

In this section you will program your first circuit using the widely available Arduino processor. You will transfer your practical knowledge of your stitched circuits onto a breadboard and begin to explore the expressive possibilities that a processor gives you.

You should end up with both a conceptual understanding and the hands-on experience needed to let you explore further with confidence.

Figure 3.75 shows the basic setup when you are prototyping a circuit on a breadboard with Arduino. There are three main components: the breadboard, the Arduino processor board, and a laptop running the Arduino programming environment.

1. The breadboard is where you physically put together LEDs, wires, resistors, switches and so on to build a functioning circuit.
2. The Arduino programming environment is downloaded onto your computer (it's free)—this is where you design the logic of your circuit.
3. The Arduino board sits between these two: connect it to your laptop with a FireWire cable. The breadboard becomes attached to the Arduino board as you link sensors to input pins and output pins to actuators with jump wires. While the boards and your laptop are connected, the laptop is providing all the power—so plug it in. When the project is complete, the Arduino board with your code stored on it will physically become part of the system (which is why the LilyPad and Flora formats are useful).

3.76a

3.75

3.75
Connecting the board to a USB port using a USB 2.0 cable (suitable for Arduino Uno, Arduino Mega 2560).

3.76a
A range of LilyPad boards and components, including a main board, buzzer, light sensor, accelerometer, button board, LED (with resistor), 3-color LED, slide switch, protoboard, and LiPower board for 5V and lithium polymer battery recharging.

3.76b
Good stitched connections. This AAA battery holder has been stitched to a fabric with conductive yarn. You can see that the metal around the holes is in good contact with the yarn, which is crucial for a robust circuit. Leah Buechley.

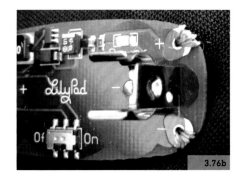

3.76b

LilyPad and Flora boards do essentially the same as a standard rectangular Arduino board, but they have been designed to be less physically intrusive once you move the project off the bench and onto the body. All the components have been designed with drill holes to make them easy to sew onto fabric, and these holes are surrounded with a metal contact so that stitching them into a circuit with conductive thread is simple. Remember to make extra stitches through these to create a reliable electrical contact.

The key steps in working with the Arduino platform are:

1. Download the appropriate Arduino application to your computer.
2. Check which version of the Arduino board you have (e.g., Uno, Duemilanove).
3. Connect the board to your computer using a USB port; the socket on the board is a tall D shape.
4. Open the Arduino programming environment and make sure the correct board is ticked under the Tools menu.
5. Make sure the correct port is selected, and download any drivers if necessary.
6. Pin out your circuit on the breadboard.
7. Program the circuit; whenever you upload an edited or new program to the board, it will overwrite anything that was there previously; it will stay there even when you remove the board from the computer.
8. Once everything works, transfer your prototype circuit into textiles and attach the Arduino, leaving the computer behind.
9. Add battery power and you're off!

Do not worry if some of this is a foreign language to you; you will learn some definitions now, and there is a glossary in this text. By the time you have tackled the how-tos, you will be confident in translating between the breadboard and textiles, and you will be flashing LEDs all over the place.

The Arduino board has pins down either side that are used for inputting data from sensors and outputting instructions to actuators such as your LEDs. Depending on which board you have, some of these are dedicated as input or output pins, and some can be told which role they will play in your program.

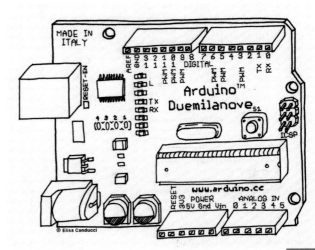

3.79

3.77

3.78

3.77
Board selection in the Arduino programming environment. Go to the Tools menu and find Board to select the one you are using. Leah Buechley.

3.78
Post selection in the Arduino programming environment. Go to the Tools menu and select Serial Port (this is most likely to be the /dev/tty option). Leah Buechley.

3.79
Diagram of the Arduino board; cable connectors are to the left, the numbered digital pins along the top edge can be programmed to be used for input or output, the pins along the bottom right edge are for analog input (e.g., sensors), and the pins to the left of those are for power and ground. Pins are the holes you slot a connecting wire into.
With kind permission Elisa Canducci.

The program is written in a window on your screen like this. Each short program is called a sketch. You write a program and give it comments to remind yourself what each bit does (you will find it useful if others have done this and you use their code, too)—use // to gray out the comments, and then they do not form part of the active program. To test your program, hit the Verify button. If you get a lot of red text in the box at the bottom, you need to check your program and try again. When it is happy, hit Upload to load it onto the board.

There are a lot of programs waiting for you to use from within the Arduino programming environment, so you do not need to understand everything before you start. For example, your first blink_LED sketch can be found by going to File > Examples > Basics > blink. All you need to do is make sure your LED on the breadboard is connected to the correct pin on the Arduino board and this will work without any programming skills from you.

However, it is good to build up some idea of what is going on, and there are plenty of tutorials online. In figure 3.82, Leah Buechley has annotated a sketch explaining what each section is doing. The basic building blocks of a program are structure (control statements, loops etc.), values (variables), and functions (like verbs—they make things happen). To mess about with your blinking LED timing, change the values (numbers) in this line:

delay(1000);

Try making this a far smaller number, or a far higher number. Change the other delay line, too. Observe the changes in flashing pattern—you altered the number of milliseconds the system waited before it ran the next line of code.

3.80
The Arduino sketch environment showing Verify (the tick symbol at left), and Upload (the horizontal arrow) commands. The page symbol means new program or sketch, the up arrow is open, and the down arrow is save.

3.81
The Arduino sketch environment finding existing programs; go to the File menu and select Examples to find a library of sample programs.

3.82
The Arduino sketch environment annotating a program. You can add comments to a program to help you remember or explain what it is doing. Use // to gray out comments so the system knows they are not part of the code.

3.83
The Arduino sketch environment program structure including control statements, functions and variables.

Exercise Eleven:
Your first LED circuit using a LilyPad Arduino

You will need:
— A computer running Arduino
— A Lilypad Main Board
— An FTDI board
— A standard mini USB cable
— A Lilypad LED
— A handful of crocodile clips
— A battery holder and battery
  (3v or 1.5V if using Lilypad holder)

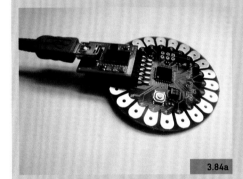

3.84a

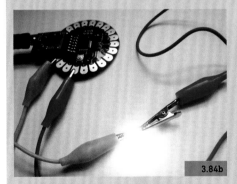

3.84b

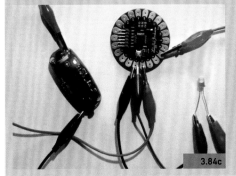

3.84c

**Now to programme an LED off the board
(figure 3.84b):**

1. Attach a resistor to the positive connector of your LED using a red crocodile clip.
2. Attach the other end of the resistor to a positive pin (one of the petals) on the Lilypad Arduino with a second red clip (the color is simply a convention, where red means positive and black or green means negative). Each petal is a numbered 'pin' in the program. Pick a digital output pin numbered between 2–13.
3. Attach the – (ground) leg of the LED to the – (ground) pin on the Lilypad.
4. To get the LED blinking, go back to the blink sketch (program) in the Arduino environment, and amend it so that the pin number you have attached the LED to is set up as the digital output (in "pinMode" and "digitalWrite")— see figure 3.85. The delays in the programme are in milliseconds and you can also try changing these values.

5. Upload the program to the Lilypad board. You may need to press the small reset button on the board so that it is ready to receive another program. Different boards and computers will have different quirks—Adafruit are good for more discussion on issues like these (see Suggested Reading).
6. To disconnect your circuit from the laptop, replace the FTDI board and USB cable with a battery. Using crocodile clips again, attach the positive electrode of a battery holder to the + pin on the Lilypad (on the left above pin 5). Attach the negative electrode to the ground (-) pin (figure 3.84c shows how the ground pin becomes shared).

The images show a 1.5V AAA battery in a Lilypad holder with on-board on/off switch. You could also try a Kitronik coincell holder with 3V battery; you may notice the Lilypad power source gives you a brighter LED; this is because the board is transforming the 1.5V supplied by the battery into a 5V output. Figure 3.84c shows a standard LED being used; if this is what you have, make sure the positive pin is connected to the longer, positive leg, and ground to the shorter, negative leg.

That was straightforward, but the LED is on the board. The next stage is to take LilyPad to the textiles. See the following online tutorials, and try the integrated project by Leah Buechley.

3.84a
Prototyping a first circuit with the Lilypad; connecting with an FTDI board

3.84b
Prototyping a first circuit with the Lilypad; blinking an LED off the board

3.84c
Prototyping a first circuit with the Lilypad; connecting to a battery source

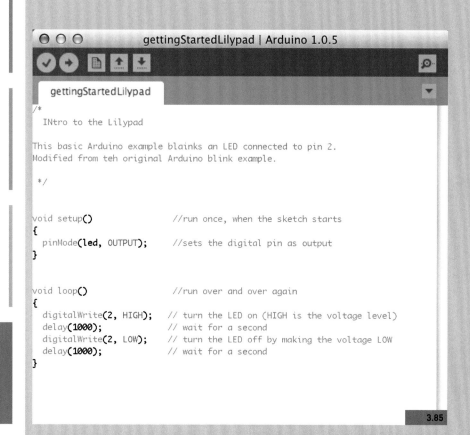

```
000                gettingStartedLilypad | Arduino 1.0.5

  gettingStartedLilypad                                              ▼

/*
  INtro to the Lilypad

This basic Arduino example blainks an LED connected to pin 2.
Modified from teh original Arduino blink example.

 */


void setup()              //run once, when the sketch starts
{
  pinMode(led, OUTPUT);   //sets the digital pin as output
}


void loop()               //run over and over again
{
  digitalWrite(2, HIGH);  // turn the LED on (HIGH is the voltage level)
  delay(1000);            // wait for a second
  digitalWrite(2, LOW);   // turn the LED off by making the voltage LOW
  delay(1000);            // wait for a second
}
```

3.85

3.85
Programming the
LilyPad.

Design with smart textiles

Exercise Twelve: Integrated practical project

To bring all your skills together, follow the online tutorial from Leah Buechley to make a cycle jacket that tells drivers which way you are going to turn. Access Buechley's project instructions here: http://web.media.mit.edu/~leah/LilyPad/build/turn_signal_jacket.html

3.86

3.86
Turn signal jacket for cycling. A push button under each wrist tells the system which way you intend to turn and turns on the appropriate set of LEDs on the back of the jacket. In night-time mode all the LEDs flash. Buechley's tutorial includes tips on sewing, circuit design, Ohm's Law and finishing so the garment is robust, and she also provides the full code for you to copy and paste into your own Arduino sketch. Leah Buechley.

3 PROJECT THREE: HE'S NOT HEAVY [BAG]

Familiar form—custom textile variable resistor—microprocessor—traffic light LED output signal function.

You are aiming to make a bag with a handle that senses when you have overfilled it.

The steps in this project are:
1. Crochet the sensor.
2. Felt the sensor.
3. Prototype the circuit and coding.
4. Design the physical circuit with the bag.

Tools and materials needed are listed under each step—it is worth reading ahead so you have what you need in advance.

Approximate timings for a beginner:
- Crocheting (including learning through mistakes)—4 hours over two days
- Felting—1 hour plus 24 hours drying
- Electronics: input pin out and code—1 hour
- Electronics: output pin out and code—1 hour
- Translating into physical circuit—4 hours

3.87
Completed bag.

Design with smart textiles

Step 1: Crochet the sensor

The first step is to make the stretch sensor handle. Images 3.93a and b show a crocheted tube with wool, elastic and conductive yarn. Its resistance measures 66.3 ohms at rest. When stretched, the resistance will drop, and we can use this to trigger an output meaning the bag is too heavy. You can choose to make the outputs a pattern of lights or a warning sound.

This project draws on Lara Grant's crochet work and Crochet Guru's post on YouTube, "Crochet in the Round." Crochet Guru was very helpful—if you have not crocheted before, be prepared to make a few mistakes and to do the work over a few times.

You will need:

- Crochet hook—5mm
- Merino wool yarn—the more merino the better (you'll see I tried more than one)
- Conductive thread—I used a 4-ply steel thread
- Elastic thread—shirring or knicker elastic
- Embroidery scissors
- Multimeter
- Crocodile clips
- Sushi mat
- Towel
- A sink and basin of cold water
- A cup of warm water
- Liquid soap

3.88a

3.88b

3.88c

3.88a
Selection of wool yarns.

3.88b
Shirring elastic.

3.88c
4-ply steel conductive yarn.

Combine the three yarns: wool yarn, conductive thread and elastic thread. Make a slip knot and slide it onto the crochet hook.

3.89a

3.89b

3.89c

3.89a
Plait the three yarns together.

3.89b
Make a slip knot.

3.89c
Slip knot on the crochet hook.

Make four chain stitches.

3.90a

3.90b

3.90c

Push the hook through the last stitch you made, just above the very bottom strand of yarn. Letting the hook do the work for you, pull the yarn through so that two loops are on your hook. Now pull the yarn through both this new loop, and the one already on the hook, leaving a single crochet on your hook. This is a single crochet (sc).

Now we need to increase the number of stitches—this is one way of increasing, and is useful here because it doesn't leave a hole at the center of the work.

Push the hook through the same stitch as before. Single crochet again. This means you have made two single crochets from one stitch. Do the same for the remaining three stitches (holes)—that is, single crochet twice in each.

At the end, make a slip stitch through the opposite end of the work, bringing the two ends together. To make a slip stitch, simply pull the yarn through both existing loops.

If you are new to crochet, it is worth practicing first with a single strand of yarn; the label on the ball will tell you which hook size will work best. This will help you get a feel for the rhythm and logic of the crochet structure.

"Single crochet" (sc) = the following steps: yarn over (yo), pull through to create two loops on the hook; yo and pull through both loops to leave just one on the hook.

If you find increasing difficult to follow, try doing Crochet Guru's tutorial first. She teaches a different way of doing it, but it helped me to understand what was happening before I went on with push_reset's Instructable.

Count the stitches that make up the round and look for the V forms that are linking together around the edge. When you push your needle into a stitch, you are going to push it through under this horizontal V. Working into each of the stitches in turn will start to build the length of the tube.

To make sure you keep working the same six stitches, count the Vs every so often. Your hook is inserted below the horizontal V. If you work the same stitch twice, or skip a stitch, the shape of the wall will alter. To open the wall up (flatten the shape) you would work more single crochets into the same stitch. To narrow the wall, you would decrease the number of stitches by single crocheting through three at a time (we'll do this to finish off). My first attempt was blue, very long, and not very uniform in shape! That's why some of the images show a yellow tube too.

Continue until the tube is about 18cm (7 inches) long. Bearing in mind you will be felting the sensor using a sushi mat, don't make the tube too long—keep it shorter than the width of the mat.

3.90a
Make four chain stitches.

3.90b
Slip stitch to join the ends.

3.90c
Build the length of the tube.

To finish off by decreasing, sc but leave the new loop on the hook. sc the next stitch too, and then yo and pull through to leave one loop. Repeat this twice more to close the tube. Finish off by cutting and pulling the yarn through completely.

Before you felt the work, measure the resistance of your sensor with a multimeter. Using the crocodile clips, attach the positive and negative electrodes to the two ends of the crocheted piece, making sure they are in contact with the conductive yarn. Switch the multimeter on and to the lowest resistance band (on this one, below 200 ohms).

The resistance will decrease when the work is stretched, and return slowly to more or less its original reading when it relaxes. This piece settled at about 66 ohms when at rest, and dropped to just over 27 ohms when stretched to 30cm.

Note that you should avoid touching the textile with your hands when stretching it as your body acts as a large capacitor and significantly affects the resistance. Instead, stretch it carefully while holding the insulated crocodile clips.

After a few minutes, the resistance of this piece returned to about 50 ohms, lower than its starting point. It continues to rise slowly if left at rest, but stops at under 60 ohms, because the form has not fully returned to the same physical resting position.

This return is not complete or reliable because of the number of stitches and connections involved (the same is even more true of knitted stretch sensors). A short narrow sensor is more reliable than a long or broad one. Some of this behavior can be dealt with in the programming by setting values as output triggers (or by building in self-learning algorithms). The physical return, and therefore the reliability of the values you are getting, can also be helped by the felting process, and that's what we're going to do now.

3.91

3.92a

3.92b

3.91
Crocheted tube almost finished.

3.92a
Decreasing to finish off, first step.

3.92b
Decreasing to finish off, second step.

3.93a

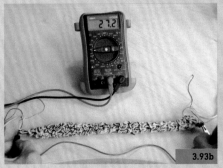

3.93b

3.93a
Checking resistance at rest.

3.93b
Checking resistance when stretched.

Step 2: Felt the sensor

You will need:
- Male and female D-sub connectors
- A sharp needle with a large eye, and needle threader
- Flat-nosed jewelry pliers
- Heat shrink tubing
- Heat gun

3.94a

3.94b

3.94c

Place the towel on a table or bench with the sushi mat on top of it. Prepare a small bowl of hot water with a few drops of liquid soap in it, plus a larger bowl of cold water. Be prepared for a workout— this process takes just under an hour.

Dunk the crocheted work into the hot soapy water. Squeeze the excess water out and place it on the mat. Now roll it, pressing down, about 200 times. Then dunk the work into the cold water to shock the fibers and help them shrink faster. Again squeezing out the excess water, scrunch the work in your hands about 75 times.

This process should be repeated at least 7 times according to Lara Grant (whose practice is all about electronic felted interfaces)—her work shrank by 0.75 inches (2cm). This piece, using the yellow merino "woolly" yarn, didn't shrink so much, if at all, but the wool did felt and the form tightened up.

Leave the work to air dry (at least 24 hours).

Once dry, this felted sensor gave a reading of about 25 ohms at rest and 15 ohms when stretched.

You can also add header wires to the ends of the textile work, as Lara Grant suggests. You can now find these components through reseller sites such as eBay, and these male and female D-sub connectors are very useful for finishing off textile components. The wire ends will fit into a breadboard so you can design your circuits and prototype with Arduino.

3.95

3.95
Checking resistance once felted.

3.94a
Materials for felting.

3.94b
Soaking sensor in warm soapy water.

3.94c
Scrunching the work up.

To finish the work with male header pins, untangle the wool from the elastic and conductive yarns. Trim the wool, leaving the other two loose ends. If the loose ends are coming out of the side rather than the tip of the work, simply draw them through to the end by threading them through a sharp, large-eye needle. Tie a small knot close to the felted work and lay the two yarns into the open crimp of the male header pin. This is fiddly, but the knot will help keep the yarns from slipping back through.

Squeeze the legs of the crimp tight shut over the yarns with the flat-nosed pliers.

Laying the yarns back toward the work, slide a small piece of heat shrink tubing over the header pin so it covers the yarns and the crimp. Hold the work in front of the nozzle of the heat gun for a few seconds—the tubing will shrink to a third its original diameter, protecting the connections you just made. WARNING! The heat gun nozzle and the air from it are very hot—do not touch!

Once the tubing is cool, you can snip away the loose threads.

3.97a

3.97b

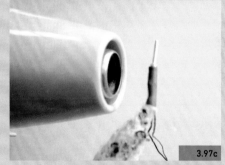
3.97c

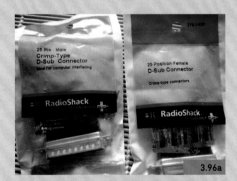
3.96a

3.96b

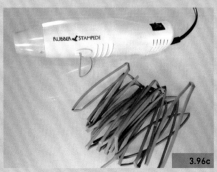
3.96c

3.97d

3.96a
D-sub connectors, male and female.

3.96b
Jewelers' pliers.

3.96c
Heat gun and heat shrink tubing.

3.97a
Laying the conductive and elastic yarns into the crimp of the D-sub connector.

3.97b
Heating the heat shrink tubing.

3.97c
Heat shrink tubing in action.

3.97d
Yarns ready for trimming.

Step 3: Prototype the circuit and coding

You will need:
— Laptop or PC running Arduino programming environment
— Your multimeter
— Low impedance resistors—e.g., 15 or 20 ohms (not included in kit below)
— The Arduino starter kit or similar, including:
  — Arduino board
  — Breadboard
  — USB cable
  — Selection of resistors
  — Jumper wires
  — LEDs
  — Plenty of crocodile clips

Read the changing voltage from the stretch sensor.

Force sensors, bend sensors and stretch sensors are all variable resistors. To connect a variable resistor with a microcontroller (e.g., an Arduino), you need a voltage divider circuit. This is not complex and will be very useful for many projects.

First measure the resistance of your crocheted sensor: this one is measuring between 21 and 21.5 ohms at rest. Then find a resistor close to this value: you can learn to read the color codes on resistors, or you can cheat and use a multimeter to test them. If the value is showing as 1, switch your dial to a higher band of values: this multimeter is banded in 100s, 1000s, kilohms and megaohms. If, on the 20k band, your resistor reads as 9.93, you have a 10k ohm resistor.

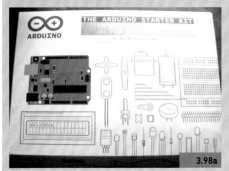

3.98a

3.98b

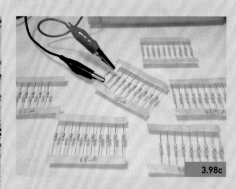

3.98c

3.98a
Arduino starter kit.

3.98b
Checking resistor values.

3.98c
Organizing your resistors.

In fact, 20 ohms or thereabouts is very low. If you have the Arduino kit as shown, it will not have a low enough resistor included in it. You can buy large bags of mixed resistors—you might want to measure these and mark the tapes as shown for later.

To create the voltage divider circuit, place your custom sensor in series with the similar (standard) resistor of roughly the same resistance in ohms, as shown in the diagram. Flex and light sensor tutorials with Arduino show the same pin-out. Follow these steps:

1. Using a crocodile clip and jumper wire, connect one end of your custom sensor to ground (GND) on the analog side of the Arduino board.
2. Place the standard resistor on the board so it bridges the conductive strips inside the board (in this case, vertically, as shown); this means the current must flow through it.
3. Connect a jumper wire from one end of the standard resistor to Analog pin A0 on the Arduino.
4. Connect another jumper wire from the 5V pin to the other end of the standard resistor.
5. Connect that same end of the standard resistor to your stretch resistor.

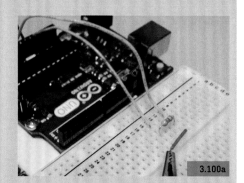

3.100a

3.100b

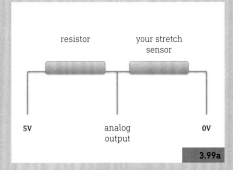

3.99a

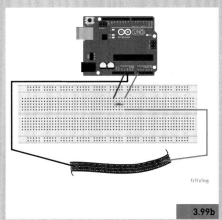

fritzing

3.99b

3.99a
Voltage divider circuit schematic.

3.99b
Fritzing pin-out of a voltage divider circuit with a textile stretch sensor.

3.100a
Placement of the resistor.

3.100b
GND and A0 pin.

3.100c
The crocodile clip connecting the sensor.

3.100c

Coding:
- In Arduino, open file > examples > basics > ReadAnalogVoltage.
- Connect your board and upload the file.
- In the tools menu, click on Serial Monitor.
- Stretch and scrunch your textile sensor and watch the values change.

This crocheted sensor gave me around 2.46 volts when I held it as you would a bag handle, and changed to around 2.16 volts when I pulled on the ends to simulate weight. Voltage will always be between 0 and 5V.

The next version of the program allows you to create some meaningful output.

It reads values coming straight into pin A0, and these will be between 0 and 1023. You may want to prototype the interaction more accurately by hanging weights on the ends of the sensor, but the values within the code can always be adjusted as you work.

NOTE: You might find that the ends of the crocheted sensor are a weak point. If the threads pull out of the D-sub crimp, or seem likely to break, try using bead caps bought from a jewelry supply store. More details on finishing the ends can be seen in the next step.

Adjust the pin-out of your board:
- Make the 5V and GND (ground) jump wires common to the whole board by plugging them into the top of the vertical rails marked + and – respectively.
- Add three LEDs as shown, with a 220 ohm resistor connecting the short (negative) leg of each LED to the ground rail of the breadboard.
- Each LED also needs a positive lead into a digital pin on the Arduino board—in this case, pins 7, 8 and 9.
- Add an open-ended jump wire to the bottom of the common ground rail to attach your stretch sensor to.
- Add a jump wire between the stretch sensor resistor and the common voltage rail.

3.101a

3.101b

3.101a & b
Traffic light board pin-out details.

Design with smart textiles

Now copy and paste the code into your Arduino sketch.

Find it online here: www.bloomsbury.com/kettley-smart-textiles

Compile and upload it to the board. You can adjust the values to suit the sensor you have made. You should now have three LEDs lighting up as the strain on the sensor increases.

3.101c
Arduino sketch reading analog input to pin 0, with scrolling output values.

KEY QUESTION

Try using a strip of conductive jersey in place of your crocheted sensor. What happens and why? What would you need to do to your code to take account of this difference in the sensor behavior? (Tip: Think about the mathematical arguments.)

Step 4: Design the physical circuit with the bag

You will need:
- An existing bag
- Fabric to match the bag, or calico or embroidery fabric if making a lining
- Medium-weight iron-on interfacing
- Snap studs
- Craft iron
- LilyPad Arduino and FTDI board, if needed
- USB cable
- LilyPad components
  - LEDs
  - Battery holder
  - Slider switch if not using LilyPad battery holder
- Battery
- Small drill bits for metal (0.8 to 3.2mm are useful sizes)
- Pendant or hobby drill
- Handheld drill tools
- Sewing needles
- Conductive thread
- Thimble
- Extra flat-nosed pliers
- Barrel-end clasp and extra trigger clasp, or alternative findings
- Sandpaper, sandpaper stick or riffler files
- Multimeter
- Plenty of crocodile clips
- Goggles

Find a suitable small bag for your handle—here, I have used a small hard-case clutch and removed the original strap. If you are going to use the existing strap hooks on the bag, check that there is no electrical connection between them before you start—the bag may have a metal frame they are attached to, which means your circuit will not work. You can get around this problem by making your own hooks and loops using strong fabric.

Collect a few alternatives to create the join between the handle and the bag. Pictured are a range of jewelry findings including pinch balls, bead caps, bar crimps, barrel cord ends and bag clasps. Check all your components for electrical continuity using the multimeter. If any do not give a reading, they may have a nonconductive finish—use sandpaper or a riffler file to expose the metal base.

3.102a

3.102b

3.102a
Clutch bag.

3.102b
Sanding connectors on clutch bag.

Collect a few alternatives to create the join between the handle and the bag. Pictured are a range of jewelry findings including pinch balls, bead caps, bar crimps, barrel cord ends and bag clasps. Check all your components for electrical continuity using the multimeter. If any do not give a reading, they may have a nonconductive finish—use sandpaper or a riffler file to expose the metal base.

I used the barrel cord ends to finish off the crochet handle; you need to find a pair with holes in them to sew through, or drill your own with a high-speed hobby drill. Make sure the hole size is large enough for your sewing needle and thread to pass through a couple of times. You can open up the holes a little with a small hand drill or a round riffler file if you need to. Now you can use the holes to sew through with conductive yarn, making a mechanical and electrical connection with the textile sensor. There are two approaches to positioning the holes—either close to the edge of the metal so you can sew over the edge, or opposite each other so you can pass the needle straight through the crocheted work and out the other side. You may need the thimble to push the needle through if the felted crochet is quite dense.

SAFETY!

When drilling, wear goggles to protect your eyes, place a wooden dowel inside the tube to support it, center-punch where you want the holes to guide the drill bit and avoid skating, and lubricate the drill bit to minimize heat. Do not drill near your electronics or your laptop—you will be creating fine metal dust. Make sure you have a first aid kit to hand in case of injury.

3.103a

3.104a

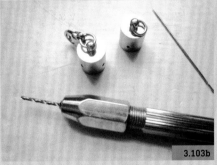

3.103b

3.104b

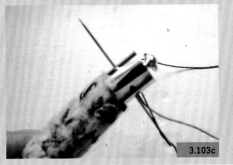

3.103c

3.103a
Crocheted sensor with selection of jewelry findings.

3.103b
Hand drilling cord ends.

3.103c
Stitching cord ends to crocheted sensor.

3.104a
Cord ends and clasps attached.

3.104b
Handle attached to bag.

3.104c
Reading the resistance.

3.104c

The barrel end clasp may come in a pack with one clasp because it is intended as a necklace clasp; fit a second one to the other end by opening up the jump ring. Holding a pair of flat-nosed pliers in each hand, twist the jump ring open. Attach the handle to the bag, and check for continuity between the two ends of the handle. (The multimeter shown does not have a continuity setting, so I am measuring the resistance in ohms.)

Now you need to transfer the circuit on the breadboard to sewable Lilypad (or other brand) hardware. If your Lilypad needs an FTDI board, as shown, make sure you have the drivers installed for it: find them at http://www.ftdichip.com/Drivers/VCP.htm. Select the Lilypad from the Arduino Tools > Board menu, and the port from the Tools > Port menu (it should include "usbserial" in the name). You should now be able to upload the sketch (code) that you used earlier.

The LilyPad has the same power, ground, and analog and digital input and output pins that you will need. Try drawing around the components or using Fritzing (Fritzing.org) to draw up circuits that start to become less orthogonal and more freeform. You can also use crocodile clips to test as you go.

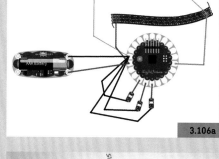

3.106a

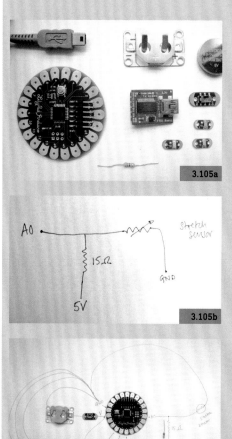

3.105a

3.105b

3.105c

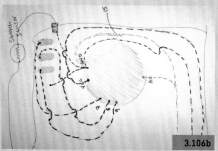

3.106b

3.105a
LilyPad components.

3.105b
Voltage divider circuit.

3.105c
Sketching the physical circuit.

3.106a
Fritzing.

3.106b
Hand drawing.

3.106c
Crocodile clips.

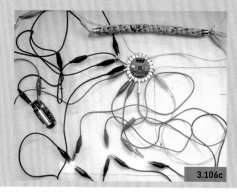

3.106c

The LilyPad power supply board will step up the 1.5V of a AAA battery to the 5V needed by the circuit. Do not use a battery supplying more than 5.5V. You can also use a 3V coin cell battery here, which is lighter and takes up less space. It will not step up to 5V, however, and you will notice your LEDs are dimmer. You might also want to add a slider switch if you use a coin cell. The 220 ohm resistors from your original circuit will be replaced by the onboard LED resistors. Make the resistor for your voltage divider sewable by making neat loops from the legs with round-nosed pliers, as shown.

Sketch out the physical circuit according to the form you are working with. In this case I have made a removable insert for the bag rather than permanently attaching the electronics. The battery sits inside one end of the closed bag, with the LilyPad against one side wall. The LEDs are on a separate flap that hangs outside the bag, and snap onto the inner lining.

Stitch the circuit onto your chosen fabric, making sure to finish ends neatly. With the multimeter, check regularly that there is continuity where you need it and no connection where there should not be.

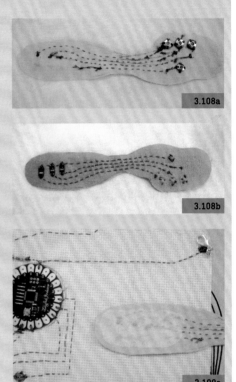
3.108a

3.108b

3.109a

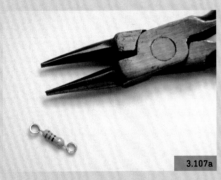
3.107a

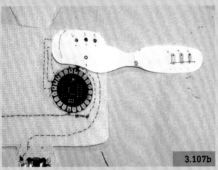
3.107b

3.109b

3.108a
Snap-on LED component (back).

3.108b
Snap-on LED component (front).

3.109a
Insulating stitched connections with interfacing.

3.109b
Insulating between two stitched connections with interfacing.

3.107a
Making a sewable resistor.

3.107b
Pattern cutting with LEDs.

Use the interfacing to keep ends in place and minimize fraying, ironing it onto the reverse of the fabric where needed. Snap studs can be used to make connections between parts—I used a different fabric for the visible part of the circuit. You could also choose to make some parts interchangeable in this way.

Once you have a complete textile circuit, you should check the values in the program again—that is, you should calibrate it. This is because you have introduced new materials with resistance into the circuit, and you will be holding the handle—each person introduces a different capacitive drain to the circuit.

Further refinements you could make:
• Do user testing to decide what "too heavy" means in use for different people.
• Redesign the connections between handle loops and inner circuit.
• Protect the hardware inside the bag with wadding or spacer fabric.
• Add automatic calibration to the Arduino program.
• Explore the mechanical relationship between the bag handle and the bag.
• Explore different bag forms and their uses.

3.111

3.110

3.110
Checking the values in the finished circuit.

3.111
The finished bag.

Design with smart textiles

Chapter summary

Suggested reading

This chapter gave you some basic practical skills and introduced you to the key principles of soft electronics. You learned about sourcing fabrics and yarns, the components found in a circuit, and some of the issues when working with conductive yarns and fabrics. You should now have a collection of your own stitched circuits with LEDs, and a range of experimental textile sensors that can be built into smart textile applications at different scales. You should understand when and why you would involve a microprocessor in your projects, and you have tried building your first wearable with a LilyPad Arduino.

Adafruit, https://learn.adafruit.com/collins-lab-soldering/transcript; https://learn.adafruit.com/collins-lab-breadboards-and-perfboards/transcript.

Arduino, "Getting Started with LilyPad Arduino." Available online: http://arduino.cc/en/Guide/ArduinoLilyPad (accessed 7 April 2015).

Buechley, L. and M. Eisenberg, "The Lilypad Arduino: Toward Wearable Engineering for Everyone" IEEE Pervasive Computing 2, no.2 (April - June 2008): 200.

Buechley, L., K. Peppler and M. Eisenberg (2013), Textile Messages: Dispatches From the World of E-Textiles and Education, Bern, Switzerland: Peter Lang Publishing.

Eng, D. (2009), Fashion Geek: Clothes and Accessories Tech, Cincinnati, OH: North Light Books.

ETH Zurich, "Thermochromic Ink & Silver Ink Video Tutorial." Available online: http://www.youtube.com/watch?v= n6EBCsuPABo (accessed 7 April 2015).

Foxtel, "Alert Shirt." Available online: https://www.youtube.com/watch?v=maHGf3LNGMs (accessed 7 April 2015).

Future-Shape, "Large-Area Proximity Sensors." Available online: http://future-shape.com/en/competencies/11/large-area-proximity-sensors (accessed 7 April 2015).

Grant, L., "Circuit Bending Orchestra for the Fairytale Fashion Show." Available online: http://makezine.com/2010/02/18/circuit-bending-orchestra-for-the-f/ (accessed 7 April 2015).

Hartman, K. (2014), Make: Wearable Electronics, Sebastopol, CA: Maker Media, Inc. Instructables.

Hughes, R. and Rowe, M. (1991), The Colouring, Bronzing and Patination of Metals: A Manual for Fine Metalworkers, Sculptors and Designers, London: Thames & Hudson.

An Internet of Soft Things. Available online: http://aninternetofsoftthings.com/how-to/ (accessed 7 April 2015).

Jseay on Instructables. Available online: http://www.instructables.com/member/jseay/ (accessed 7 April 2015).

Less EMF. Available online: www.LessEMF.com (accessed 7 April 2015).

Kirstein, T., ed. (2013), Multidisciplinary Know-How for Smart-Textile Developers (Woodhead Publishing Series in Textiles), Cambridge, UK: Woodhead Publishing Ltd.

Kobakant, "Chipmanband Workshop." Available online: http://www.kobakant.at/DIY/?p=5044. (accessed 7 April 2015).

Kobakant, "How To Get What You Want." Available online: http://www.kobakant.at/DIY/ (accessed 7 April 2015).

Lewis, A. (2008), Switch Craft, New York: Potter Craft.

Pakhchyan, S. (2008), Fashioning Technology, Sebastopol, CA: O'Reilly.

Patel, S., H. Park, P. Bonato, L. Chan and M. Rodgers (2012), "A Review of Wearable Sensors and Systems with Application in Rehabilitation," Journal of NeuroEngineering and Rehabilitation, 9: 21. Available online: http://www.jneuroengrehab.com/content/pdf/1743-0003-9-21.pdf (accessed 27 May 2014).

Platt, C. (2009), Make Electronics: Learning Through Discovery, Sebastopol, CA: Maker Media.

Plug and Wear. Available online: http://www.plugandwear.com/default.asp?mod=cpages&page_id=37 (accessed 26 May 2014).

Sparkfun, "Tutorials." Available online: https://learn.sparkfun.com/tutorials (accessed 7 April 2015).

Zeagler, C., S. Audy, S. Gilliland and T. Starner (2013), "Can I Wash It?: The Effect of Washing Conductive Materials Used in Making Textile Based Wearable Electronic Interfaces," Proc. IEEE & ACM International Symposium on Wearable Computers, Zurich, Switzerland, September 2013.

Designing your own smart textile

When working with complex and technological compositions, it is easy to get entangled in time-consuming functional details and thereby lose touch with the overall expression.

Vallgårda 2009: 69

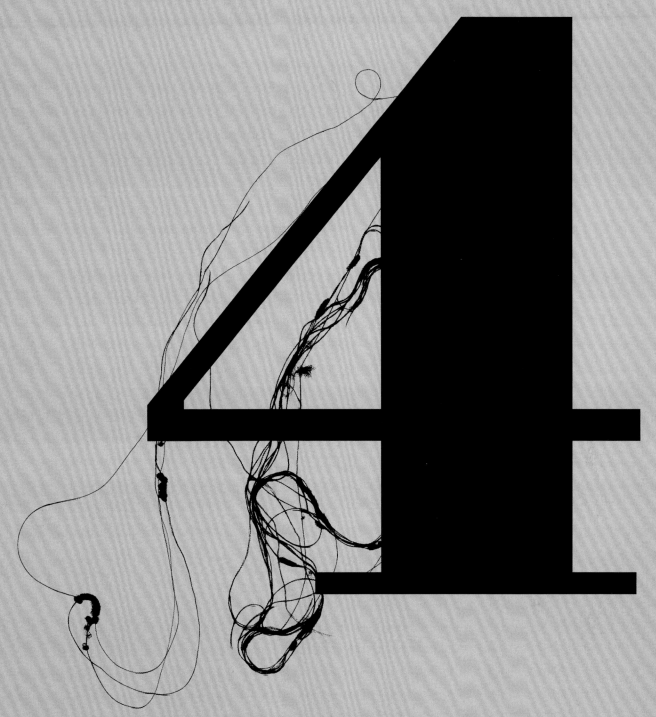

In this chapter you will be introduced to a range of researchers and practitioners who are pushing the boundaries of smart textiles, entangled with technological compositions (as Vallgårda says) without ever losing sight of the expressive potential of the work. Here you will be given access to practical experience and insights into important directions for the future of the field.

Each subsection details a project by one maker or team, with a brief introduction, a technical tip and a short list of suggested further readings. Most of these are not full projects for you to complete (although where full instructions are available online, you will be given the URL or reference for them). Instead, this chapter is intended to inspire you to try different materials, tools and processes in your own practice, and to help you to understand how material knowledge is built up through experimentation. Do not forget to document your own processes.

Case study: Lauren Bowker and THEUNSEEN

Lauren Bowker is an alumna of the Royal College of Art in London, is on the board of the European Council for the Internet of Things, and has exhibited at Paris and London Fashion Weeks. She leads THEUNSEEN, a materials exploration house in the vaults of Somerset House, site of a sixteenth-century palace and home of the Royal Academy. This location plays appropriate host to Bowker's alchemical collaborative practice, which includes chemists, pattern cutters, engineers and anatomists.
http://seetheunseen.co.uk/

Alchemy is an ancient speculative philosophy in which perfection is sought through the transmutation of material. THEUNSEEN seeks to create exquisite couture through chemical, biological and electronic science, blending art, design and performance, presented as a kind of "magick." Alchemy's concern with the relationship of the spirit with the cosmos can also be seen in the functionality of THEUNSEEN's projects, such as the Air collection, and The Eighth Sense. The consistent UNSEEN narrative of alchemy and ritual is a way to promote the lab's serious science and materials exploration. The ultimate aim is to develop seamless materials-driven technology to benefit people in everyday life.

Development of the ink
At Manchester School of Art, Bowker began to research the potential for inks and dyes with palladium chloride content, which would change color from yellow to black in the presence of carbon monoxide. Collaborating with biochemists, Bowker produced her Pollution ink, printing garments using the reversible dye to protect the wearer from contemporary hazards such as passive smoking and fuel emissions.

4.1a

4.1b

Another ink, formulated while at the Royal College of Art in London, responds to seven different parameters in the environment. Application methods depend on the material being treated and include screen printing, hand painting, spraying, and dyeing. Bowker takes a site-specific, bespoke approach to the development of pieces for individual wearers, mapping the environmental conditions in the locations where they will be worn and customizing the dye to react to those parameters.

The color changes that can be achieved in response to the seven stimuli are:

Heat—RGB or Pantone scales—reversible or irreversible change
Ultraviolet—RGB or Pantone scales—reversible or irreversible change
Pollution—yellow-black—reversible
Sound—from color to colorless
Moisture—from color to colorless
Chemicals—CMYK scale
Friction—CMYK—reversible

4.2

AIR collection

THEUNSEEN went on to present a couple capsule collection, Air, at London Fashion Week in February 2014. Air consists of three pieces: the beetle garment, which responds to heat, moisture and ultraviolet radiation; a large heat-responsive sculpture; and a wings piece, which reacted to friction and aerodynamics. The Beast garment shown in figure 4.1 is constructed of leather treated with Bowker's compound inks and dyes, allowing a mix of controlled and uncontrolled color change in the material. This piece purely responds to heat and was used during the opening of the collection in an Imbolc fire ritual: the flame retardant material was treated with the ink and the wearer set alight; once the flames had propagated, the colors were revealed.

In collaboration with Swarovski Gemstones, THEUNSEEN recently combined over 4,000 naturally occurring black spinels with the reactive ink. The stones form part of a skullcap and act as natural insulators, reacting to signals produced by activity in the brain, body temperature, skin conductivity and breathing patterns. The resulting color patterns shift throughout the day, with more orange tones occurring toward the front in the morning, and bluer patterns emerging in the evening toward the back of the head.

4.1a & b
Beast sculpture (Air collection). Leather treated with bespoke compound dyes and inks; the piece is responsive to heat, with an evolving display of color. Lauren Bowker and THEUNSEEN.

4.2
Swarovski cap with black spinel; the gemstones react to brain activity, changing color in response. Lauren Bowker and THEUNSEEN.

PRINTED CIRCUITS
Case study: Linda Worbin

The conditions for what designers are able to predict and plan for are strongly dependent on design methods, something that has evolved in parallel with material developments.

Worbin 2010: 12

Linda Worbin teaches at the Swedish School of Textiles in Borås. In her doctoral work, she developed a design methodology for working with dynamic patterns in textiles. She points out that designers are used to tools and techniques for working with static patterns, but that the expressive potential of reactive dyes means that new approaches are needed. You can think of a heat-responsive woven or printed textile as having layers of semiotic meaning, rather than a single fixed one; a single textile can give multilayered dynamic information, meaning the designer now needs to pay attention to the resolution of spatial and temporal change.

Worbin has suggested the following terms are useful for this kind of design work: *reversible*, *irreversible*, *reported* and *direct*.

A reversible pattern changes from one state into another (or others), but it will always change back to its initial expression. An irreversible pattern does not change back to its initial expression; instead it continues changing.

4.3

4.3
Woven and printed thermochromic textile; the crocodile clips at right are connected to conductive yarns woven into the fabric. They are passing an electrical current through the yarns to create heat. Linda Worbin.

4.4
Thermochromic color chart; Worbin's research has produced a large number of such charts, documenting graded ratios of pigment to thermochromic dyes in each mix, and showing results in response to a given temperature. Such charts allow designers to make more informed decisions about colorways in textile design. Linda Worbin.

4.4

A reported pattern requires a microprocessor, as it may change its expression at some other time (or even in some other site) to the interaction that triggered it. A direct pattern is similar to the term *reactive*, discussed in chapter 1—it happens in real time and in the same site as the interaction trigger (like a touch, or crumpling of the fabric). It may have been designed to have quite a specific expression, however, such as the color change when thermochromic (TC) ink reacts to body warmth. These behaviors can be mixed together, so a textile might have a reported and reversible pattern, or a direct and reversible expression, and so on. In the experiment illustrated in figure 4.5, a weave made from carbon fiber and cotton was given a screen print with TC ink (gray changing to transparent) and TC mixed with light blue pigment (gray changing to blue). In figure 4.5 the weft yarn is gray, matching the carbon fiber. The blue forms and a white horizontal linear graphic pattern appears when a current passes through the conductive carbon yarn. The power supply (4.5–12 V) is attached with crocodile clips, generating the necessary temperatures above 27°C to create visible color change. Worbin also produced color "maps" using graded ratios of pigment to binder, and different combinations of TC and non-TC pigment in layers. Her thesis documents a number of these, creating an important resource for future design work with known color change properties, reacting to quantified interaction dimensions such as how long a heat source is applied.

TECH TIPS

The general property of TC colors is that of a reversible change of color by a change in temperature. There is both a color range and a temperature range of TC pigment for textile applications; 8°C, 15°C, 27°C, and so on. Variotherm AQ Concentrated Colours is a TC pigment that gets its color-changing property from spherical particle capsules of water-insoluble film, but it can be dissolved with general pigment and water-based solvents for textile printing.

The different colors have individual fastness with respect to light and are washable at 40°C.

When designing with TC inks that react at different temperatures, Zane Berzina suggests designing for color change by applying several layers of different colors that change at different temperatures, with application of the lightest color first and the darkest in a finishing layer. She also proposes that if you design with color-changing pigment that reacts at different temperatures, you should give the highest-temperature changes the light color and lowest-temperature changes the darkest color in order to form a multicolor chromatic design.

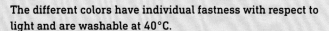

4.5 a, b, & c
Experimental thermochromic pattern; decorative patterns activated by the heat of an iron. The thermochromic ink changes, often to reveal the pigment ink color beneath it. Linda Worbin.

Sarah Kettley—
Open printed switches

Sarah Kettley is a senior lecturer in Product Design at Nottingham Trent University; she collaborates with textile practitioners and computer scientists to explore human interaction with textile interfaces.
http://sarahkettleydesign.co.uk/

Using silver-based ink Kettley included printed switches that form part of the pattern of the whole collar in *Stille*. While any pair of these could be connected to a circuit, it is the three pairs around the neck which, when touched by the wearer, complete a circuit and play digital sounds through small speakers placed in the collar. This type of switch requires a processor, for it is actually sensing a difference in potential (voltage) as a result of the body's high resistance. The Arduino microprocessor has been mounted in a small plastic box lid and supported center front. Short wires are combined with conductive yarns to create the circuit, making the best use of robustness and flexibility across the design.

Voltage divider circuits

A voltage divider is a simple circuit that uses two resistors arranged in series (not parallel) to give a lower voltage output than the power supplied (in this project a 9-volt battery). It is a very useful circuit when working with textiles and an Arduino for two reasons:
- The Arduino runs on 5 volts.
- It cannot easily read resistance (ohms), but it can read voltage input through the analog pins.

The supply voltage is divided in the ratio of the resistances in the voltage divider. If one of the resistances in a voltage divider increases, then the voltage across that resistor also increases.
So when we are working with variable resistors made with textiles, or when we are working with the body as part of the circuit (and the body is a very large resistor/capacitor), this circuit gives us the kind of output we need to trigger an actuator (lights, sound, movement). One of the resistors in the circuit becomes a variable resistor, as in *Stille*; the two silver conductive patches are open ends of a circuit, and they look very much like an on/off switch. But the current does not simply flow through the circuit and play the sound when on; because of the large resistance of the body, which closes the gap between the sliver patches, there would not be enough power to make this happen.

4.6

4.7

4.6
Stille—printed silver patches form the electrodes of three open switches, which are connected by wearers' skin when they roll their head. The body can act as part of a circuit. Author. Photo: Mike Byrne.

4.7
Stille at NIMK, Amsterdam. Only the pairs of silver "feathers" around the high neck are active.

Key questions

1. A voltage divider consisting of two 500-ohm resistors is connected across a 9-volt battery. Use the preceding equation to calculate the output voltage.
2. If the body is one of the resistors, work out what sort of value the second resistor should be to bring the output voltage within the Arduino's range of 0 to 5 volts.

TECH TIPS

Printing with silver conductive ink

Silver ink has good flexibility and can be screen printed on fabric; available from suppliers such as CreativeMaterials.com, who advise that "Best properties, for most applications, result when dried several minutes at 100°C followed by curing for 5–10 minutes at 175°C. Good properties are obtained on a variety of substrates by curing at temperatures ranging from 50°C to 175°C." Use a drying chamber, and be aware that conductivity increases when the ink is cured. A thinner is available too, which helps when printing, but you need to wear personal safety equipment to protect yourself from fumes and skin irritation.

```
+5V
 |
R1  (Sensor)
 |
 +  ——————— O  A0  (A/D input Arduino)
 |
R2  (Resistor)
 |
 =  (GND)
```

This circuit is called a **voltage divider** and the voltage at A0 can be computed as

$$A0 = [R2/(R1+R2)]\ 5V$$

Jie Qi—
Bare Conductive
painted circuits

Jie Qi spent a summer as an intern with Leah Buechley's High-Low Tech group at the Massachusetts Institute of Technology, and presented her project, *Electronic Popables*, at the TEI Conference in 2010.
http://web.mit.edu/~jieqi/Public/DREU_Site/

Exciting developments in conductive inks mean that you can work directly in sketchbooks and on flat, often flexible surfaces, or substrates, to design in a way that will be familiar to you. Pattern and color can become an integral part of an active system.

Conductive inks can also be drawn with. They have been available for a long time to the electronics community in the form of pens for spot repairs on broken circuits, but they have until recently not been viable for the creative community as an experimental medium. Jie Qi's beautiful pop-up book uses her own experimental approach to this newly available conductive drawing medium from *Bare Conductive* to build decorative two-dimensional circuits demonstrating a range of outputs such as light and movement. The pop-up genre supplies new ways to interact with switches.

4.8
Interactive pop-up book, city. Paper engineering techniques and conductive ink make interactive books possible. Jie Qi.

4.9
Interactive pop-up book, floral. The electronics in these pop-ups were created mostly using copper tape, conductive fabric and conductive paint. Earlier projects also used magnetic paint. Jie Qi.

4.10
Conductive ink for drawing and painting; the ink can also be used to cold solder components, and turns any surface into a sensor. Bare Conductive.

TECH TIPS

You might want to dilute Electric Paint to make it less viscous, and you can do this simply by adding water because it is a suspension of conductive particles in a water-based solution. But be careful—doing this will make it less conductive. Bare Conductive offers a host of tutorials on its site, including this one: http://www.bareconductive .com/make/diluting-electric-paint/ (accessed 8 April 2015).

Jo Hodge—
Thermo- and
photochromic fashion

Joanne Hodge was supported by the Arts and Humanities Research Council in her research into personal communication through textile objects. http://joannehodge.co.uk/blog/

Hodge uses screen-printed inks that react to heat (thermochromic) and light (photochromic) to enhance interaction with garments on the body. She places prints on underskirts and offers the wearer multiple choices through fastenings to make these visible at different times. She says:

> *The underskirt appears to be a clear gloss print until exposed to UV light . . . It is exciting to see the print glow brilliantly bright and turn a deep purple, but for this to occur you have to lift up the skirt, revealing more than you might normally feel comfortable with . . . To get both of these garments to change color the wearer and others will be touching, breathing on, lifting, and buttoning the garment in a variety of ways.*

4.11

4.11.
Thermochromic and photochromic inks. Hodge mixes reactive inks to explore possibilities for human interaction. Jo Hodge.

4.12
Thermochromic and photochromic inks at the CCA, Glasgow. In these garments, the inside is also printed with color-change inks; the wearer needs to pin up or lift the skirt to reveal this. Jo Hodge.

TECH TIPS

These passive forms of smart textiles do not need a microprocessor or any circuitry at all. They simply react to their environment.

4.12

KNITTED SENSORS AND ACTUATORS
Case study: Martha Glazzard

Martha Glazzard is a knit researcher working on the UK Research Council, which funded the *An Internet of Soft Things* project. She gained her PhD in qualitative design approaches to advanced material design using weft-knitted structures, exploring knowledge transfer and the characterization of knit as a discipline. Her research interests are in knitted structures, material and structural properties, function-focused design, practitioner approach, and practice-led qualitative assessment. https://marthaglazzard.wordpress.com/author/marthaglazzard/

Aeolia
This project combined expertise from fashion, textiles, electrical engineering, interaction design, and craft. The project worked first of all with commercially available rubber-carbon stretch sensors held in knitted channels (and in the other garments, couched embroidery channels, and channels created in woven structures with floats—see figure 2.11) before Glazzard developed her own approach to creating knitted stretch sensors for a "cello garment" (figure 4.13).

This knitted fabric acts as a variable resistor, using the change in number of contacts between stitches when stretched to create changes in resistance across the material. The sensor data that is gained from this is very "noisy," however, and not reliable enough in this form for medical or other critical applications. This project made creative use of this problem, filtering the sensor output from the movement of the cellist's bowing arm in real time using Ableton software, and feeding values back into the interactive sound system as part of a dynamic performance feedback loop.

4.13
Knitted stretch sensor. Long narrow knitted forms gave more reliable data than wide ones; this data was fed back into software that was able to filter it and make it usable.

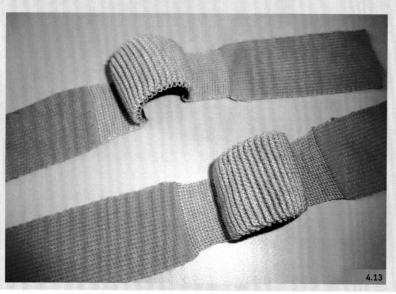

4.13

4.15

4.14
Autoclave in situ; thermochromic inks are changed by the bands of knitted copper wires. Martha Glazzard.

4.15
Autoclave process; testing the current and ink reactions. Martha Glazzard.

Autoclave

Glazzard collaborated with scientist Nisha Rana to produce the knitted artwork shown in figure 4.14 for the 3M Health Care award in the category "safeguarding health by preventing infection." *Autoclave* uses conductive heating elements and thermochromic inks to exert the sterilizing properties of heat on bacteria-covered agar plates. When the copper wires that are knitted into stripes in the fabric are warmed with the circuit, the thermochromic ink fades away to reveal a different color.

Auxetic structures

In her doctoral research, Glazzard drew on traditional textile design methods to examine the potential functionality of *auxetic* structures. Materials with this kind of structure are said to have a negative Poisson's ratio, meaning they expand in a direction transverse to applied stretch (they appear to become fatter rather than thinner when they are stretched lengthwise). An important aspect of Glazzard's work here was her recognition of *tacit knowledge*—the embodied understanding she had of the

knit process and knitted fabric structure. This allowed her to demonstrate the aesthetic, tactile and subjective design qualities alongside the more normal goals of auxetic functionality and testing criteria. She then developed this in playful explorations of three-dimensional printed rubber and plastic materials to create similar geometric structures with very different surface and functional properties, such as porosity, scale and stretch characteristics.

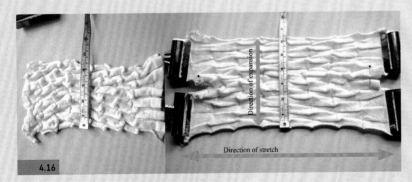

4.16
Measuring auxetic behavior; an auxetic structure expands along both its length and breadth at the same time. Different knit structures had different auxetic characteristics. Martha Glazzard.

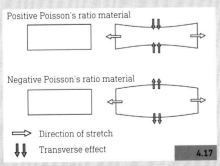

4.17
Communicating auxetic behavior. Auxetic materials are of interest to many different fields, which value information delivered in different ways. Martha Glazzard.

4.18
3D printed auxetic structure; Martha translated the knowledge she had built up in creating knitted auxetics to collaboratively program a 3D printer to build an auxetic structure in two types of rubber material. Martha Glazzard.

Anna Persson—
Using heat to change
a knit structure

Dr. Anna Persson completed her PhD at the University of Borås in 2013. Her thesis was titled "Exploring Textile Materials for Interaction Design," in which she investigated reversible and non-reversible changes in textile structures for communicative and expressive ends.
http://smarttextiles.se/en/textile-interaction-design-explores-new-expressions/

Anna Persson has explored using heat as a way of changing the surface and structure of knitted fabrics through *shrinking, breaking, stiffening, texturizing* and *warming*. In the project *Touching Loops*, three different interactive textiles can change their visual and tactile expression: when you touch the textile with your hand, it warms up, and the different fibers change their structure, shrinking, breaking or hardening. The most successful experiments were those where the conductive fibers were introduced in rows, and which did not have large areas of plain knitting.

4.19

4.19
Heat change fabrics; embedded textile sensors react to touch by heating up areas of the fabric; the heat is enough to deform or even melt polymer yarns used in its construction. Anna Persson.

TECH TIPS

The first experiment combines a silver-coated copper yarn and Pemotex yarn in a ridge pattern with plain knit areas. Fine rows of conductive yarns separate the areas of the textile surface, sensing and transmitting the information as heat. When current is applied, the knitted patterns change size by shrinking in relation to the amount of heat and the surface area where heat appears. The metal fibers are generating the heat, while the Pemotex yarn (100 percent polyester) melts (and is nonreversible).

In the second sample a Jacquard pattern combines shrinking polyester monofilament, a Grilon yarn and a silver-coated copper yarn. Grilon is a lowmelt nylon, Co-PA (copolyamide) multifilament typically used in industry for molding knitted fabric into a shape. At between 80 and 90°C, this thermoformable yarn will melt, becoming a bonding and adhesive agent. Rows of ridge patterns are interlaced on the surface design, building its texture as a structural frame. In this case, the surface does not change texturally, as it did in the previous design experiment. Instead, applying heat through the conductive yarns on the material's ridges produces a transformation in the surface from soft to hard by stiffening specific areas.

The third piece is constructed with partial knitting and ridge patterns, and the yarns used are Pemotex, a Grilon yarn, and the silver-coated copper yarn. The pattern uses a Jacquard 2 × 2 net technique. The rows of Jacquard are separated in a computer program to control the placement and size of the breaks in the material. When exposed to heat, the transformable yarns melt, leaving the loops of conductive yarns. The rows of conductive yarns sustain the shape of the loops, transforming the textural effect of the surface from a two-dimensional to a three-dimensional pattern by breaking.

Amit Gupta— Galvanic skin response with knitted circuits

Amit Gupta is a researcher at Colab, a collaboration for design and creative technologies at the Auckland University of Technology (AUT), New Zealand. Gupta is highly experienced in the design and production of fine-gauge knitwear, whole garments, and intricate CAD fabrics, and is a CAD knit and Shima Seiki programming specialist, including advanced fabric construction and pattern development.
https://colab.aut.ac.nz/projects/emotionally -intelligent-knitted-textiles/

For different intelligent clothing applications, different knit structures can be chosen to suit confining pressure and conductivity requirements. Conductive knitted fabric of specific stitches can be innovatively used as powerful devices for intelligent uses, such as monitoring sensors and heat generators.

Gupta is interested in the potential of the emotional responses of people to textiles through the sense of touch, and for his PhD, he is working on knitted circuits for monitoring health signals. In the example shown in figure 4.20, Gupta is aiming to keep the conductive yarn away from skin contact for two reasons: it affects the accuracy of readings taken by the system (the body acts as a very large capacitor, creating a voltage drop across the circuit), and for some people, the metals in the yarns may cause irritation. Although the galvanic skin response sensor cannot identify a particular emotion on its own, the sweat glands are controlled by the sympathetic nervous system, so moments of strong emotion such as happy, sad, and so on will produce a higher voltage, indicating higher levels of stress or excitement.

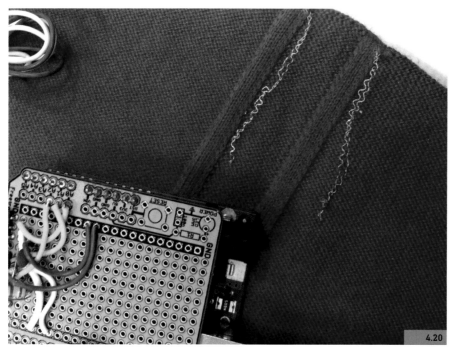

4.20
Knitted galvanic skin response sensor; the conductive yarn had to be knitted into the structure tightly to minimize fraying. Amit Gupta.

TECH TIPS

One strand of conductive yarn (conductive yarn carries electricity from a battery to light-emitting diodes (LEDs) or other components—it is like a wire without insulation) is plaited inside the back of tubular knit construction (sandwiched between front and back bed knitting). Various knitting techniques have been used to achieve the desired result, such as intarsia, plaiting, tubular knitting and interlock knitting. Conductive yarn must be knitted tight to ensure a proper connection because after wear and tear, it tends to fray, and the stitches can become loose. The single strand of conductive yarn is enough to carry full current on a 65 centimeter by 80 centimeter knitted panel. The resistivity of all conductive threads increases drastically with length, making them inappropriate for long connections. I have used a 1 megaohm resistor to overcome this issue; it is placed between the send pin and the receive (sensor) pin for absolute touch to activate.

This prototype used:
One LilyPad Arduino
One 0.1 microfarad capacitor
One 1 megaohm resistor
One NeoPixel (RGB)
One end of conductive yarn (stainless steel)
Two ends of wool blend (2/60 Nm)

Skin conductance, also known as galvanic skin response (GSR), is a method of measuring the electrical conductance of the skin, which varies with its moisture level. Skin conductance is used as an indication of psychological or physiological arousal. Two electrodes are knitted at the bottom of the panel, where the user places two fingers, and an RGB LED lights up according to the person's conductance. In this case, one end of conductive yarn was connected to the 5-volt battery and the other to one of the analog input/output pins, and then to the ground. It is essential to use a capacitor and a resistor to eliminate unwanted noise. The output data was converted into voltage and was measuring between 0 and 5 volts. Different colors are associated with the output:

0–1 V = White
1–2 V = Blue
2–3 V = Green
3–4 V = Yellow
4–5 V = Red

Ebru Kurbak and Irene Posch— The knitted radio

Ebru Kurbak is an artist, researcher and educator based in Vienna, Austria. She studied architecture at the Istanbul Technical University. Irene Posch works at the University for Applied Art in Vienna within the artistic research project Stitching Worlds, and is a PhD student at the Vienna Technical University. The Knitted Radio was nominated for the New Technological Art Award and exhibition at The Zebrastraat, Ghent, BE on November 7, 2014.
http://ebrukurbak.net/
http://www.ireneposch.net/

Ebru Kurbak and Irene Posch work together to explore the political dimensions of knitting. The Knitted Radio is designed to be hand-knitted, with instructions made available democratically. Other projects such as Drapery FM and Punch Couture have involved knitting machines and punch cards. These projects enable the creation by home crafters of electronic components made from scratch using textiles. By writing and sharing instructions in the familiar form of a knitting pattern, but including conductive yarns, they reach out to new communities of makers so they may knit their own resistors, capacitors and inductors.

The Knitted Radio was developed with the support of the Federal Chancellery of Austria and the Province of Styria, at Eyebeam Art + Technology Center in New York, and comprises an open source FM radio transmitter in the form of a large patterned sweater. It is envisaged as a way for individuals to express themselves in electronic space without fear of censorship.

Looking at Kurbak and Posch's pattern pieces for the sweater (figure 4.28), you can see the electronic values written on each, along with the physical dimensions. The sleeve on the right, for example, should be a resistor with a final impedance value of 27 kilohms. The coil forms part of the other sleeve. Full instructions are given on Kurbak's website, along with details of other projects.

4.21
Stitch pattern for a sweater designed to be a complete FM radio transmitter after a battery, audio source and transistor have been attached; without these, it is electronically undetectable. Ebru Kurbak and Irene Posch.

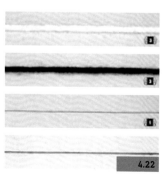

4.22
Yarn specifications in knitting pattern, including enameled copper wire (CW) with colored wools (CC and MC). Ebru Kurbak and Irene Posch.

4.23
Radio as personal expression; radio frequency creates a field around the person, and can be individually expressive. Ebru Kurbak and Irene Posch.

4.24

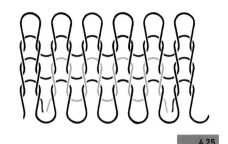

4.25

4.26

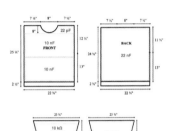

4.27

4.24
Radio components; resistors, capacitors, a coil, a transistor, battery, and connector for an audio source. Ebru Kurbak and Irene Posch.

4.25
Knitting a coil. A coil is created by wrapping a conductor around a core. Here it is made by knitting a few plain stitches using an insulated copper wire. Ebru Kurbak and Irene Posch.

4.26
Charge/discharge. The coil in this project consists of uninsulated copper wire wrapped tightly around a Steradent tube. A magnet inside the tube is free to move up and down within it when shaken, creating electric potential (voltage). John Richards.

4.27
Possible distribution of knitted radio components across the sweater pieces. Ebru Kurbak and Irene Posch.

4.28
Knitted components. If the knitting pattern is followed, the same components can be repeatedly made. Ebru Kurbak and Irene Posch.

4.29
The finished sweater does not look unusual, and returns some power to the individual. Ebru Kurbak and Irene Posch. Photo: Mahir M. Yavuz.

TECH TIPS

A radio is made up of resistors, capacitors, a transistor, a coil, a battery and an outlet to connect to a power source. This sweater incorporates these components, some of them as textiles, so that wearers can transmit their own sounds over a radius of up to 6 meters. Anyone tuning in on the right frequency will be able to hear the transmission. The pattern asks for wool, insulated copper wire, and stainless steel yarns, and Kurbak and Posch explain how to knit the copper coil to generate a magnetic field. A coil is made up of a conductive wire wound around a nonconductive core; see also John Richards' Dirty Electronics in the Suggested reading section for instructions on creating a Faraday generator to drive sound modules, using magnets and copper wire, and the feature interview with Tilak Dias in Chapter 1 to learn more about knitted heating elements.

4.28

4.29

Ramyah Gowrishankar— Conductive yarns for knitting

As an MA student at Aalto (Helsinki), Ramyah Gowrishankar asked how it might be possible to integrate electronics into fabrics in such a way that they were specific to the medium of textiles, and further, how the versatility and material familiarity of fabrics might allow a dialogue between user, artifact, and the surrounding environment. To approach these questions, she created a series of knitted soft "triggers," or objects, found in their "natural habitats." They are parts of possible soft devices, and they can be put together in different ways.

Like all of Gowrishankar's work, this program of study is thoroughly documented and generously shared (see the Suggested Reading section). http://narrativize.net/

Gowrishankar found that the directionality produced by the knitting machine meant that the trigger concepts could be more effectively built if they were broken into parts to assure the working of the soft circuitry. Instead of thinking about a flat circuit layout, the designs became portions of the circuit that would later come together as a trigger. This often affected the form and shape of the triggers. Examples of separate parts included the "sensors," soft cables, and pockets for holding batteries. LilyPad microcontrollers and power sources were detachable, and parts were assembled with loose ends trimmed and glued to avoid short circuits. Hand or machine sewing was used for secure assembly.

1 Knit the different parts of the trigger. For this one, there were 2 same-sized discs and a long knitted strip to be attached between.

2 Knit in the loose threads with a needle and glue to secure them.

3 Cut away the extra thread to get a neat look.

4 Attach the parts together roughly first with pins.

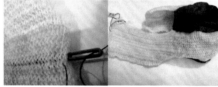
5 Insert the conductive yarns and other components in the appropriate places.

6 Stitch the parts together using yarn and a needle. Remove the pins afterwards.

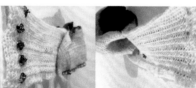
7 Sew in the metal snap-buttons at the end of data lines that need to be connected to the microcontroller.

8 Stitched and ready - but still inside out.

9 Invert for right side out.

10 Program the microcontroller and test the trigger.

4.30

4.30
Building a knitted "trigger" composed of different parts, including sensors, cables and pockets for batteries. Ramyah Gowrishankar.

TECH TIPS

- Silver-coated Statex yarns were found to be much better for knitting as they matched the thickness of the normal yarn, were stronger, and unlike the steel fiber yarn, they did not fray while knitting.
- Higher-resistance threads were better for making potentiometers.
- The stretchy conductive thread worked well with the smaller knitting machines. However, it was often found to break in the industrial knitting machine if not combined with another normal fine yarn. These conductive yarns were not stretchy by themselves, but when knitted with normal yarn they assumed the elasticity of the overall knitted structures.
- Stretch-sensitive conductive thread (Shieldex Nm50/2) was found to work best for a width of around fifty rows when incorporated directly in the circuit without a microcontroller interpreting its values. Making the stretch sensor too long required the fabric to be stretched to an unnatural extent in order to produce a significant change in current flow. On the other hand, shorter lengths let too much current pass even when not stretched.

- Low-resistance yarns were ideal for making power connections. The thin conductive yarn from Sparkfun has medium resistance and was ideal for shorter-length power connections. Being much thinner, it hid better between the layers of the knitted fabric. The Sheildex yarns were easier to knit with than the Bekinox steel fiber yarns because the Sheildex ones were better twisted and did not fray or break easily while knitting with the thin needles of the machine. The Bekinox thread often broke and stretched when knitted.
- Page 83 of Gowrishankar's thesis includes Arduino code for the triggers.

WOVEN DISPLAYS AND COMPONENTS
Case study: Barbara Layne

Barbara Layne is director of Studio subTela and a professor at Concordia University in Montreal. She leads a team of researchers in crafting woven structures with microprocessors, sensors, and light and sound output, including scrolling text for real-time communication, and dresses that convey the drama of storm chasing in print with LED arrays.
http://subtela.hexagram.ca/Bio.html

Studio subTela has worked on both wearable systems and installations and is working with architect Mahesh Senagala to plan large-scale architectural constructions with outputs that will respond to touchpads in garments. Soft switches are incorporated into aprons, ready to be plugged into existing portable devices such as mobile phones and tablets. The driving research theme behind this work is social dynamics and the interaction of the human and cloth.

The Tornado Dress features a mimaki print of a tornado, photographed by Nebraska storm-chaser Mike Hollingshead. Mimaki produces specialist industrial inkjet printers for wide-screen applications such as billboards, interiors and apparel. A funnel cloud and lightning bolts are printed on the linen fabric, while the lining has been embroidered with conductive threads and electronic components, including super-bright white LEDs. Three small photocells on the outside of the dress detect ambient light, and depending on the quantity of light that is sensed, different flashing patterns are triggered in the LED display, reminiscent of lightning effects that can accompany severe weather situations. Layne's team is now working on a second Jacquard weaving based on an image by Mike Hollingshead, which will include sound triggered by the movement of the viewer. Earlier work leading up to the Tornado Dress includes Lucere, a Jacquard wall hanging of a white-on-white landscape. The sound and light of two woven lightning bolts are triggered by the viewer, suggesting the distant illumination known as heat lightning.

4.31
Tornado Dress. The print used in this dress is wide screen, achieved on a specialist Mimaki printer.
Studio subTela.
Photo: Mikey Siegal.

4.32

4.32
Lucere. The bright white LED lighting
is triggered by the viewer's proximity
to the work. Studio subTela.

This is an example of soft switches organized as an array using the orthogonal arrangement of woven threads; this allows sensing of the location of human touch through capacitance. Using the changing location data as a finger moves across contact points gives a "drawing" output rendered in LEDs. The input and output textiles communicate using wireless XBee, and the system evolved to become the black dress shown in figures 4.34 and 4.35, with the input textile array in the sleeve.

In the white dress shown in figures 4.36 and 4.37, the embroidered "keyboard" of this dress is actually a display rather than an input device. An iPad is connected wirelessly to the dress, and the letters of the keyboard display become illuminated as a second person types on the tablet. The back of the dress is connected with two silver ribbons, which clip together to switch the dress on.

Layne trained as a textile designer rather than a fashion designer, so she has always been interested in the structure of the fabric and how electronics can be integrated into them. Most of the work of the subTela research studio is hand-woven, and references the way circuit boards are also designed using x- (weft) and y-coordinates (warp). New work is being made with a Tajima laying machine, which creates double-faced fabrics, keeping positive and negative threads away from each other; this requires a knowledgeable weaver—you need to know when to pick up a thread to create the circuit you want. The thread used by the studio comes from Germany; it has a silk core spun with copper and tinned with silver. Its original use in ceremonial wear for the military, church officials and royalty has led to an interest in historical costume, which will further inform innovative design development.

4.33
Soft switch development. The array of horizontal and vertical conductive yarns is connected to a microprocessor that can recognize which two yarns are being simultaneously touched. This effectively creates a touchpad. Studio subTela.

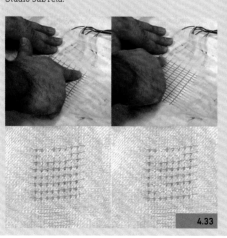

4.33

4.34

4.34
Dress with touchpad system (input). The touchpad has been integrated into the sleeves of a dress. Studio subTela.

4.35
Dress with touchpad system (output). The drawn or written input from the touchpad is wirelessly communicated with a wall mounted textile where it is recreated using LEDs. Studio subTela.

4.35

4.36
Keyboard Dress.
Studio subTela.

4.37
Keyboard Dress—detail.
The letters on the textile
keyboard light up when
another person types on
a nearby tablet.
Studio subTela.

4.38
Tajima laying machine. Fiber laying
technologies mean yarns can be
precisely placed on a substrate;
common applications include reinforced
composites created by selectively
adding layers on top of previously laid
fibers. Studio subTela.

4.38

4.36

4.37

TECH TIPS

The Keyboard Dress is a new work, which illustrates the nonlinear nature of the design process very well. This idea began as a skirt, then became a courier bag before becoming a dress. Layne started work in this field fifteen years ago, and the process has changed as new forms of components and technology become available—previously it would take a long time to prepare each LED for attachment to the fabric by hand, but now LEDs with holes for threading through are common. Now the production of a garment can take sixty hours, but it is the design work, testing and troubleshooting that take the time. Garments need to be battery powered, but installation pieces can be connected to mains electricity, which makes them easier to exhibit for long periods of time. When incorporating wireless connectivity, Bluetooth has been replaced with XBee, a newer and more reliable protocol. Finally, everything produced by the studio is hand-washed; the battery needs to be removed first, but all the other technology can be gently washed.

Lynn Tandler—
Weaving with metal

Lynn Tandler holds an MA in Constructed Textiles from the Royal College of Art and works jointly as a textile designer and academic researcher. http://www.lynntandler.com/

Lynn Tandler was inspired by her brother's blacksmithing practice to start working with metal yarns. Watching him work with this material as if it were just as malleable as cloth, she started to create textiles in a new way, drawing on metalsmithing techniques such as forging and patination. Tandler points out that metal fibers, or fine wires, have different material properties just as a weaver will expect different yarns to have different behaviors depending on their composition, and she aims to respect the material for what it is, building on existing properties. As an example, different metals, woven in the same way, will give different draping characteristics, and surface texture will be an outcome of the material itself. These fabric collections are exclusively produced for Tandler by a weaving mill in Italy, are 100 percent recyclable, and need only wiping rather than washing.

In the metal fabric collections, Tandler has challenged structures and the use of materials by reversing the construction roles of soft textile threads and metal wires: the construction of the metal fabrics mostly relies upon the interlacement methodologies of textile threads, which allow drape, softness and reversibility upon bending and folding of the metal fibers. In her PhD work she is now taking this approach further into developing new weave structures that contribute enhanced properties to fabrics independent of the properties of the fibers and yarns that they carry.

Working with fashion designer Marie Cunliffe, Tandler creates menswear entirely from woven metals, rolling, folding and forging the edges of the fabric to avoid sharp ends. The fabrics can be cut as normal, but they can also be formed on the body, as they hold their shape. The experience of wearing metal garments includes a new appreciation of wear and of the traces habitual gestures will leave. In Marie Cunliffe's fashion collections, Tandler's metal satin weaves are used for their weight and sculptural properties, creating large, voluminous forms and dramatic shadows contrasted with shimmering reflection. Metal fabrics will "remember" movements through an emerging patina, and Tandler has explored graduating the metal content of her satin weaves to allow fabric to absorb habitual movements, like the lines on the palm of a hand. Individual patterns of behavior and wear might be seen to develop over time into an expressive personal patina.

4.39

4.39
Weaving metal fiber. Different metal
fibers handle differently when working.
Lynn Tandler.

4.40

4.40
Lynn Tandler fabric used in Marie
Cunliffe fashion collection to create
sculptural forms and unique handle.
Photo: Marie Cunliffe.

TECH TIPS

One of Tandler's contributions to the field is her research
into the application of metal patination techniques to textiles,
creating a new form of dyeing materials. She followed
recipes in Hughes and Rowe's (1991) *The Colouring, Bronzing
and Patination of Metals* to re-create the samples seen on
the cover of their book. Each metal sample became a woven
swatch, producing a "new organic" color palette.

4.41
Patination samples. Patination is
the coloration of metals through
chemical reaction, such as the green/
blue finish of copper as it oxidizes
in air. Introducing other chemicals
and controlling the amount of oxygen
available to the reaction are ways of
achieving different patinas.
Lynn Tandler.

4.42
Patination dye cards. Color change as a
result of aging in conductive fabrics is
usually seen as a problem; Lynn Tandler
has made the process repeatable and
offers a range of textile finishes as part
of her studio practice. Lynn Tandler.

Anna Piper—
Working with third
generation smart fibers

Anna Piper is a PhD candidate at Nottingham Trent University. She takes a simultaneous approach to textile and garment construction, integrating hand and digital technologies. She researches embodied knowledge and design innovation through traditional hand weaving practices and digital weaving techniques.
www.annapiperdesign.com

Anna Piper is a specialist in weaving whose research focuses on the design and production of garments constructed on the loom. She combines digital and hand-loom techniques to create vibrant graphic woven textiles inspired by traditional dressmaking techniques and the relationship between sport and fashion. In particular, Piper is interested in the production of integral garments, a term often found in knit production, but very rarely in weave. Traditionally, the loom itself dictates the cut of a piece of woven cloth—cultural examples include the kimono and the sari—and Piper draws a comparison here with initial woven prototypes using e-fibers, such as the Georgia Tech Wearable Motherboard, or "smartshirt" (1999). Her approach is to internalize her understanding of yarns' properties through repeated handling, close proximity, and time to allow design concepts to emerge through the practice. In this way, she is building expertise in the weaving of new composite yarns, including e-fibers that will sidestep the current reliance on elastic fibers for fit.

Piper worked with "third generation" e-fibers as part of the Advanced Textile Research Group at Nottingham Trent University; using conventional unadapted looms for complex production, she collaborated to produce the demonstrator for the group's embedded e-fibers (see p 20 for more details). Through crafts practice, Piper has now begun to build embodied knowledge of the fibers, including an understanding of its constraints, functionality and visionary potential. She has begun to explore the pattern, proportion, color and construction it lends itself to, developing a dialogue between maker and material.

The demonstrator garment developed with PhD student Anura Rathnayaka incorporates a new yarn with LEDs smaller than the size of a pinhead integrated into its structure. This process produces a smart textile, which retains the fabric's basic characteristics of being tactile, flexible, machine washable and able to be tumble dried.

4.44

4.43

4.43
Anna Piper weaving. The knowledge gained through practice with tools and materials becomes embodied.
College of Art and Design, Nottingham Trent University.

4.44
Anna's design process includes highly stylised graphical sketches informed by the orthogonal nature of weaving.
Anna Piper.

Designing your own smart textile

Intelligent Textiles Ltd.

Intelligent Textiles Ltd. (ITL) is a UK company started by engineer Stan Swallow and textile designer Asha Peta Thompson in 2002. They have come to specialize in minimizing weight and removing risk from the design of soldiers' combat uniforms.
https://www.youtube.com/watch?v=B7NxMz80iv8

Initially supported by a research grant from Brunel University's Design for Life initiative, which paid for a custom loom built in Switzerland, Thompson and Swallow developed woven fabric keyboard technology. Having won substantial development grants from the MOD (Ministry of Defence), they have since begun to focus on the requirements of the modern foot soldier. The main issue ITL seeks to address is the weight carried by soldiers using many different electrical devices and their associated power sources. Their approach is twofold: where possible, replace cables with fabric connections, and centralize the power source, much as in a domestic electrical ring main system. Additional benefits include comfort, increased shock absorption, time saved in replacing batteries, and the ability for devices to share data across the same system (a "personal area network" or PAN). ITL iterated designs for a textile harness to act as a central power unit to multiple devices by standardizing on-body connections and creating complex woven textile arrangements to replace the capability of a computer's printed circuit board. ITL is an interesting case study because the company has been in operation for over a decade, and it has been well documented in the press. Thompson and Swallow have given interviews not only on the multidisciplinary process, but also on the different funding streams that have supported the business, and the intellectual property negotiations that have been necessary to shift it from academic research to commercial reality.

4.45

4.45
Wheelchair cover with textile pressure sensors to detect and prevent pressure sores. Asha Peta Thompson.

4.46
Flexible woven keyboard. Intelligent Textiles Ltd.

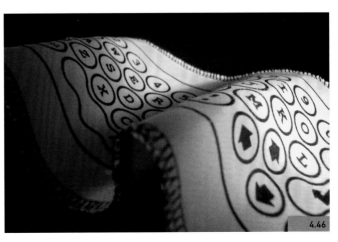

4.46

Heat generated by the system is more efficiently dissipated by the two-dimensional arrangement of conducting material, in contrast to the bundled wires in a conventional system, and the MOD's concerns with electromagnetic detection can be alleviated either by the integration of a woven ground grid or by screening materials layered with the system after construction. One of the most crucial aspects of this approach is that of "redundancy." In engineering and human-computer interaction, this means the use of lots of conductive pathways rather than just one, so that if a failure occurs, the whole system is not severely affected. In terms of usability, redundancy also means building in more than one way to find information for the user. In ITL's design, there are between twenty and one hundred such pathways.

Multidisciplinary communication

The communication problems experienced by Thompson and Swallow are not unusual. First, they found that although they could see the potential in bringing their fields together, effectively they "spoke different languages"; Thompson has said that their stubborn personalities allowed them to persevere and create their own hybrid language of electronic and textile terminology. In communicating their work with other fields and markets, they also found confusion between craft and science; while they understand their work as exacting and complex, the promotion of it as "craft," based on the use of a wooden loom, feels inadequate. The most powerful communication tool is always the object itself, although even this can be misunderstood, as it has sometimes seemed to clients as just too fantastical, and the implications of the technology have taken time to sink in.

4.47

4.47
Application of the fabric in the Ranger Vest. The fabric allows for flexibility in the placement of functions on the body, and a conductive fiber grid layer is used to shield the soldier from detection. Intelligent Textiles Ltd.

4.48
Multifunctional fabric. Power can be transmitted both vertically and horizontally as conductive yarns are placed in both warp and weft directions. Intelligent Textiles Ltd.

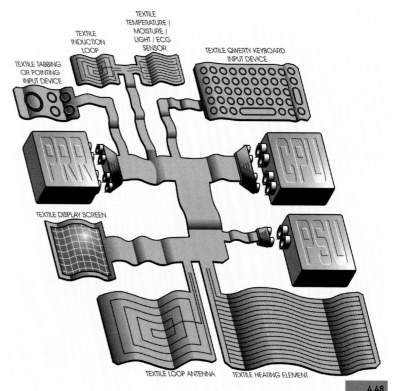

4.48

TECH TIPS

BUSINESS MODEL AND INTELLECTUAL PROPERTY
Ownership of intellectual property has been key
to the creation of the business. It was originally
owned by Brunel University; in 2000, Thompson and
Swallow put all their savings together to buy back
the patent rights with a view to developing their
technology as far as it could go. With intellectual
property ownership in place, they thought the MOD
might want to take over the rights, but found in
fact that they were easy to work with and were only
interested in access in order to see the benefits of the
technology's application. Thompson also learned to
instill in clients a sense of value in the product, and
found that charging £500 for a sample was a simple
way of achieving this. The process of protection is
time consuming: the pair spent six months drafting
the initial thirty-page application and undertook their
own novelty search. Now they spend up to £40,000 a
year on maintaining intellectual property protection,
despite continuing to draft their own documents,
which a patent attorney then checks and files. The
company now owns seventeen patents filed with the
Patent Cooperation Treaty and with the European
Patent Office, and applications have also been made
in the United States and Canada.

TECHNICAL INFORMATION
By precise organization of conductive and
nonconductive fibers in the warp and weft fibers of
the weave, a range of flexible electrical components
can be built reliably. Permanent separation or
permanent connection can be achieved, as well as a
connection when pressure is applied to the fabric.

- Typical maximum electrical currents are 1 to 5
  amperes.
- Thermal imaging tests have shown that
  approximately 10 millimeters of fabric width is
  required for each amp of current, to guarantee a
  temperature rise of less than 1°C.
- The textile can transmit power and/or data both
  horizontally and vertically, as conductive pathways
  are introduced in both warp and weft directions
  and manipulated during the weaving process into
  arbitrary two-dimensioned network geometries.
- The technique allows for two-sided routing with
  "vias" creating connections between the layers.
- A power supply can be attached at any point across
  the surface of the fabric, and any number of power
  take-off points may also be attached.

eCrafts Collective—
Card weaving

The eCrafts Collective is Ramyah Gowrishankar and Kati Hyyppä, who combine traditional crafts and electronics. Based in Helsinki and Berlin respectively, the pair travel to meet people face to face, learn traditional textile crafts, and put a twist on them with electronics as part of the mix. In this example, eCrafts Collective demonstrates how to use card (or "tablet") weaving, found in the construction of traditional Latvian belts. https://ecraftscollective.wordpress.com/

Hyyppä and Gowrishankar were inspired by this technique to think about interactive possibilities for traditional Latvian belts. Perhaps touch could be a trigger for subtle responses in the belt, or it could harvest energy through the wearer's movement.

They started playing with EL (electroluminescent) foil, which has a light-emitting surface, experimenting with it as a warp thread. However, it was stiffer than the other threads and did not bend or twist well, breaking easily. Further experiments included inserting two-dimensional EL shapes into the weave using the backstrap loom method, in which the warp threads are picked individually by hand for each row. This method allows for altering the pattern on the go and creating negative spaces within the pattern between the red bulkier threads, making room for EL foil cutouts to be fitted in.

4.49
Tablet woven Latvian belts; the wide range of patterns and colors reflect different regions, and are worn with traditional costume. eCrafts Collective.

4.50
Setting up a loom between the body and a fixed point such as a door handle. eCrafts Collective.

4.51
The tools for card weaving are simple and easy to make using everyday materials. eCrafts Collective.

Cards with punched corners and rounded edges

Thick stick and rope to secure the loose yarn end

Two small sticks to keep the belt straight while weaving

Paper knife used to push the weft tight; as a reed of a loom

This is an ancient technique for making a strong strap quickly. A five-foot strap can be woven in a couple of hours. You don't need a loom, only cards with holes in the corners, and about two hundred feet of cord.

Society of Primitive Technology, adapted from Bart & Robin Blankenship, 1996

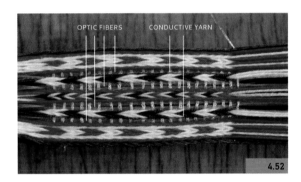

4.52

4.54

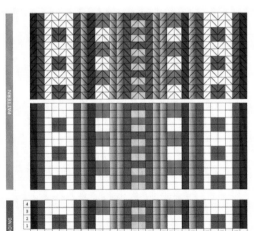

4.53

4.55

4.56

4.52–4.56
Cosmic belt—tablet weaving with electronic components. Conductive yarns (intended as antenna to pick up electromagnetic waves) and optical fibers (for light ouput) were introduced in an exploratory reinterpretation of the Latvian belt. eCrafts Collective.

TECH TIPS

CARD WEAVING A REPEAT PATTERN

Card weaving is a technique that uses a stack of cards as a loom through which long yarns are threaded. These warp yarns can be lifted or dropped by rotating the appropriate cards, usually by a quarter or half turn, after which the weft thread, wound round a shuttle, is passed through. Repeating this action weaves the belt and reveals the patterns.

The tools needed for card weaving are easy to make using everyday materials. The cards can be made from old cardboard pieces by cutting them into palm-sized squares and punching holes in each corner. The loose ends of the yarns are knotted and secured around straight sticks—these could be anything from twigs to broken chopsticks. There are different ways of making patterns, depending on how the cards are rotated (see the Further reading section for more on these), and more complex patterns can be created with hexagonal or other polygonal shaped cards. Repetitive patterns, covered here, are woven by rotating all the cards simultaneously by a quarter turn in the same direction and passing the weft through the shed after each turn. In this technique the pattern is based on how the yarns are threaded, as the rotation of all the cards remains the same.

You will need:
- 8 loom cards
- 1 shuttle (about 2 inches long)
- 2 different colors of yarn

1. Cut your warp threads: 2 x color a; 2 x color b, each about 6 feet long.
2. Pass the warp threads through the corner holes in one of the loom cards, keeping the same colors next to each other.
3. Tie the threads horizontally about 5 feet apart to secure the end of the work.
4. Turn the loom card to create a striped cord.
5. Cut another fourteen warp threads and thread up the remaining seven loom cards.
6. Arrange all the cards in a deck, with the same colors in the same holes.
7. Prepare the shuttle with a few yards of thread for the weft.
8. Leaving a length of weft thread hanging on one side, pass the shuttle through the shed to secure the eight cords together.
9. Without squashing the loom cards too tightly as a pack, rotate them all together a quarter turn to make the new shed.

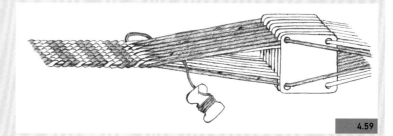

4.59

---- Construction line
—— Cutting line

4.57

4.58

4.57
Tablet weaving basics; preparing the weft threads, wound around card shuttles. Shelagh Lewins.

4.58
Tablet weaving basics; preparing the cards or tablets. The warp threads pass through the four corner holes. Shelagh Lewins.

4.59
Tablet weaving basics; the shed is the gap between warp threads that the weft is passed through. Shelagh Lewins.

Feature interview:
Joanna Berzowska

Joanna Berzowska is an Assistant Professor of Design and Computation Arts at Concordia University in Montreal, where she is a member of the Hexagram Research Institute. She is the research director of XS Labs, where her team develops innovative methods and applications in electronic textiles and responsive garments. http://www.berzowska.com/

I clearly remember something you said at the ANAT ReSkin media lab in Canberra, way back in 2007; in guiding the ReSkin participants, you urged us to aim for "conceptually rich" outcomes. Can you tell us a bit about this idea?

In my twenty years of experience in this field, I have worked with talented artists and designers in their first interactions with electronic technologies, in the context of smart textiles and wearables. These artists and designers bring to the table years of previous work that is complex and conceptually challenging. Their experience with materials and materiality is very nuanced and mature. I have witnessed, however, that in their first interaction with electronics, they forget the complexity of their previous work and revert to a very simplistic model, influenced by consumer electronics. They start thinking of "function" in lowercase, instead of "FUNCTION" in uppercase. Their years of conceptual accomplishment evaporate and they start making simplistic work with very linear interaction scenarios. I mean, how many "hug jackets" have we seen? There is nothing conceptually rich about a "hug jacket." Why do these artists and designers not engage ideas

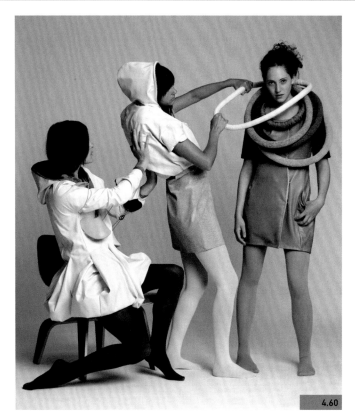

4.60

that are political, difficult, controversial, or perverse? Is it because electronics are supposed to have a well defined "function" where there is only one way to interpret the interaction, as opposed to the multiplicity of perspectives inherent in a nonelectronic piece? We have this false belief that electronic work can only be interpreted in one way: the correct way. Digital work, however, should also have FUNCTION, which includes concepts of beauty, pleasure, confusion, anger, despair, as well as create discourse in a political, socioeconomic, cultural, or philosophical sense.

My projects at XS Labs often demonstrate a preoccupation with—and a resistance to—task-based, utilitarian definitions of "function" in the electronic. My definition of "FUNCTION" simultaneously looks at the materiality and the magic of computing technologies; it incorporates the concepts of beauty and pleasure. I am particularly concerned with the exploration of interactive forms that emphasize the natural expressive qualities of transitive materials. I focus on the aesthetics of interaction, which compels me to interrogate and to re-contextualize the materials themselves. The interaction narratives function as entry points to question some of the fundamental assumptions we make about the technologies and the materials that we deploy in our designs.

What have been the important concepts in your own work?

Throughout the past fifteen years, I have been very interested in questions of memory (human and computer memory), the contrast between our desire to remember and our need to forget. We tend to idealize the ability to record every moment, whether through images, narrative, or biometric data, and we don't know yet how meaning will be constructed from these vast repositories of data. Clothing is one of the most intimate things that we interact with in our daily lives. Because of its extremely close relationship to our body, our (nondigital) clothing is able to witness some of our most intimate interactions; it is able to record our fear and excitement, our stress and our strain, through the collection of sweat, skin cells, stains and tears. It becomes worn over time and carries the evidence of our identity and our history. Without proper contextual filtering, our digital memories (the computer "data") become simply a huge repository of facts and figures, devoid of meaning.

I have also been fascinated with the potential of programming materiality. First of all, when a material integrates computational behavior, how do we "program" such a material? We do so by determining the length, the shape, and the placement of the material in a composite system (in this case, the textile). We program a functional fiber by cutting it to a specific length and positioning it in the cloth so as to deliver the desired functionality. Changing its shape or orientation will change its behavior, not only in how it behaves visually, but also in how it behaves computationally. The second, more profound, implication is that the language of aesthetics and design (parameters such as shape, color, or visual composition) becomes conflated with the language of programming. Designers have historically been "programming materiality" in a metaphoric way, controlling physical and aesthetic parameters so as to give rise to emergent forms and interactions. Designers today, in addition, can program their materials and their objects in a computational way, which traditionally involves a nonmaterial and nonintuitive set of processes.

How do concepts and technology come together? In what ways does technology inspire concepts for you?

A core component of my work involves the development of enabling technologies, methods, and materials—in the form of soft electronic circuits and composite fibers—as well as the exploration of the expressive potential of soft reactive structures. Many of my electronic textile innovations are informed by the technical and the cultural history of how textiles have been made for generations—weaving, stitching, embroidery, knitting, beading, or quilting—but use a range of materials with different electromechanical properties. I am really interested by the soft, playful, and magical aspects of these materials, so as to better adapt to the contours of the human body and the complexities of human need and desires.

You are an experienced educator in wearable technology and interactive textiles; can you talk a bit about helping students to approach hardware, software, and the less tangible aspects of technology as materials to add to their creative palette?

I have developed two courses specifically for the Department of Design and Computation Arts at Concordia University: "Tangible Media and Physical Computing" and "Second Skin and Soft Wear." Each course deals with different aspects of physical computing and tangible media in a fine arts context. In both courses, I introduce concepts of soft computation and intimate reactive artifacts as artworks. I emphasize the concept of

4.61

4.61
Itchy. Inductive generators transform kinetic energy (movement) into electrical energy stored in a cell on the body. Joanna Berzowska, XS Labs.

memory (contrasting computer memory and personal, interpretive memory), and explore how responsive or interactive objects can create a new medium for annotating architectural space and objects, for leaving traces of presence, and for recording personal histories. In recent history, a scientific revolution has been redefining our fundamental design methods. Materials such as conductive fibers, active inks, photoelectrics, and shape-memory alloys promise to shape new design forms and new experiences that will redefine our relationship with materiality and with technology. I focus on analog electronics and materiality as an entry point to construct more complex narratives and interactions. At the core of this pedagogical practice is a strong emphasis on developing a nuanced, personal approach to working with electronics and physical computation.

What are you excited about now in the field? (Your work with Maksim Skorobogatiy is referenced elsewhere in the book—see Chapter 1, figures 1.11 and 1.12 , for example.)

I am very interested in the development of future functional fibers, as well as all questions around the area of the Quantified Self movement. In the last five years, I have been working with Professor Maksim Skorobogatiy to develop a new generation of composite fibers that are able to harness power directly from the human body, store that energy, or use changes in energy to change their own visual properties. The core technical innovation involves shifting this functionality entirely within the fiber itself. The goal of this project, entitled "Karma Chameleon," is to develop a prototype for an all-fiber–based textile that can harness, sense and display energy. Conceptually, this constitutes a radical deviation from the dominant model of a textile substrate with integrated mechano-electronics to a fully integrated composite substrate, wherein the fibers themselves (a) harness human-generated energy, (b) store the energy directly inside the fibers, and (c) use that energy to control a fiber-based actuator (such as fiber illumination and color).

At the same time, I have been working with OMsignal, a Montreal startup developing wearable technology products that focus on wellness and well-being. Responding to the growing need in our society to find balance in our lives, our first product is a shirt that tracks various biosignatures through textile-based sensors and offers a variety of engaging biofeedbacks to help improve well-being, increase self-knowledge, and reduce stress.

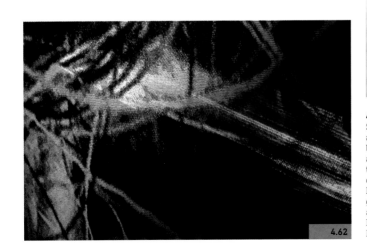

4.62
Sparkl Textile. Light is both transmitted and reflected in the fibers, and different layers of imagery and color are revealed as the "sparkl" panels respond to the angle and intensity of light; the colors can be changed dynamically by controlling the relative intensity of guided light (through the fibers) and ambient light in the environment. Photos: Joanna Berzowska & Marc Beaulieu © XS Labs 2010

4.63
Sparkl Dress. The sparkl work was a collaborative effort by Joanna Berzowska, Marguerite Bromley, and Marc Beaulieu. The panels are woven on a computer-controlled electronic Jacquard loom with cotton, linen, and PBG fibers that reflect one color when side illuminated with ambient light and emit a different color when transmitting white light. Photos: Joanna Berzowska & Marc Beaulieu © XS Labs 2010

EMBROIDERED SWITCHES
Tessa Acti—
Transmitter/receiver

Tessa Acti specializes in digital embroidery design, and she worked as a research assistant on a UKRC-funded project to develop embroidered electronic antennae systems for high-frequency communication between 2010 and 2013. https://ntuadvancedtextiles.wordpress.com /2012/05/24/introducing-tessa-marie-acti/

Acti's MA work had led her to develop a creative practice based on the limits of a multihead embroidery machine, working with stitches up to half a meter long. Through extensive experimentation and analysis she has developed a working methodology that questions the pioneering value of what is essentially a commercial production machine. Her approach explicitly demonstrates the valuable tacit knowledge of the makers in relationship with their technology with regard to multihead processes, digital embroidery techniques, yarn counts and fabrics and how they interact with production machines.

It was this knowledge that proved useful to the three-year collaborative program of research with Professor Tilak Dias and the Department of Electrical and Electronics Engineering at Loughborough University in the creation of functional embroidered antennae for the military, search and rescue teams, and emergency services.

4.64

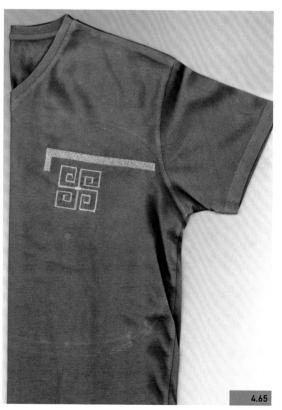

4.65

4.64
Embroidered antenna. Such innovations are tested against existing standard technologies; Loughborough University tested for gain and efficiency of the fabric antennas compared to a reference copper patch antenna. Different stitch geometries give different technical results. Loughborough University and Nottingham Trent University.

4.65
Embroidered antenna development. Loughborough University.

Designing your own smart textile

TECH TIPS

Throughout her work, Acti has articulated both methodological and technical insights:

METHODOLOGY

- The technician is privileged, and may be an explorer or a designer, rather than an artist. Technicians have the luxury of time with a technology.
- Production is a sensory process; the digital may be creative through playfulness with the mechanical and the software.
- Hand skills underpin good digital practice and allow a personal narrative to develop.
- Textile machinery and software offer different limitations.
- Different practices have different criteria and languages—what is "function"?
- Errors are not always human, and "digital" does not guarantee accurate results.
- Craft means negatives may become positive in exploratory phases, and challenges may be created as well as solved.
- It can, however, be difficult to remember that craft knowledge is not trivial.

TECHNICAL

- The aesthetics of the work impact on embroidered functionality and vice versa, requiring trial and error.
- Density of stitch, speed, and placement are all variables that will affect the functionality of the textile antenna.
- Silver or copper threads were most successful for wireless communication (and were commercially available), but they were not designed for embroidery.
- It was necessary to modify the machine, or to omit some yarns.
- The trim is usually omitted when digitizing, but is left on here to allow attachment to garments using nonconductive edges.
- Manipulation continues after machine's role in production.
- Challenges for production included conductivity, electromagnetic properties of the yarn, yarn characteristics, and metal needles and needle damage. It was not clear what the implications might be of the electromagnetic properties of the yarn in automated production.

Ramyah Gowrishankar and Jussi Mikkonen—CAD embroidery with flexible substrate components

Ramyah Gowrishankar is a doctoral student and member of the Embodied Design research group at Aalto University, where Jussi Mikkonen is the interaction lab manager. Together Ramyah and Jussi organized the Textiles Interaction Lab as part of the 2013 Arcintex network workshop, where this work was shared.

http://mediafactory.aalto.fi/projectpage/mfprojectid_33/

The surface mount electronic components (light sensors, resistors, LEDs) in figure 4.66 have been soldered to a flexible substrate printed with copper. These are trimmed to size before being tacked with fabric glue to the design. The same outline shapes are prepared as elements that can be dropped into your embroidery CAD file. This means the electronics can become an integral part of an embroidered design. With the finished file prepared correctly, the multihead, threaded with conductive yarn, will stitch into the substrate, creating a stitched circuit.

4.66

4.66
Using a digital embroidery system to stitch in custom electronic components. The electronic components have been mounted on a thin flexible material that can be stitched through by the embroidery machine.
Ramyah Gowrishankar.

PATTERN CUTTING AND FABRIC MANIPULATION
Case study: Rose Sinclair

Rose Sinclair is a designer/practitioner/ educator, and she considers herself a "multifaceted designer or hybrid designer," by which she means using and bringing different elements from other design disciplines into her creative practice. She teaches at Goldsmiths University in London, and works with companies such as sewing machine specialists Brother UK, Frankfurt-based fashion software company SpeedStep, and UK-based heat press specialists Adkins. http://www.sinclairconsultancy.co.uk/

Sinclair is particularly interested in the relationship between the analog practice of craft, in this instance knitting, and the practice of technology, in this instance the knitting machine and the related CAD software, and how for practitioners, aspects of the language of the analog and the digital interfaces are shared or mirrored and reinterpreted. She is also interested in the emergent communities of practice and how knowledge and practice are exchanged within them.

She also recommends Brother digitization products; you can find a comparison of embroidery digitization packages on websites such as Wikipedia. Sinclair uses Brother's embroidery machines because the same software package can be used for all the embroidery machines in the range, and designs created can be formatted using the standard industry .dst format. Depending on the machine being used, design ideas can also be resized on the machine itself, reworked or drawn directly on a graphics tablet, then transferred directly to the machine. Some models have "print and stitch" capability, which combines a printed background with embroidery to create a three-dimensional effect.

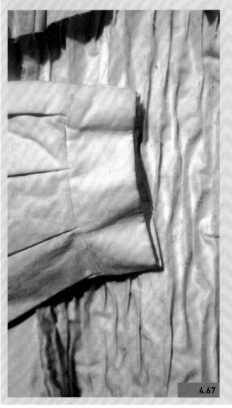

4.67

4.68

4.67
Repeat fabric manipulation for garment construction. Approaches like this explore the characteristics of fabrics and what they add to a garment form. Construction. Rose Sinclair.

4.68
Fabric manipulation for garment construction. Rose Sinclair.

Designing your own smart textile

In approaching manipulating textiles in studio practice, Sinclair starts with pattern cutting, looking at one technique at a time, such as the use of darts, as a form of contouring and three-dimensional shaping and encourage an approach to structural manipulation of existing material. Forms are trialed using Bondaweb and other weights of fabric interfacing, combined with different weights and types of fabrics, and through repeats and draping on fifth-scale blocks. The learning and design journey is recorded visually using photographs and video. Surface texture and color are also explored. Only after this do the students or clients consider garment or other three-dimensional construction, or other methods leading to new opportunities for the development of textiles on the body, or in other spaces.

IDEAS TO TRY

1. Make a similar dart structure using a range of different fabrics to experience their characteristics: understand the handling characteristics (e.g., an organza will produce a different effect from wool felt).
2. Use laser cutting or die cutters or a vinyl cutter (fitted with a textile blade) to create interesting layers to manipulate structure.
3. Use hand-carved or digitally routed blocks (cut on a CNC machine) to create your own print block.
4. Use a vinyl cutter to create your own intricate stencils for printing; take inspiration from traditional Japanese hand-cut stencils.
5. Screen print/stencil with Bare Conductive paint to create expressive circuits, combined with other e-textile technologies and materials.
6. Take the same design and change it for each interface from digital embroidery to laser to router to vinyl cutter to knitting machine to textile software. What are the variables or the challenges?

Delia Dumitrescu— Architectural approaches

Delia Dumitrescu was an architect before undertaking both her MA and PhD in "Relational textiles: Surface expressions in space design." She has undertaken a number of collaborative projects in the course of completing her doctoral studies at the University of Boras (Sweden), exploring heat, light, and movement as materials for spatial design. https://www.materialthinking.org/people/delia-dumitrescu

Dumitrescu describes the collaborative approach with Anna Persson, Hannah Landin, and Anna Vallgårda as "interfering" in each other's fields. For Dumitrescu, the outcome has been a series of reactive and interactive knitted samples, a "material library," intended to inspire the architectural community, as well as a bank of technical knowledge necessary for their production. She is interested in the relationship between structure and surface expression, creating three-dimensional structures with knitted fabrics, transforming the material through felting, the use of conductive yarns, and manipulation of different yarns such as Pemotex, which can be knitted while soft and flexible, then shrunk with heat.

Through these manipulations, the fabric becomes three-dimensional and lends itself variously to the transmission of light, or to movement in interaction with people. Scale, pattern and texture are all changed, and a range of different expressions become available for spatial design. Dumitrescu claims that knitting has great potential in this area because, unlike weaving, for example, it lends itself so well to three-dimensional approaches, although, as she points out, the architectural discipline may not know the difference. Knitting also offers fantastic potential in its fluidity—fabric can be formed dynamically during the making process, whereas a woven fabric needs to conform to the parameters of the loom and predetermined (and time-consuming) warp setup. Thus, a three-dimensional knitted fabric can be made to order and be produced without a need to cut it later. It lends itself to a creative, sketching type of process, or even "painting" as Kaffe Fasset has claimed.

While at Boras, Dumitrescu has been able to play with many of the machines there, which all do slightly different things and allow for different approaches. The large circular knitting machines are capable of knitting stiff materials, while the Japanese Shima Seiki and the German Stoll machines can manage metal yarns; the Shima in particular is flexible and is good for three-dimensional shaping.

4.69
Touching Loops. Pemotex is a flame resistant melting yarn, which means that the constructed textile can be stiffened with heat treatments: you can try using a heat gun, an oven, or an iron. Delia Dumitrescu and Anna Persson.

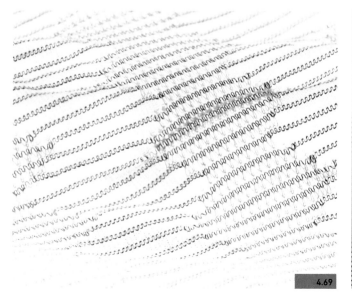

4.70
Textile Forms in Movement. Exploring new dynamic materials from surface construction up to the interaction context provides an understanding of the expressive possibilities they may generate for space design. Delia Dumitrescu, Hannah Landin, Christian Mohr.

Dumitrescu worked with Felecia Davis (see page 188) on an architectural installation, comprising a series of large tubes produced on the circular knitting machine. The intention was to demonstrate how pattern can be introduced after the fabric has been knitted, but one of the key outcomes was an understanding of how tension changes in a knitted fabric at large scale. The programming of the machine was done again to take this into account, but the issue showed that making models on a smaller scale will not always reveal the technical problems (and opportunities) associated with designing for larger spaces. These included the conductive loops in the design touching each other where they were not supposed to, creating short circuits and faulty interaction, and the need for increased current and therefore a redesign of the circuit to take account of the distance and increased resistance involved.

TECH TIPS

The three-dimensional shapes have been knitted using an alternative version of the knitted patterns in one of the surfaces in the example Tactile Glow. Stitch transfers from the front bed to the back bed have been used to effect the shaping of the textile form, and the transfers are combined by decreasing and increasing stitches in a single direction. The shapes use an interlock structure. When flattened, the shapes are rectangular, and each rectangle is divided into smaller triangles by diagonal lines and mediating lines. Each triangular shape formed in this process is knitted using an interlock pattern in the front bed, while the dividing lines are rows knitted as single jersey in the back bed. The areas of single jersey are knitted on every other needle and form lines separating shapes. These areas are less dense in order to enable the background light to make a difference on the surface of the textiles. Two threads of soft Pemotex yarns have been knitted together to form the overall shape. When knitted, the yarns are soft in order to be able to perform precise stitch transfers without breaking the loops. After knitting, the textile is heat pressed at 100°C, which causes it to shrink by 40 percent and stiffen, that is, features similar to those of a nonwoven textile. Thereafter, the textile is folded along the separation lines and heat pressed again to allow it to maintain its three-dimensional shape.

4.71
Textile Forms in Movement. Different knitted structures were augmented with programmable servomotors to create movement. Delia Dumitrescu, Hannah Landin, Christian Mohr.

4.71

Felecia Davis and Microsoft— Textile Mirror and the tangible visualization of big data

Felecia Davis is an Assistant Professor at the Stuckeman Center for Design and Computation at Pennsylvania State University and is the director of SOFTLAB. She is a PhD candidate at Massachusetts Institute of Technology (MIT), as part of the Design and Computation Group.
https://stuckeman.psu.edu/faculty/felecia-davis

Felecia Davis is an architect who works with textile interfaces to explore our relationship with interior space. Her Textile Mirror responds to a person's mood through a change in surface texture. The aim is to reflect the person's current mood and, if they are stressed, help them to relax by changing that texture to a calmer form.

The fabric surface is constructed with laser-cut felt, with insulated Nitinol wire sewn along the seams. In their academic paper, Felecia and her coauthors state that "Nitinol is a combination of nickel and titanium that can be trained at 900°F into a shape at the high temperature. After training the metal can be cooled and unfolded. Heating the wire with a hair dryer will return the wire to the shape it was trained." For a design like this, felt is useful because it is quick to work with, needing no finishing at the edges. It is soft to touch and is relatively resistant to heat, important if you are using an actuator like Nitinol that is heat responsive. In this design, the felt was placed over the Nitinol, but you can try different thicknesses of industrial felt and score grooves in it, for example, to vary the design. Some designers have found that the weight of the felt can have an impact on how quickly the wire is able to return to its original position. For the Textile Mirror, the Nitinol wires were also protected with heat shrink tubing, and the felt was laser cut before being sewn together with a sewing machine.

4.72
Textile Mirror details; laser-cut felt with shape-memory alloy wires.
Felecia Davis.

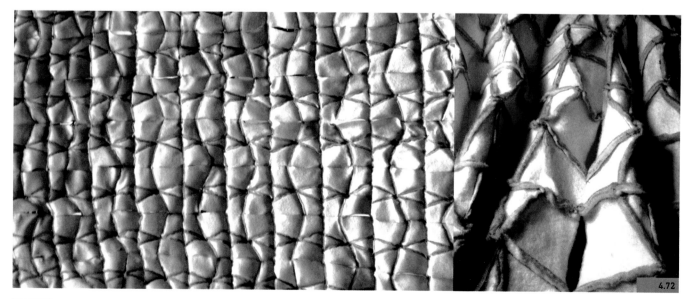

4.72

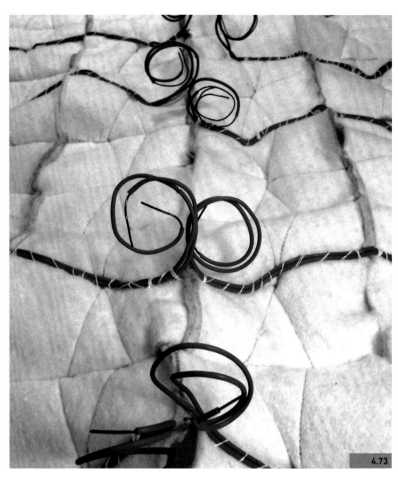

4.73
Nitinol wire in felt. The
wires have been couched
or laid onto the fabric
surface.
Felecia Davis.

TECH TIPS

Nitinol memory wire at 0.762-millimeter diameter was
used as an actuator for the felt fabric because of its ability
to change shape without having to use motors. The wire
was trained on a steel jig in a ceramic oven at 500°C for ten
minutes and left to cool slowly to room temperature in its jig.
The slow cooling allowed us to use less current in the wire
to actuate it, thus keeping the wire cooler when actuated.
Our pattern used 35-centimeter wires looped to and formed
on a jig. The current we ran was between 2 and 3 amps with
3 amps as the highest.

PLAYFULNESS WITH OTHER COMPONENTS
Case study: Paola Tognazzi

Paola Tognazzi is an artist and physical interaction designer; she studied industrial design at the IED of Milan, and Philosophy at the University of Bologna, and set up her company, Wearable_ Dynamics, with the aim of designing interactive tools for the development of ergonomic full-body interfaces. http://www.wearabledynamics.com/

"I focus my research on how to create 3D printed garments tailored to shape shift and react to your movements while they are on your body. For this I used the interactive tools I developed in my company Wearable_Dynamics, with which I explore how to use sound and visuals to navigate and create personal intimate environments using 'dynamics data' of the wearer. At the department of Wearable senses, University of Eindhoven, I developed a research about body-informed 3D printed fashion: how to make a wearable garment, using the technology of 3D printing, able to react and accommodate physical movement, allowing the wearer to participate in the design of the shape through their own personal dynamics. The results are being integrated in a jacket by the Dutch fashion designer Pauline van Dongen."

"In the investigation process, first I analyzed how to put in communication about the wearer's movement to the 3D printed material; the second step was how to design a 3D printed shape, which would change the direction, thickness, and volume as well as the structural characteristics of the 3D printed material sections connected to the body dynamics. Analyzing geometric properties for textile designs, using a tool made in Processing code, I extrapolated different functionalities and reactive behaviors of the textiles that connect to the dynamics of your body in motion or at a standstill."

How did I do it?
"*Step one* is to develop a pattern that reacts to movement. In order to pattern the textile correctly, I used a kind of 'kinesthetic relativity theory,' or a method of proprioception in order to communicate and combine dynamics data with design mechanisms, which also allow me to embed 'triggers' within the material. By applying dance and choreography techniques, I was able to develop simulations of pattern designs, which react to different directions of push and pull, so that the pattern transforms, thus changing the behavior of the textile. This was done using physical exploratory techniques and building low-tech prototypes to test them.

4.74
Materials-informed "dynamics data" development. The body plays a central role in prototype development and evaluation. Paola Tognazzi.

"For *step two*, I used code. In Processing I coded the design from scratch, then I connected the code to the tool Wearable_SuperNow. Wearable_SuperNow is an interactive multi-user tool for live performances and installations. It uses iPhones/iPod Touch or the Wii as controllers of the W_dynamics system, which tracks and analyzes the movement data, transforming it into interactive audiovisuals. With this I tested the change in behavior of the textile design according to the variations of the directions of the body movement. The designing part of the process was done in Processing. Because the Object 500 3D printer needs specific format files (i.e., .stl), we then used Grasshopper to reproduce the design and create the .stl files to 3D print the patterns."

What's the difference between Processing and Grasshopper?
"Grasshopper is specific to 3D print, used a lot in architecture. Processing is used for interactive installations as it's a pure code language; you can use it for almost everything, also for 3D printing. It started as an easy version of Java, created to allow artists to code and create quick prototypes, but is now used also by engineers. In Processing you have to code everything by writing, which, although it requires a bit more time, also gives you more control and understanding of what you are doing, and above all you can really put your personality into the work. Grasshopper doesn't use writing language but connecting boxes (like Max and Pure Data)—you first draw the shapes and surfaces in Rhino and then import them into Grasshopper. Personally I find it a bit annoying having to use two different windows simultaneously—it's not very ergonomic. Grasshopper also has less processing power, and if the file has a lot of elements it gets slower and crashes easily. Although it's much faster, as you don't need to code the drawings, if you need to make specific changes to the composition, it's not that easy. I'm not an expert in Grasshopper so I cannot say if it's not possible or if it's just a question of being really experienced in it. Given this and the time limitations—it was a short research period—I stuck with Processing. From what I've seen around though, it seems Grasshopper uses a lot of randomness, with which you can produce eye-catching design but at the same time because of the randomness they all look similar. The trickiest part, though, is that if we are speaking of wearable garments, that is, garments that have to fit moving bodies and be dynamic, randomness does not work.

We had a Grasshopper workshop at the beginning of the process, and the first thing the teacher said when we presented him the ideas of the designs we wanted, was: If you have a specific design in mind, Grasshopper is not the tool for that. So I guess at the moment Grasshopper can only do raw sketches (raw meaning not precise and specific), which does not mean not pretty.

Paola Tognazzi Drake, http://www.wearabledynamics.com

Boriana Koleva—Aestheticodes for textile interaction design

Boriana Koleva is a researcher in the field of human-computer interaction (HCI) at the University of Nottingham, UK and has been developing the Aestheticodes concept for some time. Having demonstrated that visual code recognition does not have to look like a bar code or a QR code, she began to experiment with Aestheticodes on different materials, including fabric.
http://aestheticodes.com/boriana/

The graphics in figure 4.75 use a code structure recognized by a smartphone with the Aestheticodes app loaded onto it. The developer will decide what happens when a code is recognized—in the design trial with restaurant Busaba Eathai, codes in graphics on placemats led to seasonal and daily menus online, while those on empty plates sent a signal to the waiting staff to bring the bill to the table. These visual codes are built into a larger product service system, which also needs to be carefully designed with stakeholders.

When using other materials to make these codes, new problems arise, and the research team is still working on these. Examples include the glare from ceramic plates interfering with pattern recognition, shadows in textiles with raised surfaces, and levels of contrast when introducing color. Line quality also plays an important part, as does the quality of the camera phone being used in relation to the resolution of the pattern. Recent explorations with lace versions of the original illustrative designs highlighted new design problems with textile structure, as previously white areas became gaps in the fabric. A solution was found using a mesh background, which was not "seen" by the camera.

4.75
Graphic designs for Aestheticodes. Visual recognition codes can become part of graphic designs so they are less obvious to the human eye, but still readable by a camera phone.
Kaoru Parry.

4.76
Embroidered Aestheticode with smartphone app. The app is searching for a readable code in the embroidery motif; codes can be associated with online content such as web pages to combine physical and digital experiences. Amanda Briggs-Goode and Tessa Acti.

TECH TIPS

To create your own Aestheticode, download the app—it will let you make up to five different codes. To draw a graphic code, you must follow a system of lines, spaces, and marks—these, in order, are what the software looks for. A code is described using a sequence of numbers, for example, 4, 3, 3, 3, 2. This means there are five spaces in the pattern, all attached to a continuous line, and there are 4, 3, 3, 3, and 2 marks in them.

1. Copy the simple flower in figure 4.77 with the marks inside the regions as shown.
2. The marks inside the regions translate into a code written as 1:1:1:1:2.
3. To troubleshoot, check the space between outside lines that enclose spaces, and the marks inside the space—if they are too close, the camera on your phone may not "see" it. You are not allowed to leave any empty regions, either.
4. Try drawing a different pattern for the same code.

4.77
Simple Aestheticode 1:1:1:1:2. Visual recognition codes follow rules concerned with continuous lines, enclosed spaces, and the number of marks within those spaces.

Yemi Awosile—
Acoustic vibrations

Yemi Awosile holds an MA from the Royal College of Art; her work is informed by cultural insights translated through textiles and material processes. As part of a playful workshop at the Institute of Making in London, she led a group of researchers to experiment with wood, rubber, fabric, plastic and paper, also supplying threads, needles and a small speaker kit available from Technology Will Save Us. http://yemiawosile.co.uk/

Different fabrics propagate sounds to different effect. The structure of the fabric, its weight, and the composition of the fibers all make a difference to its acoustic properties. How you attach the fabric to a structure, and if it is formed to deliberately amplify sound waves, for example, in a cone or cylinder, will all change the outcome.

4.78

4.78
Acoustic vibrations workshop, Institute of Making. We hear sound when vibrations occur within 20–20,000 Hz, or cycles per second. Touching a vibrating speaker to other surfaces causes these vibrations to be transmitted, and different forms and materials "sound" different. Yemi Awosile.

4.79–4.80
Acoustic vibrations workshop, Institute of Making. Yemi Awosile.

4.79

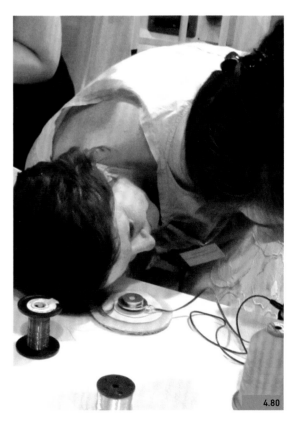

4.80

TECH TIPS

Purchase a Technology Will Save Us speaker kit, and plug it into your MP3 player. Follow these steps:

1. Build your own custom amplifier out of electronic components. Then design your own set of speakers to house it.
2. Attach the exciter to your amplifier and explore how it turns any material into a resonating surface. Play with different sizes, shapes and materials and see how your favorite band sounds through paper or plastic.
3. You will not only learn how to solder but you will start to understand how circuits work and what role each component has. You will then explore some of the principles of sound as you test your exciter on different materials.
4. Design and construct a bespoke speaker to fit your needs using any material from wood to acrylic, from a cereal box to a balloon!

Then extend your play to fabric to think about how sound might work in a textile system. Place the small speakers inside and behind different forms to listen to the changes they make. Think about how they might be controlled on the body, and what they might express.

Of course, textiles are also used for damping sound. Philips, in collaboration with Kvadrat, for example, is developing soft sound panels for interiors to manage sound quality and levels. Textiles are stretched over aluminum frames and backed with foam with moderate acoustic properties. Panels can be purchased for different acoustic and visual properties; they are used in meeting rooms, large public spaces such as airport lounges, and in hotel interiors.

Eef Lubbers—
Making thermochromic fibers

Eef Lubbers is a masters student at TU/e Eindhoven, in the department of Industrial Design. She has been inspired to create her own thermochromic yarns and is developing methods to weave dynamic color-changing fabrics with them. http://www.eeflubbers.com/

To hand-make these yarns, Lubbers looks for suitable commercially available braided round yarns; she then pulls a conductive fiber through the center to create a core that can be heated with a current high enough to cause resistance and heat. By painting the outer surface with different thermochromic inks, she can then make the yarns change color. Working with color-change yarns allows for the construction of open textile structures such as lace, as opposed to the more usual thermochromic print technique applied to a surface.

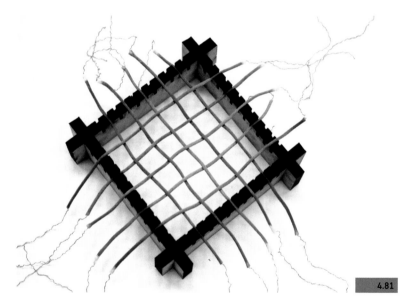

4.81

4.81
Weaving color-change yarns. Lubbers constructed a frame to prototype compositions of her color change yarns. Eef Lubbers.

Marina Castán, Gerard Rubio and Miguel González— Wearable Fashion Orchestra

Marina Castán is Professor and researcher in fashion and textiles at ESDi (the at Escolar Superior de Disseny in Barcelona). Gerard Rubio is a Barcelona-based designer working at the intersections between open source, 3D printing and knit technology; and Miguel Gonzalez is a fashion designer, teacher and member of the ESDI Unit Trends and Fashion (University Department of Theory and Development of Design ESDI). http://medialab-prado.es/person/marinacastan

The Wearable Fashion Orchestra is a collection of five dance costumes that behave as a group of musical instruments. Each one has a distinct sound, allowing the wearers to become musicians. It merges dance, music and fashion in a very intuitive and dynamic way by using a simple electronic system embedded in the garments.

The orchestra is an evolution of the Sound Embracers project (Gerard Rubio, Cristina Real, Sara Gil, and Gerda Antanaityte), in which sound is generated through body movement when the fabric is stretched. It works with the Arduino platform, which translates the body movement (by the means of a sensor made out of conductive thread) into sound sent out via four speakers embedded in the garment.

4.82

4.82
Fashion Orchestra. Fabric stretch sensors in the costumes send changing data signals and are transformed into sound output that can be "performed" by the dancers. Marina Castan, Gerard Rubio and Miguel González.

TECH TIPS

Each garment incorporates a knitted stretch sensor made out of conductive thread (of stainless steel fiber), attached to the neoprene by creating a kind of tube. We used the same fabric used for the garments, passing the sensor through it. That way we were able to keep the stretch sensor and the wires in the right place inside the garment. An Arduino Fio microcontroller with a lithium battery was placed between the shoulders, inside a pocket made of spacer fabric that isolates the dancer from the electronics while giving a nice feeling to the skin. The most difficult part of the project was to create the WiFi network that allows us to connect to the computer where the sound is generated. XBEE modules are used in every garment to create a reliable and fast (real time) data transfer.

The Arduino Fio is basically an Arduino controller without the programming device installed on it. This makes it smaller and cheaper and means you can leave a module in each garment or other physical "node" you design to form a wireless network. Because the programming device is not on it, loading a program from the Arduino IDE (Integrated Development Environment—the sketch interface on your computer) is slightly more complicated to begin with. You can use either wired or a wireless method, and Cytron offers comprehensive tutorials in how to achieve both (see the Suggested reading).

Chapter summary

Suggested reading

This chapter aimed to inspire you to bring your own textile processes into contact with technical challenges. Many of the contributors here are postgraduate students or young researchers, who have generously shared insights into their experimental approaches. The field is still developing and there is plenty of room for makers like you to take it further.

Worbin

Berzina, Z. (2004), "Skin Stories: Charting and Mapping the Skin: Research Using Analogies of Human Skin Tissue in Relation to my Textile Practice," PhD thesis, University of the Arts, London.

Kooroshnia, M. (2015), "Creating diverse colour-changing effects on textiles," Licentiate thesis, University of Boras, Studies in Artistic Research No. 11. Available online: http://bada.hb.se/handle/2320/14363 (accessed 8 April 2015).

Worbin, L. (2010), "Designing Dynamic Textile Patterns," PhD thesis, University of BorasStudies in Artistic Research No. 1.

Awosile

Kvadrat Soft Cells on the Philips site:

http://www.largeluminoussurfaces.com/luminoustextile

Reading Materials workshop documentation:

http://vimeo.com/user10683076

Supplies and basic steps:

http://www.techwillsaveus.com/

Yemi Awosile's website:

http://www.yemiawosile.co.uk/

Kettley

Creative Materials (2007), "Flexible Electrically Conductive Adhesive," available online: https://server.creativematerials.com/datasheets/DS_124_33.pdf (accessed 8 April 2015).

Engineered Conductive Materials (2010), "Membrane Switches," available online: http://www.conductives.com/membrane_switches.php (accessed 8 April 2015).

Munich University of Applied Sciences (2011), "Ducky in the Dark—Interactive Book," available online: http://www.the-interactive-book.com/components.html (accessed 8 April 2015).

Sparkfun (2015), "Voltage Dividers," available online: https://learn.sparkfun.com/tutorials/voltage-dividers (accessed 8 April 2015).

Sparkfun (2011), "Force Sensitive Resistor Round 0.5," available online: https://www.sparkfun.com/tutorials/269 (accessed 8 April 2015).

Starting Electronics (2013), "Measuring DC Voltage using Arduino," available online: http://startingelectronics.com/articles/arduino/measuring-voltage-with-arduino/ (accessed 8 April 2015).

Jie

21st Century Notebooking. Available online: http://www.nexmap.org/21c-notebooking-io. (accessed 8 April 2015).

Bare Conductive. Available online: http://www.bareconductive.com/. (accessed 8 April 2015)

Carter, D. and J. Diaz (2011), *The Elements of Pop-Up: A Pop-Up Book for Aspiring Paper Engineers*, New York: Simon and Schuster.

Jie, Q. and L. Buechley (2010), Electronic Popables: Exploring Paper-Based Computing

Through an Interactive Pop-Up Book, TEI'10, January 24–27, 2010, Cambridge, Massachusetts.

Jie, Q., (n/d) Circuit Stickers. Available online: http://technolojie.com/circuit-stickers/, and https://www.crowdsupply.com/chibitronics/circuit-stickers. (accessed 8 April 2015).

Hodge

Jo Hodge (2013), "Joprints," available online: http://joannehodge.co.uk/ (accessed 8 April 2015).

Glazzard

Glazzard, M. and P. Breedon (2013), "Exploring 3D-Printed Structures Through Textile Design," in *Research Through Design 2013 Conference Proceedings, 3–5 September 2013*, 51–54, Newcastle upon Tyne and Gateshead: Baltic Centre for Contemporary Art.

Glazzard, M. and P. Breedon (2014), "Weft-knitted auxetic textile design," *Physica Status Solidi (b)*, 251 (2): 267–72.

Kettley, S., *Aeolia*. Available online: http://sarahkettleydesign.co.uk/2013/02/20/aeolia/ (accessed 8 April 2015).

Kettley, S. & M. Glazzard (2010), "Knitted Stretch Sensors for Sound Output," extended abstract, *Proceedings 4th International Conference on Tangible, Embedded & Embodied Interactions*, Massachusetts Institute of Technology, Boston,.

Persson

Dumitrescu, D. and A. Persson (2009), *Touching Loops*, exhibited at Responsive by Material Sense, Hanover and Berlin, Germany, April–June 2009, and at It Is Possible, Avantex, Frankfurt, Germany, June 2009.

Persson, A. (2013), "Exploring Textiles as Materials for Interaction Design," PhD thesis, University of Boras Studies in Artistic Research, No. 4.

Uppingham Yarns. Available online: http://www.wools.co.uk/index.php?_a=category&cat_id=99 (accessed 8 April 2015).

The Yarn Purchasing Association. Available online: http://www.yarn.dk/gb/ (accessed 8 April 2015).

Gupta

Gupta, A. (2013), "Emotionally Intelligent Knitted Textiles: Emotional sensing and responsive action." Available online: https://colab.aut.ac.nz/projects/emotionally-intelligent-knitted-textiles/ (accessed 8 April 2015).

Coyle, S. and D. Diamond (2013), "Medical Applications of Smart Textiles," in T. Kirtsein (ed.), *Multidisciplinary Know-How for Smart Textile Developers*, 420–33, Cambridge, UK: Woodhead Publishing Ltd.

Kurbak and Posch

Ebru Kurbak (2014). "The Knitted Radio." Available online: http://ebrukurbak.net/the-knitted-radio/ (accessed 8 April 2015).

Waag Society (2014), "Open Knit Machine Workshop." Available online: https://www.waag.org/en/event/openknit-machine-workshop (accessed 8 April 2015).

John Richards (2012), "Charge/Discharge." Available online: https://vimeo.com/47413553 (accessed 8 April 2015).

Gowrishankar

Gowrishankar, R. (2011), "Designing Fabric Interactions: A Study of Knitted Fabric as an Electronic Interface Medium," MA thesis, Media Lab, Aalto University, Helsinki.

Gowrishankar, R. (2011), "Informal user testing for fabric trigger prototypes." Available online: www.defint.wordpress.com (accessed 8 April 2015).

Layne

Suites Culturelles (2014), "Montreal Fashion Innovation and Technology—Barbara Layne." Available online: https://suitesculturelles.wordpress.com/page/3/ (accessed on 19 December 2014).

Tandler

www.e-fibre.co.uk

www.Lynntandler.com

Hughes, R. and M. Rowe (1991), *The Colouring, Bronzing and Patination of Metals: A Manual for Fine Metalworkers, Sculptors and Designers*, London: Thames & Hudson.

Piper

Park, S., Gopalsamy, C., Rajamanickam, R., and Jayaraman, S., "The Wearable Motherboard™: An Information Infrastructure or Sensate Liner for Medical Applications," in Studies in Health Technology and Informatics, IOS Press, Vol. 62, pp. 252–258, 1999.

Intelligent Textiles Ltd.

Electromagnetic field shielding materials:

www.lessEMF.com.

Intelligent Textiles Ltd. (2004), Patent: "Electrical components and circuits constructed as textiles," US 8298968 B2. Available online: http://www.google.com /patents/US8298968. (accessed 9 April 2015).

Swallow, S. and A. P. Thompson (2010), "Intelligent Textiles: Reducing the Burden," in *Infantry: Capability, Burden and Technology*, 50–55, London: RUSI Defence Systems.

World Intellectual Property Organization, "Digitize Your Clothes: Look Smart in Intelligent Textiles." Available online: http://www.wipo.int/ipadvantage/en/details .jsp?id=2610 (accessed 28 October 2014).

eCrafts Collective

Crockett, C. (1991), *Card Weaving*, Loveland, CO: Interweave.

http://katihyyppa.com/eweaving-belts/

http://ecraftscollective.wordpress.com/belt-weaving -project/cosmic-e-belts_v2/

http://ecraftscollective.wordpress.com/belt-weaving -project/belt-weaving-techniques-learning-from-the -masters/

http://www.shelaghlewins.com/tablet_weaving/TW01 /TW01.htm

Society of Primitive Technology (1996), "Card Weaving." Adapted from Bart & Robin Blankenship (1996), *Earth Knack: Stone Age Skills for the 21st Century*. Layton, Utah: Gibbs Smith. Available online: http://www .hollowtop.com/spt_html/weaving.htm (accessed 9 April 2015).

Acti

Briggs-Goode, A. and K. Townsend (eds.) (2011), *Textile Design: Principles, Advances and Applications*, Cambridge, UK: Woodhead Publishing Ltd.

Sinclair

Gardiner, M. (2013), Designer Origami, Melbourne, Australia: Hinkler Books.

Hallett, C. and A. Johnston (2014), *Fabric for Fashion: The Swatch Book: Second Edition with 125 Sample Fabrics*, London: Laurence King Publishing.

Iwamoto Wada, Y. (2002), Memory on Cloth: Shibori Now, Tokyo: Kodansha.

Nakamichi, T. (2014), *Pattern Magic*, London: Laurence King Publishing.

Rutzky, J. and C. K. Palmer (2011), *Shadowfolds: Surprisingly Easy-To-Make Geometric Designs in Fabric*, New York: Kodansha USA.

Sinclair, R. (ed.) (2014), *Textiles and Fashion: Materials, Design and Technology* (Woodhead Publishing Series in Textiles), Cambridge, UK: Woodhead Publishing Ltd.

Wolff, C. (2003), *The Art of Manipulating Fabric*, Iola, WI: Krause Publications.

Brother sewing machines, http://www.brothersewing .co.uk/en_GB/home (accessed 19 November 2014).

Matthew Gardener, http://www.matthewgardiner.net (accessed 24 November 2014).

Oribotics, http://matthewgardiner.net/art/On_Oribotics (accessed 24 November 2014).

PE Design 9, Trial version, http://www.brother.com /common/hsm/pednext/pednext_trial.html (accessed 19 November 2014).

SophieSew, embroidery and design software, http:// sophiesew.com/SS2/index.php (accessed 23 October 2014).

Dumitrescu

Brett, D. (2005), *Rethinking Decoration: Pleasure and Ideology in the Visual Arts*, New York: Cambridge University Press.

Dumitrescu, D. (2010), "Interactive Textiles Expression in an Architectural Design—Architecture as Synaesthetic Expression," *Design Principles and Practices: An International Journal*, 2 (4): 11–28.

Dumitrescu, D. (2013), "Relational Textiles: Surface Expressions in Space Design," PhD thesis, Swedish School of Textiles, University of Boras, Sweden.

Ingold, T. (2007), *Lines: A Brief History*, London: Routledge.

Spuybroek, L. (2005), "The Structure of Vagueness," *Textile: The Journal of Cloth and Culture*, 3 (1): 6–19.

Davis and Microsoft

Davis, F., A. Roseway, E. Carroll and M. Czerwinski (2013), "Actuating Mood: Design of the Textile Mirror," *TEI 2013*, February 10–13, Barcelona, Spain.

Koleva

http://aestheticodes.com/

http://aestheticodes.com/wp-content/uploads /2013/09/Aestheticodes_Designer_Pattern_Book.pdf

Castán and González

Excerpt of the Project:

http://vimeo.com/107462260

SoundEmbracer Project by Gerard Rubio, Cristina Real, Sara Gil and Gerda

Antanaityte, project website:

http://soundembracers.tumblr.com

Tutorials for the Arduino Fio and XBee wireless communication:

http://tutorial.cytron.com.my/2012/12/03/getting -started-with-arduino-fio/

Vallgårda, A. (2009), "Computational Composites: Understanding The Materiality of Computational Technology," Ph.D. thesis, IT-Universitetet i København.

Developing your practice

Designers embarking on the development of products within the hybrid mix of smart textiles and wearable electronics must research fiber types and constructions and their applications, found beyond the limits of the traditional fashion sector.

McCann and Bryson 2009: 79

CHAPTER OVERVIEW

In this chapter, you will find a range of ways to think about how you work now, and how you might need to work in the future, to find a professional place within the field of smart textiles. These tools have been developed by others, but they are not fixed in stone—you should take the basic principles and play with them so that you can better understand the value of your unique skillset, and recognize how you will work best as part of a larger team. Picking up from chapter 2, you will develop your understanding of the interdisciplinary nature of smart textiles, and you will look at the implications of this for evaluating products and marketing.

The case study of Sarah Walker in this chapter shares the experiences of a young textile designer experiencing these issues for the first time and describes the design process. You will also learn about the different models of intellectual property, innovation and design protection relevant to this field, and you will find out how regulations and standards are being developed in Europe and the United States to support commercialization. The chapter ends with a discussion of the design innovation challenges facing UK-based industry according to textile consultant Mike Starbuck.

5.1
Interactive Media Design
(now Digital Interaction
Design). Year 3 students
2008–9.

5.1

THE T-SHAPED DESIGNER

The "T-shaped" designer is a well-known concept in product design; it represents good depth of knowledge in one discipline or practice, complemented by a broad awareness of other methodologies, skills, and an outward-looking approach to social issues or the matters of concern that might drive our work in the first place.

Conceived by David Guest, the idea was popularized by Tim Brown of IDEO throughout the 1990s, lending itself to the call for Renaissance men and women and people who would fit well with other disciplines in a team. We still teach T-shaped design, but it has been around long enough to attract some criticism and to be further developed by others. Visual metaphors are useful for thinking about how you work, how the field of smart textiles is evolving new hybrid practices, and how we need to consider teaching and learning for such environments in the future. Here are some others:

Shortened T	(and others) What does it mean if we play with the form?
I-shaped	Grounded in issues; broad skills, but mostly one specialty
*-shaped	From Unix symbol for "anything" = "any shaped"
X-shaped	"Me" at the center
H-shaped	Two areas of specialty

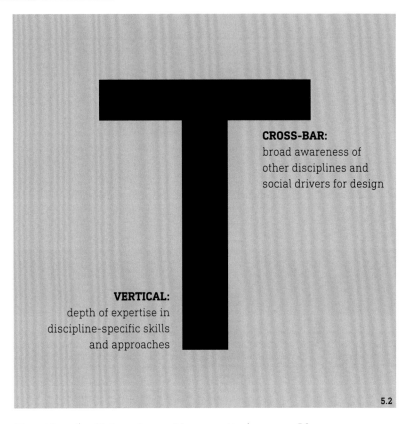

CROSS-BAR:
broad awareness of other disciplines and social drivers for design

VERTICAL:
depth of expertise in discipline-specific skills and approaches

5.2

Steve Mann (godfather of wearable computing) and Sara Diamond (of the Banff Centre and OCAD) visualize the X shape as being an excellent conduit, a "cross-fitting" to facilitate workflow with others. They variously label the arms of the cross to play with the concept. Mann goes on to discuss the "tree-shaped" designer, with a strong trunk, and growth both above and below ground; this metaphor represents "forests" of designers and the development of new "branches" of existing practice and inquiry.

5.2
Model for the T-shaped designer; you need to be aware of your core strengths as a designer, and the broader subject areas that will help you connect with other professionals.

IDENTIFYING VALUES AND FRAMING YOUR PRACTICE

In a short space, this section covers reasons for considering your values as a designer and some simple exercises that help you to do this. Increasingly, the concept of *phronesis* can be found creeping into areas of interaction design and pervasive and ubiquitous computing, and we should therefore pay it some attention as we create smart textiles that will no doubt become an integral part of bigger connected systems. Phronesis refers to a composite kind of knowledge—at once technical and academic—but it also means more than this. Importantly, phronetic designers are aware of the ethical issues in their own practice, and in how their work may affect the world, for the good (or bad) of

humanity. They are capable of "judgements and decisions made in the manner of a virtuoso social and political actor" (Flyvberg 2001), and they may be as politically aware as they are mindful in their material practice. The need for this type of designer is growing in importance as the boundaries of design itself expand and even dissolve altogether. Projects that aim to redesign entire provinces, improve the experience of patients in an emergency ward, rearrange materials at the molecular level, or reimagine global financial ecosystems are no longer all that surprising. The implementation of smart textiles, as a contributing platform in an "internet of things," needs to be just as carefully considered.

There are different kinds of design projects, and it is easy to continue working as you always do, especially if you are good at it, without paying too much attention to the bigger picture. But reflection makes you a far better designer, and here you will find out about three simple tools for doing this:

1. Personal practice timelines
2. Framing projects
3. Repertory grids of practice

5.3

Design shapes much of the world we shape and that shapes us.

Tony Fry 1994:39

5.4

5.3
The future; it has been said that the best way to predict the future is to invent it. Design is an inquiry into what might be.

5.4
Personal visual timeline; a useful if time-consuming way to reflect on your design practice. Try using digital photo applications to achieve the same overview.

Personal practice timeline

This is simple, if a bit time-consuming, but it is very powerful. Find images of your own work, and arrange them physically in chronological order along a wall or large roll of paper. It will become immediately obvious when you were being most productive and which work was most meaningful to you. Look for the recurring themes.

Exercise Twelve: Framing your practice

Draw this table in your sketchbook. List four recent projects you have worked on and identify whether they were conservative, pragmatic, critical or radical. Did they fit the descriptions? Might you need to redefine any of the categories, or create a new one?

Framing your projects and practice

In 1995, the architect Richard Coyne discussed design for information technology from four different perspectives: conservative, pragmatic, critical and radical. Using these labels, you can "frame" your practice—it will help you recognize your habitual goals and will allow you to question them. If you find you always design for the status quo, what would it be like to do a project from a critical perspective? Can you "translate" a pragmatic project so that it becomes radical?

Conservative in this context means that your work tries to maintain an existing situation (it does not mean good or bad!); it assumes people are essentially the same at different times and in different places.

Pragmatic tends to refer to a user-centered approach, in which the people who will be using your designs have some say as part of the design process; it assumes people have different values according to their cultures.

Critical means work that tries to raise awareness of some issue; it is often not made for commercial reasons, and it is intended to ask questions of the status quo; it draws attention to the mechanisms at work in society, especially where power is concerned.

Radical is hardest to define, but it refers to work that challenges fundamental aspects of the field or practice (for example, if we embed computation into jewelry, it becomes "useful" in a way this class of objects has not been before).

Table 5.1
Table of Dimensions. Practice each approach to design. Translate one project from pragmatic to critical. Try a completely new approach to your next project. After Richard Coyne 1995.

	Project 1	Project 2	Project 3	Project 4	Project 5
Conservative					
Pragmatic					
Critical					
Radical					

Repertory grids of practice

Repertory grids (rep grids) are used in psychology to try and understand how someone is making sense of the world. It is based on the observation that humans like to use pairs of descriptive constructs to compare experience; an example would be describing one of your acquaintances as distant and others as friendly. The distant–friendly pair becomes a dimension that can be used to comparatively describe new acquaintances. Although rep grids are more often used to try and assess users' preferences for certain designs, they can also be used to reflect on practice, revealing attitudes to risk, aesthetics, materials, use of digital tools for creativity, collaboration, or any other aspect of design practice that comes up. Working with this tool in a group can help to elicit the topics and help you talk through what the results might mean for you. Creating a grid with the first few topics and dimensions can help bring out more information, and it may be that you create more than one grid before being satisfied that all the relevant topics are being covered, and that the constructs have been refined well enough.

The basic steps in working with this type of grid are:

1. Elicit the terms to be used in the descriptive constructs.
   For example, Risky–Safe; Good job satisfaction–Boring; Highly skilled–Repetitive

2. Decide on the topics (elements) to be examined.
   For example, being self-employed; innovating materials; designing for manufacture

3. Rating the topics against the constructs.
   Can be visual (gradation of color, or using different symbols); more often a Likert scale from 1 to 5

4. Discuss, share or analyze the final grid.
   If used with large groups, statistical methods are often used, such as counting the frequency of recurring topics; if reflecting on your own practice, a more qualitative approach will be appropriate, and if working with others, you could look for agreement and difference in the use of terminology as well as in how you feel about your field of practice.

Constructs (Emergent Pole)	ELEMENTS								Contrasts (Implicit Pole)
1									5
1									
2									
3									
4									
5									
6									
7									
8									
9									
10									
11									
12									
13									

5.5

5.5
Repertory grid template; a technique useful for finding out about tacit (difficult to describe) knowledge, expertise, and attitudes.
t-h-inker.net (part of the Creating Knowledge through Design & Conceptual Innovation Project).

KEY QUESTION

Bearing in mind the preceding exercises, how would you characterize your own design process in relation to the larger world and society?

WORKING ACROSS DISCIPLINES

One of the key themes of this book is the importance of working across fields of practice, and the broad range of skills and knowledge that are involved in smart textiles development. One way to engage with this is to attend residencies, media labs and workshops in which people from different disciplines are brought together. Organizations such as Arcintex (Sweden), Steim and V2 (The Netherlands), ANAT (Australia), and the e-Textiles Summer Camp (various locations) frequently run this type of event, and they are usually well represented online in Flickr streams or blogs (see Suggested reading at the end of the chapter, as well as Resources in the appendix). Some of these are designed for postgraduate students, while others are open to the public; some are aimed at practitioners funded by arts councils, and you will also find some attached to larger conferences. Costs will vary; try your local Hackspace or Makerspace for more informal drop-in learning.

One thing to be aware of when attending these is that the projects you create may be difficult to run when you are back home—if a workshop is jointly delivered by a specialist in MIDI for sound output, and you create a textile interface to input gestural data, you may end up with something you cannot demonstrate once the event is over.

Tips for making the most of your experience include:
- Take video of your final collaborative works in action.
- Make sure you have some high-resolution photos of the development process.
- Get everyone's contact details (for later collaboration, but also permissions to use images).
- Collect as much information as you can on the parts of the system you are not learning about—for example, can you download software while there?
- Join or set up shared discussion spaces for troubleshooting later (e.g., with Arduino board setup).

It is easy to assume when you are outside looking in at another discipline that it is homogeneous; that is, as a textile designer, you may think you need just one technical partner to collaborate on projects. Similarly, interaction designers looking at textiles may not make a distinction between knit and weave specialists. This is normal, but one important aspect of this (which is a result of silo-ed education systems) is the separation of programming from electronics engineering (not many people do both). There are a number of high-profile, small, innovative teams in smart textiles and wearable technology, such as Cute Circuit and Intelligent Textiles Ltd., which might lead you to expect that all you need to do is find that ideal partner in practice. But the reality is usually more complex and involves a wider network of contacts.

5.6
Cross-disciplinary collaboration is usually necessary to achieve robust working textiles systems. This printed and laminated textile by Sara Robertson is being wirelessly networked by Steven Battersby as part of a textile residency on the Internet of Soft Things project 2015.

Another assumption is that traditional skills-based practices are undertaken in solitude, that the work is not distributed, or even that it is all one kind of work. In what is often referred to as the jewelers' bible, Oppi Untracht (1985) illustrates how different approaches to jewelry relate to each other, and how the different trades rely on each other; there are specialists in polishing and stone setting, casting and fabricating, as well as in conceptual design. He called this a "convocation," a coming together of different subdisciplines to create a kind of ecology of allied professional practices. This ecology or convocation of practice is still emerging in smart textiles.

Because the ability to work in teams is so crucial to this kind of work, it is useful to have an awareness of the kinds of roles and personalities involved. The Belbin (2009) model of teamwork is based both on people's understanding of the jobs they are expected to do and on their attitudes about working with others. It recognizes that different types of individuals have different valuable contributions to offer, and that the potential of a synergistic team is far greater than that of an individual. The recognized behavioral roles are: plant, resource investigator, coordinator, shaper, monitor/evaluator, teamworker, implementer, completer/finisher, and specialist. Each is understood in terms of his or her team contribution and allowable weaknesses; so for example, a shaper is someone who is challenging and dynamic, with the drive to overcome obstacles, but who may sometimes provoke or offend others in a team. Be aware that everyone normally draws on more than one team role.

On the other hand, the Myers-Briggs Type Indicator describes personality type using a series of dimensions, which indicate an individual's interpersonal attitude and approaches to information gathering, decision making and planning. For example, the judging–perceiving dimension describes the person's preference for dealing with the world in a more or less orderly or flexible way. A popular and simple way to experience different personality roles is Edward de Bono's (2009) Six Hats exercise. Using props to allocate attitudes to a task means you can roleplay; use this exercise to critique your own work and drive a project forward or to reflect on your usual personality type and behavior in a team. Wear the white hat to gather the facts, the green hat to think creatively, and the black hat to consider any risks in a project.

In relationships between practices, the outputs of one practice will often be taken up by another as part of its process; in this view, practices (such as weaving, coding and ethnography) are interrelated and almost "alive," as they exist beyond the lives of the individuals who are engaged in them. Smart textiles, like wearable computing, can be seen as a collection of related practices that are emerging, evolving and stabilizing, and this has an impact on how you see your own role within what is a very dynamic environment.

MARKETS, THE AUDIENCE AND CRITERIA FOR SUCCESS

The concept of wearable technology and its enabling materials of conductive yarns and fabrics have been around for decades, but critics point out that nothing has really changed since Maggie Orth's Firefly Dress and squishy musical instruments of the late 1990s. This is open to debate—it could be argued that the LilyPad Arduino has brought tinkering with textiles to a whole new community, and is responsible for engaging more females in electronics; or that industry has been solving manufacturing problems such as washability or robustness where hard components meet soft. But perhaps the underlying issue is with the expectations of different audiences, raised by the promise of high-profile projects.

Wearables and smart textiles have grown up at the same time as social media—every step of early student projects was blogged religiously—the field is growing up in public, and the public wants to know what smart textiles are really for. There is skepticism that the world needs smart textile products at all, particularly if they do not work reliably, or are hard to care for. They have even been described as a technical solution still searching for a problem. The annual Gartner Hype Cycle (2014), compiled by a large market research company, helps to tell the story of technologies as they evolve from exciting technical novelties into mainstream products. The graph shown is the general form of the hype cycle— you will be able to find annual emerging technology hype cycles online.

Smart fabrics are subsumed into the Gartner report on Smart City Technologies, and in 2012 they were shown climbing the "peak of inflated expectations"; at the same time, Gartner published an *Innovation Insight* report on smart fabrics, pointing out their role in big data, and implications for "improved employee productivity and well-being." The need to balance the benefits and costs of adoption is highlighted. As of July 2013, wearable user interfaces were just beginning to come down the other side of the peak of inflated expectations and into the "trough of disillusionment"; however, since then, media coverage of wrist- and head-worn devices has been intense, with the launch of Google Glass, Nike+, Samsung Gear, and Pebble products. New forms such as smart jewelry are already creeping into mainstream markets, and by the time this book goes to print, wearable user interfaces are likely to be climbing the "slope of enlightenment."

A recent Arts and Humanities Research Council Network project in the UK focused on the difference between invention and innovation, where invention is the production of original technical knowledge and innovation is a process of value creation involving manufacture and marketing. There are different models of innovation that need to be considered when talking about smart textiles; if innovation depends on people, time and different channels of communication, then thinking only about fashion, say, or only about medical use value will not be enough. All of these channels need to be recognized as part of the larger process of innovation in this case.

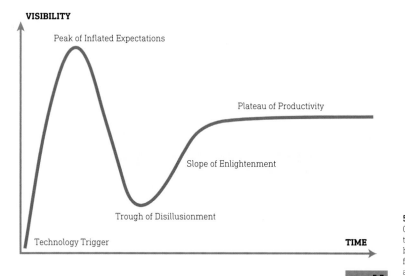

VISIBILITY

Peak of Inflated Expectations

Plateau of Productivity

Slope of Enlightenment

Trough of Disillusionment

Technology Trigger

TIME

5.7

5.7
Gartner Hype Cycle. Technologies tend to follow a pattern in the public mind, based on media-fed expectations, followed by actual experiences of use and consumption.
Gartner Inc.

A report from researchers in smart textiles for biomedical applications (Park and Jayaram 2010) points out the "painfully slow" transition of smart textiles from research to reality; it considers technology success factors, such as reduction of cost and improvement of service, and adoption of innovation factors such as relative advantage, compatibility and trialability. The report then suggests a three-step program to demonstrate the overarching value of smart textiles and get them into the market by establishing robustness and readiness of components and systems, demonstrating need through contextual effectiveness of design concepts, and conducting a comprehensive cost-benefit analysis.

But Berglin (2013) points out the commercial activity bubbling beneath small fashion and arts-led businesses, which are creating awareness, solving technical issues and developing expressive approaches to design, if not creating lucrative markets. Ultimately, the question consumers will have is, "Where can I buy this?" IDTechEx (2014) identifies the first wave of wearable technology as being characterized by electronics on the ear and the wrist, the second as being about connectivity, smart watches, skin patches and VR headsets, and the third as being all about e-fibers in e-textiles.

Elena Corchero's Lost Values brand is an excellent example of an early business venture in this field. Corchero's exploratory craft-led work as an MA student took her to the Distance Lab, an incubator for digital technologies in Scotland. Here she worked with teams to develop commercially feasible products, going through the European CE marking process for product conformity with her Loopin kits for kids, then raising venture funding, developing a brand, and innovating simple textile products for the mainstream in the form of LFLECT, reflective yarn incorporated into fashionable cycling gear.

If you are thinking about how businesses in this new sector operate, a useful tool is the Business Model Canvas template. This is freely available online at http://www.businessmodelgeneration.com/canvas. It lays out the relationships between the value proposition, the activities, partners, marketing, and customer segments on a single page; you can use this to analyze how existing businesses work and to design your own potential business ideas. The same team also publishes "Business Model You," which can help you reflect on the value of your own skillset in smart textiles for a range of potential clients.

There is a difference between approaching this work as research, as art project, and as commercial venture—objects in each of these processes play different roles, and problems can arise when, for example, things made in the name of research are expected to perform as if they are mainstream products under warranty. Different practices will value your work differently too—the contemporary jewelry community is interested in conceptual rigor, while traditional silversmiths are interested in workmanship—so expect different questions and feedback depending on your audience, and be clear what the work was meant to achieve.

5.8
Business Model Canvas. This template helps you to think about the "offer" your business makes to customers, and to identify the relationships you will need to build to make it work. businessmodelgeneration.com.

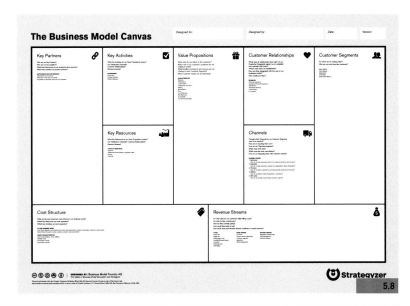

SELLING YOUR SKILLSET

For a long time, textile designers (as opposed to textile engineers) did not understand the value of their expertise to other, often engineering-led disciplines. This is beginning to change, but it still has a long way to go. A lot of textile design education can still be described as modernist, in that it champions the creative vision and aesthetic expression of a single individual. In fact, artistic flair is only part of the story. Of course you need to be able to develop different aspects of textile expression—weight, hand, color, surface, structure—and you will be able to communicate these product concepts effectively. But the experiential and technical knowledge involved in the different textile specialties are also very valuable to smart textiles and wearable development collaborators. Working out how to characterize this kind of knowledge and then communicate that with other disciplines will be an important aspect of your professional development.

Exercise Thirteen
Identifying textile knowledge and process

Use one of the tools outlined in the previous sections to help you understand your own processes, and how they may differ from other disciplines. Examples of things that might differ include attitudes about playful exploration with materials, the role of a design brief in the process, or even what a product is (is a fabric swatch a product?). Once you have thought carefully, you will be better able to focus the message you want to get across about your work.

The standard formats of communicating creative work (printed CVs and a large folio of loose sheets carried to an interview) have diversified hugely, and they depend much more on an online presence than before. But the principal strategy in communicating your practice has not: be aware of the expectations of your audience, and orient your communication to them. Put together the best portfolio you can to display your talent. Given that you will have diverse audiences, preparing and carefully managing a live folio online is paramount. Here you will see a handful of examples that achieve a professional level of representation of creative smart textile development, before we make some further suggestions for you to try.

Online and digital formats

Oscar Tomico's presentation for the Smart Textiles CRISP (Creative Industry Scientific Programme) project is a beautiful example of communication of smart textile projects, published using Issuu. Professional photography is used to create a coherent mood, with older users presented respectfully wearing smart textile project outcomes. The catalog uses simple statements and questions to orient the viewer to the images on the page. These allow the catalog to outline very elegantly the research questions and the design processes being used in the project. Single design concepts are highlighted with dedicated pages.

The catalog is available as a high-quality print publication and as a PDF file on Issuu. This obviously means there is no possibility of tactile engagement with the textiles themselves, but the models throughout are demonstrating touch and interaction with the garments, suggesting the quality of the knitted materials.

The online PDF format allows you to combine written details on skills and experience with the visual folio, and you can have more pages than a standard two-page CV or resume. However, be aware of your reader's precious time; browsing textile folios on Issuu, this author found one at a massive 178 pages.

Moving images: These typically use common formats such as .MOV, .AVI, or Quicktime. If you need to use a single PDF or PowerPoint file to submit work digitally, you may be able to add standalone movies to a file. Take a look at examples like Cute Circuit on Instagram.

Websites: Websites should have clear navigation and should be available for view in common browsers such as Google Chrome, Internet Explorer, Firefox and Safari. A Facebook page or WordPress site are very effective ways of preparing work online without the need for specialized web development.

5.9
Presentation of wearer in CRISP project. The knitted garment is part of the Vigour collection, which incorporates stretch sensors and an app for physical rehabilitation. Oscar Tomico, Eindhoven University of Technology.
Photo: Joe Hammond.

5.10
Boudicca website, platform13.com. The presentation of your business across online and offline media should be consistent and communicate something of the feel of your practice. Zowie Broach.

Sometimes finding the words to describe your specialty can be hard. Di Mainstone has evolved her fashion practice to describe herself as a "movician"—creating body-centric sculptures designed to initiate movement and storytelling. Much of her work involves sound output, to such an extent that she has become one of 100 "momentum" ambassadors for Sennheiser's project on personal sound journeys. Some labs, brands or "houses" treat words quite differently. Boudicca, an innovative fashion brand, takes a very poetic and holistic approach to its brand; the website reads like a portfolio, emphasizing process as a central interest. It takes a multimedia approach, incorporating music, digital and stop-frame animation, photography, visual research and sketches. Little of Boudicca's fashion is "smart," but it is extremely interactive in that it engages the wearer and the viewer in creating new images and uses multiple layers of technology to create intangible garments. Everything about the essay's mini-site, for example, is quite tangible and personal, from the recognizable blue-tack creases in the corners of the "paper" to the need for the viewer to enter a password (which is provided at the bottom of the screen). Danielle Wilde's website uses a simple format, which allows her to add projects and ideas easily without the viewer having to click through menus. Everything is present on the front page, but the layout remains visually exciting and inviting. Everything is a link to more details, videos and information on projects and collaborations. Further, Wilde has effectively integrated key research questions and professional accolades as part of the page design, creating a kind of immediate resume.

Including the tangible in the digital

Employers and academic courses are interested not only in your product ideas, but in your working process. It is assumed that you work in sketchbooks, whether these are physical, digital, or a mixture of both, and that you have some kind of explorative materials practice. This should always be documented and included in any kind of portfolio. You can scan sketchbook pages and collages, photograph large physical works, and film processes in action. Just be aware of the difference between the printed or on-screen version of a beautiful image and the raw power of a messy, physical page. Do not make it too beautiful.

You can also show people touching and interacting with your work. "Embodied" videos are enjoying a moment in some textile and crafting communities; these try to convey the immediate experience of either making or playing with smart textiles or other materials. Maria Blaisse has always made excellent examples, featuring her simple wearable forms in rubber and felt and her large open-weave structures.

5.11
Fabrics on hangers.
Explore creative methods
for organizing and
presenting your practical
work. Ink & Spindle.

5.11

Physical formats

Self-publishing sites such as Blurb allow you to create
professionally bound volumes of images and text.
These sites will usually provide you with a choice
of templates or a simple editing package to design
your own "book." If you are good with packages such
as InDesign already, many will accept files you have
prepared yourself. Prices vary, as you can select the
quality of paper, number of pages, size and format,
and whether the book should be hard- or soft-bound.
See examples at http://www.blurb.co.uk/portfolio-
book. Business cards do not need to be bland, either:
Moo cards allow you to upload artwork so that every
one of your cards is different—a portfolio in a tiny box.
Alternatively, make a book of stickers.

Drawing on standard textile display methods, you
could also consider making your own folded card
headers to go over hangers, create a swatch book,
or use luggage tags to record technical details
attached to samples.

Case study:
Sarah Walker

Sarah Walker finished an MA in textile design and innovation at Nottingham Trent University in 2013. Her BA was in multimedia textiles, focusing on fabric manipulation, three-dimensional surfaces, and digital processes such as laser cutting. Work from her undergraduate years was featured in Technothreads, curated by Marie O'Mahony. Now at the start of her doctoral studies, Walker has been reflecting on how her route through higher textile education has shaped her attitude toward material, process, and research methodology. In particular, she recounts her experience as an intern at the Belgian Textiles Open Innovation Centre, TIO3 in Ronse, Belgium, during which she collaborated with an interior architecture design student for the first time.
https://www.linkedin.com/in/sarahkwalker

Multimedia textiles

In the domain of smart textiles, there is often a focus on knit, print, embroidery and weave—the standard specialties to be found in most textile courses. Each promotes a particular way of thinking and knowing, of understanding material and form, and of working with specialized technologies in production. Multimedia, on the other hand, can include any of these, as well as existing materials and fabrics. It is characterized by exploration of new technology processes, combinations of disparate techniques, and a questioning about the very nature of textiles themselves. Outcomes tend to be focused on the quality of a surface and the interaction between two and three dimensions. The most well known publications that reflect this approach in the interactive and technical textiles field are the books by Marie O'Mahony (2008) and Sarah

Braddock-Clarke (2012), in which many examples are wonderfully illustrated (see Suggested reading). However, it is not a practice that is often discussed as a different way of thinking, and it is this that makes Walker an interesting case study here.

Risk taking on the MA

Walker continued to take a proactive approach to her studies while on her masters course, successfully applying for the Paul Smith scholarship to Bunka Gakuen University in Tokyo, and later undertaking an internship at TIO3 in Belgium, also coinciding with the Arcintex research network event held there in 2013. This caused her to return to the MA studio in Nottingham just one month before her final show. The fact that Walker was doing cross-disciplinary work meant that a proactive approach to research was necessary in order for her to understand and translate that information back into her own work. She found that she needed to situate herself as textile designer in those different environments, and adapt to using new languages and tools.

5.12
Technothreads. Multimedia textiles like this can include many different processes in one piece, such as weave and print. Sarah Walker.

Such opportunities are not always available in UG (undergraduate) courses, which can be closely structured; Walker found the open structure of the MA to be the perfect platform for her exploratory approach to textile innovation. She does, however, recognize that much of this comes down to personality—she made a point of getting involved in as many opportunities as possible, such as a multidisciplinary module run out of the product design subject area. Now in the position of leading a project on this, and pitching its value to the next cohort of MA students, she realizes that she might be quite unusual in her attitude. Her approach to the whole MA experience was ambitious—she sought to understand the textile design process, but she also wanted to challenge it, open it up, and restructure it.

Having come through the multimedia route, and with a growing interest in smart textiles, she made the difficult decision not to make any products for her final submission: no garments, footwear or interior products. This challenged the standard notion of what outcomes should be—what would she present if not things? But her explorations into spacer fabrics with CAD embroidery, regular patterns using electronic components, combined with product design concept boards, demonstrated a way of thinking about design rather than design as a solution to a given brief, and were the best way to represent smart textiles. These boards showed how the textiles Walker had developed might be variously applied within different design sectors: automotive, fashion, and sportswear.

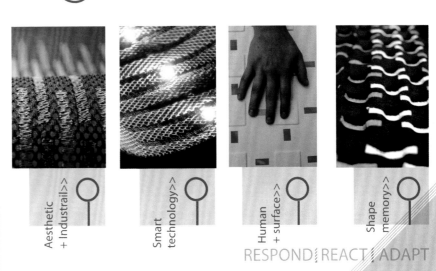

5.13
Final Textile Designs (MA). Walker organized her material explorations into four categories to guide the viewer and tell a story of the design as research. Sarah Walker.

5.14
MA show featuring concept design boards. Smart materials and fabrics can be applied in different product sectors; this expo layout explained the opportunities clearly. Sarah Walker.

Learning across disciplines

This approach to the culmination of her Masters study was influenced greatly by her residency at TIO3, which aimed to provide students from around the world with new experiences in developing interactive textile concepts. Walker was paired with Karolien Notaerts, an interior architecture design student at Design Museum Ghent in Belgium, and together they spent a month developing the hiddenblinds concept.

Hiddenblinds became a series of screens activated via a tablecloth: the blinds want to be part of an environment, to be integrated and interactive. They are a way to create a private space, but also a way of communication. The user can choose the position of the blinds and direct their opening and closing. The project focused on creating poetic experiences in environments using smart textiles. Approaching the project as a piece of research, Walker and Notaerts asked the following questions:

• How can hiddenblinds be created with smart textiles?
• How can hiddenblinds interact with public space?
• How can hiddenblinds manipulate human behavior?

These three questions occurred on three scales: the textile, textile and environment, and textile and human. Using a design-led methodology, the women sought to answer these questions through practical tests and observation with print testing on a range of transparent fabrics, laser cutting and interactive circuit development. Openings, movement and pulling up were considered outputs for the blinds. Actual-size prototypes were made and tested with the public in a local café.

Tio3 Internship>> *Hidden blinds*

>>Prototype: 3 screens activated via table cloth

>>Digital embroidery communication symbols

>>Push button

>>Motor activation

>>LED sequence

>>Arduinoo programmed motion sensor

'smart textiles become human and virtual become real' maison caro

RESPOND REACT ADAPT

5.15

5.16

5.15
hiddenblinds at TIO3; a design concept for a network of smart textiles in a domestic environment.
Sarah Walker.

5.16
Testing at Vooruit Café. User feedback is an important part of smart textile development.
Sarah Walker.

The test in Vooruit Café showed that a way for the user to communicate with the blinds was needed, and a tablecloth was introduced to the system as the input interface. The print developed for the blinds was quite organic, which would fit into different environments, and with the addition of a motion sensor and an Arduino, Walker and Notaerts also created a more indirect sort of communication from people passing by.

Toward academic research in smart textiles

Three months into her PhD, the expectations of Walker's supervision team and the researchers on the project she is attached to are causing her to reflect on her approach to textile design. Academic research funding is usually dependent on a well-defined project proposal, with a research question, methodology and expected outcomes clearly articulated. In the UK at least, there is now also a healthy tradition of practice-led research, which may include artworks as deliverable outcomes. Walker's project does not yet fit either of these definitions—she is still working out what role, if any, making will play in her research.

What she has defined is her tendency to treat all experience as learning through explicit reflection—that is, she keeps notebooks and diaries, blogs and sketchbooks. She is collecting evidence of her changing thinking as she engages with researchers in computer science, product design and mental health, as well as embroiderers, pattern cutters and knitters, and she is defining her own very interdisciplinary practice. She understands how important it is to be able to communicate this practice in research teams, and with nonacademic research partners too. Everyone she comes into contact with has their own expectations of "textiles," "textile research," and any other term relating to practice—Walker's skill lies in being able to communicate such practice visually to a wide range of other disciplines.

MANUFACTURING IMPLICATIONS

Current PCB and microchip manufacturing can be achieved at nanometer scales with great reliability at relatively low cost; this is in marked contrast to textiles, which are flexible, meaning such levels of accuracy cannot be matched. While traditional textile manufacturing in principle is suitable for the integration of conductive yarns and fabrics, and while some standard haberdashery parts can be used as conductive connectors, there are a number of issues that cause problems when processes are scaled up for industrial manufacture.

You have already heard about metal fibers that can create problems through the buildup of uneven tension in yarns through working, the buildup of electromagnetic fields in processing, the blunting of cutting edges against metal materials, and the migration of conductive filaments within sensitive electronic manufacturing machinery: all of these mean that processes cannot be simply automated, but require high levels of human monitoring.

In fact, smart textiles represent a radical innovation problem, in that they are not an incremental development of an existing product; instead, they require technology management, IP management and market development as well as proof-of-concept or semi-industrial–scale demonstrators. Such radical development involves high levels of uncertainty about such fundamental aspects of manufacture as the settings on machines, potential modification of parts or new monitoring systems. It requires a systems engineering approach, in which there is continuous engineering development in line with production. Ger Brinks, of MODINT, a credit management service organization for the German fashion and textiles industry, proposes that we think about the bigger picture and aim for "smart industries" rather than continuing to develop smart products that cannot be manufactured in a cost-effective way. Without this, smart textiles are never likely to move up the Technology Readiness Scale (also called the Technology Readiness Index, or Level). At best, they currently sit at around 4 or 5 on the 1-to-10 scale, in which components can be validated in a lab or relevant live environment. To move them up from this to 6 or 7, in which the production system can be demonstrated, is very ambitious. This step-up would require an

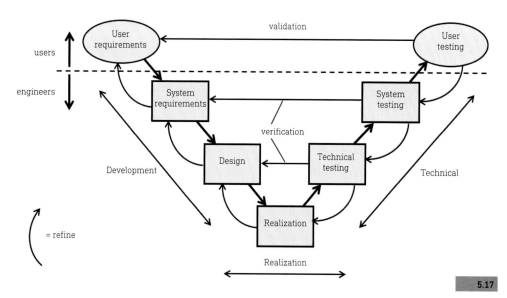

5.17
System engineering. Smart textiles are not feasible as an industry without considering the complete system of production and consumption. Saxion University.

5.17

inventory of useful materials, including the new combinations and composites involved, through iterations of continuous improvement engineering and the kind of system requirements engineering already found in mechatronics. Connectors cannot degrade after only one day; instead, testing systems for smart textiles need to be developed to test components and subsystems tens if not hundreds of thousands of times, so that databases of materials and construction parameters can be drawn up to guarantee function.

Fundamental research still to be done includes the development of energy harvesting and storage; this is very complex work, but if systems cannot store energy, the wearable concept is likely to fail. Saxion University is part of a European project called Texenergy, which is investigating the feasibility of flexible solar cells for wearable rechargeable batteries.

SMEs (small to medium enterprises) do not have the funds for research and development, so one way forward is collaboration. Universities in some instances are natural sites for shared resources such as finishing machines at Borasin Sweden, and a textile machinery research network led by Loughborough, in which participating universities share facilities and expertise with industrial partners. This allows students to undertake research for industry as part of their courses.

5.18

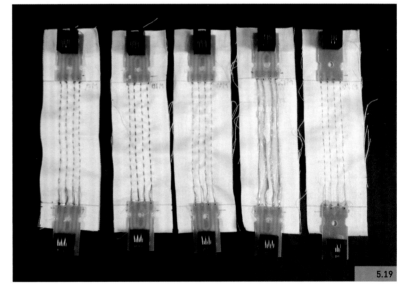

5.19

5.18
Testing conductivity; a systematic approach allows you to make informed decisions about yarns and fibers.
Saxion University.

5.19
Testing rig. It is often necessary to develop custom testing rigs for novel areas like smart textiles.
Saxion University.

DESIGN MANAGEMENT
AND OPEN INNOVATION

Innovation can be described as comprising theoretical conception plus technical invention plus commercial exploitation (Trott 2011); it is more than simply a great idea or a novel technology, and it involves, above all, time and people.

Businesses in the smart textiles field may be well-established manufacturers of existing textile products dating back to the Industrial Revolution, or they may be small startups with a novel idea. Whatever the profile of the company, it needs to nurture a culture that can support new ideas and concepts, and it needs to put in place the processes that can then make them successful.

A decision also has to be made between the costly and time-consuming protection of intellectual property through patenting and the speed and excitement of open innovation models. Smart textiles and wearable technology are caught between the two, with many basic structures and processes being shared by the open source hacker community online, but also with large industry players protecting their assets.

Open innovation, in which problems and approaches to solving them are shared among collaborating companies, needs to be carefully managed, but it can be very powerful. Members of the EU Matrix project (in multirisk and multihazard assessment), for example, shared ownership of the core technology developed, but individual members were able to file patents for related work; management of the project included extensively minuted meetings to prevent any intellectual property rights issues from arising subsequently.

Meanwhile, Devan Chemicals in Belgium creates innovative sustainable properties and functionalities for textiles; Devan has six existing patents and another five pending. They invest 10 percent of their annual turnover in research and development (R&D) and collaborate regularly on scientific research projects with a range of partners, with a focus on user health, comfort and protection. They apply a "SmartNets" approach to transforming ideas into innovations, recognizing the roles that different kinds of knowledge play, the ways in which ICT (information and communication technology)

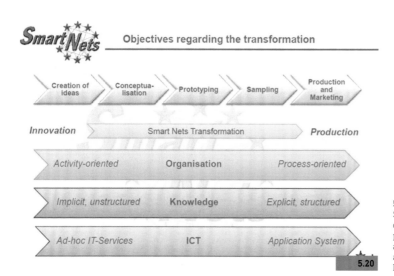

5.20
SmartNets innovation model: creation of ideas > conceptualization > prototyping > sampling > production and marketing. The innovation process also needs to be designed. Devan Chemicals.

services need to be developed, and how pockets of motivated activity are transformed into business-oriented processes (see figure 5.20). Outcomes include new niche markets in home textiles (bedding, upholstery, carpets), apparel (underwear, shirts, sportswear), and technical textiles (medical, filtration, workwear). In order to make this work as a business strategy, Devan takes a long-term view on investment in innovation, expecting commercialization of R&D in three to five years, and with no expectation of immediate returns. They deliberately adopt open innovation as a mindset, offsetting the increasing complexity of each contributing science field and diversifying risks. Within the company, employees are encouraged to explore networks and seek partnerships with academia and research institutes. As in the Matrix project, there is an understanding that IP will have to be shared to make this work. One example of a product outcome of this process has been Probiotex, a mix of probiotic bacteria applied to textile fibers to help reduce allergic reactions to dust mites in products such as mattress protectors, quilts, ticking, foam, pillows and upholstery.

Established high street brands face these as well as organizational problems. Those that have their roots in the Industrial Revolution of the nineteenth century will have been through restructuring processes as a result of trends in globalization, outsourcing manufacturing to cheaper labor sites across the world. In doing this, most have sold off what textile and garment manufacturing resources they once owned in their original countries. Now that developing countries are beginning to charge more for their labor, there is no longer such a compelling financial argument for this model, and the very mass-production modularity that made it attractive in the first place through economies of scale is now causing problems for companies seeking to innovate with smart textile industrial processes. Smaller companies that have retained control over local manufacturing are finding it easier to redesign their systems and reskill workforces, working directly with the machinery as well as their customer bases. This concurrent design approach appears to be one of the most promising ways forward, and it also creates a need within industry for textile designers who are well versed in smart textile techniques.

Case study:
Debbie Davies

Debbie Davies worked as a television producer for a number of years before being employed by The Centre for Creative Collaboration (C4CC), an initiative of the University of London, as an artist in residence. She is a design entrepreneur who founded the Acton Street company to develop commercially feasible garments with light emissive technology.
http://www.ddavies.me/

Here, Davies discusses the issues she faced when she launched her light-up dresses and skirts using electroluminescent (EL) wire. An artist working across a variety of disciplines, Davies makes interactive art and exhibits in Berlin, Germany, and at Burning Man, a festival held in Nevada. Her work includes interactive textile dolls called *Stabby Man*, and she runs a fashion label called *Acton Street Designs*, under which she makes the garments that light up. While at C4CC, she attracted a diverse group of people to share their interest in electronics and science, such as the Open Source User Hardware Group, Homecamp, Dorkbot MzTEK, and Codasign. Working as the label Acton Street, Davies set herself the difficult goal of bringing into existence a fashionable product that was washable, wearable, comfortable and stylish. She was determined to avoid making another wearable that required the user to carry a backpack of batteries with them, was not washable, or that made them "look like a Christmas tree."

EL wire and inverters

The route to achieving this was not simple: different colors of EL wire shine less brightly than others, and Davies experimented with at least thirty different inverters (EL wire runs off AC not DC, so you need an inverter to change the current from DC to AC); it took a long time to find anything that had been designed to save on space. She says, "no electronics engineer ever made electronics with a fashion designer in mind." Hiring an electronics engineer to design a custom inverter proved expensive, and assumptions about the design differed—while an on/off switch is the norm for the high street consumer, an engineer might not think it is important. Paying attention to what is important to whom in collaboration and innovation management is crucial. Hacking together an inverter, a switch and a battery yourself, as Davies ended up doing, is possible, but you will then face the prospect of having to have it CE marked so you can sell it. Davies reports that it can cost approximately £3,000 to get an electronics kit like hers CE tested (for more on quality assurance and testing, see the Regulations and certification section that follows). In addition, if you sell items with batteries sewn in, like *Stabby Man*, the law requires you to help your customers to dispose of the batteries safely should they wish for your assistance. Different countries have different legislation, too.

5.21

5.21
Silk skirt with EL circle. Davies invested time with factories to build the necessary skills and new production processes needed in commercializing these garments. Debbie Davies. Photography: Mark Stokes.

Materials and their impact on the design

Davies also had to negotiate a good price for her material supplies. It is fine for a one-off project to pay retail prices on materials like EL wire, but not when creating a product for sale. She originally found fixed lengths of wire in the UK, with a large battery pack and inverter attached (and difficult to remove). Suppliers of EL wire where the length could be specified were expensive, and so Davies turned to a supplier in the United States; it worked out to be cheaper for her to import the goods from the United States and pay duty on the wire than it did to pay UK prices. Eventually, she returned to the UK supplier, who agreed to match the US supplier prices. Following this, the EL wire's main manufacturer closed, and production was moved to a factory in China. The new EL wire was far less stiff, which greatly affected the form of the skirts. It was also important to make the electronics removable. Technically, if the connector is protected, a garment with EL wire in it can be dry-cleaned—but dry cleaners will not be easily convinced of that. Davies knew she wanted to use silk to diffuse the light and to appeal to a more aspirational fashion consumer. The silk that worked best was a Dupion with minimal slub, prewashed by the supplier. Davies has washed her dresses over fifty times without damage to the silk, although there is shrinkage of between 3 and 10 percent that needs to be taken into account.

Manufacturing

The design was for a shift dress that could hide the electronics easily while still being flattering. An award from the Manufactory Advisory Board enabled Davies to manufacture in India, where the silk supplier was, where the price of production was cheaper, and where tie-dye was a specialty. Most factories operate on large production numbers— the contact Davies was given usually dealt with orders of 3,000 or more—but business depends on creating good relationships, and Davies was able to negotiate a small run of just 150 items, to be developed collaboratively. All stages of the process had to be anticipated. For example, where EL wire crosses a seam, you need the seam to be closed and ironed in the direction the wire is traveling in. A factory that caters to the mass market will understand that most people want an open seam—anything different in the production process has to be closely supervised. While they will be experts in standard garment construction, creating a garment with embedded electronics requires new areas of expertise, and the process will not be traditional. On the other hand, people are excited to see components like EL wire, and a lot of time may be spent showing people what has been made and answering questions. For Davies, it was important to be on the factory floor when the samples were being made because she was able to anticipate problems as and when they arose.

A final word from Davies

"I now have a great education around what not to do, and I did achieve my aim. I had done what I set out to do, I had made a dress that lit up, it looked sophisticated, it was subtle, it was practical, you could replace the batteries easily, and you could wash it. I had overcome my lack of knowledge around electronics, and I overcame my lack of understanding as to how garments are made—I spent months looking at different inverters, not to mention time spent learning how to solder and the expense of it all. But the more you learn, the more able you are to communicate with others. You garner more respect, too, and people are more willing to go the extra mile because they know you have. I also learned that making hardware is no different to making a dress, or a sculpture, or writing a story; there is more than one way to do it, and there is more than one way or one kind of technology you can deploy to make something light up. If you are armed knowing a few of those options it can make for a better conversation with those who want to collaborate with you on your projects."

REGULATIONS AND CERTIFICATION

Standardization is a current issue for smart textile innovators, although it is more achievable in this field than in wearable technology, which involves more varied permutations and possible complex combinations of technologies in the final product. Some companies who want to purchase new high-performance textile garments, such as for the fire department (in Belgium), find that there is a risk involved for them, as they are responsible for the health and safety of the staff who will be relying on the products. Insurance can become difficult or expensive to put in place without industry standards, and this is where another European project has stepped in, to provide the cover needed to these sectors, so that functionality can be certified and market demand established. Enprotex recognizes that for the consumer of such garments, standards are fragmented: electronics can be certified, and so can garments, but there is a lack of standards in testing for smart garments. While the research institutes can lead on this, standardization committees tend to be manned by traditional companies, and the process is long and difficult. This affects a number of sectors.

Another example is the hot melting industry, where workers need protection from extreme temperatures. There are International Organization for Standardization standards for skin temperature measurement, comprising over ten items, but core body temperature measurement is harder to achieve. The Prospie project is working to deliver sensors in garments to trigger local warnings and an integrated system for remote warning and rescue, based on sensor data on hypo- and hyperthermia in advanced personal protective equipment (PPE). The US Food and Drug Administration (FDA) handles regulatory processes that are rigorously applied and are relevant to health and medical applications of smart textiles. Applicants need first to identify an existing classification that the product fits within, which can be challenging in this new field. No medical device can be marketed in the United States without FDA approval. Oekotex publishes and checks sustainability standards in textile products. The STeP certification system analyzes and evaluates production conditions with respect to the use of environmentally friendly technologies and products.

5.22

5.23

5.22
The CE mark, meaning the product has passed a series of regulatory safety checks for the European market.

5.23
The FDA logo. Any product claiming to be medically beneficial needs FDA approval. US Food and Drug Administration.

5.24
Confidence in Textiles certification. Oekotex.

5.24

Feature interview: Mike Starbuck

Mike Starbuck is a UK-based textile innovation consultant, whose role has changed along with the industry. Globalization of the textile and garment retail and manufacturing industries has taken him to work in the United States, Australia, Europe, and the Far East. Here he talks about the impact of globalization on UK manufacturing and innovation.

Mike, you have had an interesting career—can you tell us something about how the industry has evolved?

Globalization has absolutely been the biggest driver of change in this industry. Speaking from a Western perspective, manufacturing moved offshore as the established high street retail brands found low-cost labor elsewhere. This meant that the loyalty of the manufacturing base also moved offshore, creating the need for new quality assurance processes. More than this, design was then outsourced in the same way. Quality became harder to control, as offshore manufacturing serviced the world, not only the UK. There has been a strange role reversal, as the established high street retailers have now become desirable as business assets to powerful manufacturing bases.

What has been the impact on our high street today?

Well, the internet and e-commerce affects every part of the process. It offers huge scope for the product offer, including lower overheads—so the manufacturing base that was once dedicated to the retail sector can now sell itself—the manufacturing base has become a competitor for the high street retail brands. So we see falling sales, with retailers trying desperately to attract people back into the stores. You can see different approaches—for example, Burberry is able to retain a customer base who shop for quality and personal service.

Primark is owned by British Sugar, which means they can sell reasonable quality goods at a far lower margin than some other retailers—about 30 percent rather than the more normal 80 percent. This gives them an advantage, and you can see them upgrading their stores now to attract both young customers and people looking for good customer service— things that the internet can't offer.

And how is textile engineering involved?

It always has been—and the next level of innovation has to happen not only in performance but also in design. There is an important link between the product and the fiber, which is really obvious in shapewear and lingerie. It's all about moving forward old technology to improve the product. My own background is in knitting innovation, and I have done everything from design management to design and development; there just cannot be any business without innovation, it's as simple as that. The product has to work, the process and material has to be cost effective, and there has to be a market ready to display the product. And then, each kind of product has its own areas of expertise— to knit a sock is not a simple thing—so, knitted garments, socks, underwear, shapewear—each is really specialized.

What are the implications for the future of textile innovation?

There are basically two ways to innovate—through product development, or through the cost of manufacturing. For example, I worked with a stretch covers business, which diversified into apparel by using new yarns. Globalization has removed that opportunity by separating manufacturing from the business, so now it needs to come back in a new way: brand, manufacturing and sales all need to come back to sit within a single business. In fact you could say this is the Victorian model that many of the large British high street brands began as.

Is this business model difficult to achieve now?

Yes—the expertise has gone, and if a company finds manufacturing expertise overseas it is hard to bring people to the UK to work. So in fact universities have a key role to play in training for textile innovation—we can look to Italy, a real center just now for textile innovation, where you could say old knowledge has new heads. What young people and textile graduates need is to get experience working within this complex situation before branching out, because it's not an easy time to launch new product types that also need new manufacturing processes.

Thank you, Mike. Could you give us an example of a particular project or process that you found inspiring?

Of course—well, I was working with a knitting business in Mansfield (the East Midlands, UK), and we were involved with ICI/DuPont; they had brought out a new carpet yarn, which wasn't fully resolved—in fact, that was the positive thing about it—it allowed more diversification and development. A carpet yarn is traditionally a round cross-section, but this was a new cross-section, which gave new qualities of light reflection when the yarn was cut off—not seen before in carpets. Not only this, but the yarn offered other unexpected characteristics like a silky handle, moisture transportation, and antistatic, and it led to the design and development of very successful lingerie products like bras, panties, shapewear and slips. That Diablo yarn became the basis of the Tactel brand, which went truly global in the 1970s and 80s. I think you can see in this example the relationship between all those different aspects I spoke about—the knowledge in the different product sectors, in the textile engineering through manufacturing, to the brand and market.

Chapter summary

Suggested reading

This chapter discussed the variations in "multi" and "inter" disciplinary working and asked you to reflect on your role in a team through thinking about your own values and creative practice. It introduced markets for smart textiles, and the issues in communicating your skillset and design intentions to different audiences and potential employers. You also learned about the tension between the open source community in smart textiles development and the closed nature of intellectual property in the commercial sector. Finally, the chapter discussed design management in a global innovation economy and the challenges smart textiles pose for outdated manufacturing business models.

Belbin Associates (2009), *The Belbin Guide to Succeeding at Work*, London: A & C Black Publishers Ltd.

Berglin, L. (2013), "Smart Textiles and Wearable Technology: A Study of Smart Textiles in Fashion and Clothing," a report within the Baltic Fashion Project, Swedish School of Textiles, University of Boras. Available online: http://www.hb.se/Global/THS /BalticFashion_rapport_Smarttextiles.pdf (accessed 9 December 2014).

de Bono, E. (2009), *Six Thinking Hats*, London: Penguin Books.

Boudicca (n.d.), "Essays." Available online: http://www.essays.boudiccacouture.com/essays .htm?password2=essays (accessed 9 December 2014).

Braddock-Clarke, S. and J. Harris (2012), *Digital Visions for Fashion + Textiles: Made in Code*, London: Thames and Hudson.

Corchero, E. (2014), "Lost Values Creative Lab." Available online: http://www.elenacorchero.com/ (accessed 9 December 2014).

Coyne, R. (1995), *Designing Information Technology in the Postmodern Age: From Method To Metaphor*, Cambridge, MA: MIT Press.

"Enprotex Innovation Procurement for Protective Textiles" (n.d.). Available online: http://www.enprotex .eu/ (accessed 9 December 2014).

Flyvberg, B. (2001), *Making Social Science Matter: Why Social Inquiry Fails and How it Can Succeed Again*, Cambridge, UK: Cambridge University Press.

Fry, T. (1994), *Remakings: Ecology, Design, Philosophy*, Sussex Inlet, Australia: Envirobook.

Gartner Hype Cycle (2014), "Gartner's 2014 HypeCycle for Emerging Technologies Maps the Journey to Digital Business." Available online: http://www.gartner.com /newsroom/id/2819918 (accessed 10 February 2015).

Hemmecke, J. and D. Divotkey (2012), "Repertory Grids as Knowledge Elicitation Method of Tacit Assumptions in Design Artefacts," First Multidisciplinary Summer School on Design as Inquiry, Kiel, Germany, September 3–7.

Hemmings, J. (2005), "Defining a Movement: Textile & Fibre Art." Available online: http://jessicahemmings .com/index.php/defining-a-movement-textile-fibre -art/ (accessed 13 January 2015).

Hemmings, J. (2014), "Smart Textiles Archive." Available online: http://jessicahemmings.com/index .php/tag/smart-textiles/ (accessed 9 December 2014).

IDTechEx (2014), "Wearable Technology" (various reports). Available online: http://www.idtechex.com /reports/topics/wearable-technology-000052.asp (accessed 9 December 2014).

McCann, J. and D. Bryson (2009), *Smart Clothes and Wearable Technology*, Cambridge, UK: Woodhead Publishing Ltd.

Moo Cards (2014), "About Moo: Printfinity." Available online: http://uk.moo.com/about/printfinity.html (accessed 9 December 2014).

The Myers and Briggs Foundation (n.d.), "MBTI Basics." Available online: http://www.myersbriggs.org /my-mbti-personality-type/mbti-basics/ (accessed 9 December 2014).

O'Mahony, M. (2008), *TechnoThreads: What Fashion Did Next*, Dublin: Science Gallery.

Orth, M. (2013), "The Short Life of Colour Change Textiles." Available online: http://www.maggieorth .com/Short_Life.html (accessed 9 December 2014).

Osterwalder, A. and Y. Pigneur (2013), *Business Model Generation: A Handbook for Visionaries, Game Changers, and Challengers*, Hoboken, NJ: John Wiley and Sons. Template available online: http://www .businessmodelgeneration.com/canvas.

Park, S. and S. Jayaram (2010), "Smart Textile–Based Wearable Biomedical Systems: A Transition Plan for Research to Reality," *IEEE Transactions on Information Technology in Biomedicine*, 14 (1): 86–92.

Putten, C. van (2013), *Maria Blaisse: The Emergence of Form*, Rotterdam: nai010 Uitgevers.

Rodgers, P. and M. Smyth (2010), *Digital Blur: Creative Practice at the Boundaries of Architecture, Design and Art*, Faringdon, UK: Libri Publishing.

Rogers, E. M. (1995), *Diffusion of Innovation*, New York: Free Press.

Saxion University of Applied Sciences (2014), "Chair Smart Functional Materials." Available online: http:// smarttex-netzwerk.de/images/PDF/Symposium2014 /Brinks_Saxion-NL.pdf (accessed 9 December 2014).

Tomico, O. (2014), "Smart Textile Services." http:// issuu.com/fadbarcelona/docs/opendesigntomico (accessed 9 December 2014).

Trott, P. (2011), *Innovation Management & New Product Development*, Harlow: Pearson Education.

Untracht, O. (1985), *Jewelry Concepts and Technology*, New York: Doubleday.

Appendix: further reading and resources

Glossary

Actuation
An output from a system; includes such things as light, sound, and movement. Uses actuators such as light-emitting diodes (LEDs), speakers and motors.

Addressable
A digital system sends instructions to components. A pixel on a screen is addressable because it can be sent instructions to change state.

Affect
Refers to human emotion. In HCI terms, affective computing means attempts to make systems that understand or react to emotions.

Analog
In computing terminology, analog (analogue) refers to a state change with continuous, nondiscrete values. In technology terms, analog is often used to describe older, physical technologies like paper, contrasting them with digital technologies.

Arduino
A popular system of hardware and open source programming environment for creative projects and prototyping purposes.

Arduino XBee
A wireless communication module for the Arduino hardware system.

Auxetic
A three-dimensional structure that expands in two directions simultaneously in a single plane.

Baud rate
A measurement of the pulses per second in a digital signal.

Big data
The use of massive amounts of similar types of data collected from many anonymous sources to reveal large-scale behavioral patterns.

Biocompatible
Material that is not harmful or poisonous when implanted in the body.

Breadboard
A solderless base for prototyping circuits.

Capacitance
A potential force (voltage) stored by an object or component.

Circuit
The functional combination of a power source, resistors and diodes to produce output through the flow of current.

Cloud (storage)
The remote management of data on servers, made available to users using different devices over a network.

Colocated
Input and output occur in the same place.

Composite
A material made up of at least two other component materials, taking advantage of their different performance characteristics, such as strength or flexibility.

Conductor
A material through which electrons flow freely.

Continuity
When two or more components allow current to flow, there is continuity. If a break in the system is introduced, there is no continuity.

Couching
A textile technique commonly used in embroidery to attach a bulky material such as a cord to a substrate, typically by stitching over it to hold it in place without piercing it.

Course
A horizontal series of knitted stitches.

Current
The rate of flow of electrons in a circuit, measured in amps, symbolized by A.

Digital
A system such as a switch with two possible states: on or off. Also referred to in programming as high or low, or a 1 or 0. More complex digital systems make use of many series of such states.

Digitization
The process of preparing a design for embroidery using CAD software, specifying stitch type, density and other parameters.

Elastomeric
A material with the elastic properties of rubber.

Electroactive polymer (EAP)
A polymer that changes shape or moves when a current is passed through it. Can have large deformation while able to move other objects. Sometimes called artificial muscle.

Electrode
The contact point at which current enters or leaves a system.

Electrodeposition
The use of electron flow to plate or grow a substance on an electrode.

Embellishing
Techniques used in textile surface development, such as applique, needle felting and needle punching. Specialist embellishing machines are often used.

Extrusion
Transformation of a material through a drawplate to create long, continuous filaments.

Findings
A jewelry term for functional fastenings and connectors.

Forging
The transformation of a solid material, usually metal, through the repeated, strategic application of force, often using heat to soften the material first.

FTDI
A board that adapts a USB to a serial connection.

Haberdashery
The fashion and textile term for supplies such as threads, ribbons, braids, cords, buttons and other fastenings.

Hacker
In some cases a negative term referring to one who gains illegal access to protected websites and systems. Now also used to describe a grassroots movement of open source hardware, do it yourself, and tinkering, usually with creative or educational goals.

Handle/Hand
The drape and mechanical characteristics of a fabric; the subsequent human perception of the fabric in the hand and on the body.

IDE
An integrated development environment (IDE) is an application in which developers edit code and debug and compile programs.

Impedance
Resistance value.

Input
The action or environmental state that causes a system to react.

Insulator
A material that does not conduct electricity.

Integral garment
An integral garment is seamless, often manufactured using knitting techniques, with fully fashioned form and differentiated areas of tension.

Interfacing
A nonwoven fabric laminated or sewn to another to add local strength or structure.

IOT (internet of things)
A vision of a world embedded with computational functionality and wireless, real-time communication. Previously referred to as ubiquitous computing.

Jacquard
A weaving technique that allows individual warp threads to be lifted. Originally "programmed" using punched cards, this technique allows complex and often figurative patterns to be woven.

Jig
A custom tool that allows repetitive manufacture of a desired form.

LiIon battery
A lithium ion battery has the same electrochemical makeup as a LiPo battery—both refer to lithium ion polymer.

LiPo battery
Lithium polymer batteries are rechargeable and typically used in mobile phones. "Polymer" may refer only to the casing, not the composition of the battery.

Maker
A term that has come to mean an individual who tinkers with electronics or undertakes craft projects, often with sustainable or political goals. The maker movement champions individual creativity.

Mathematical modeling
The simulation of real life situations using mathematical rules. Used to predict behavior of a material or system.

Microprocessor
A computer processor on a microchip that can be programmed to accept input, store small amounts of data for processing, and return output values.

Modality
A term found in experience design and interaction design, referring to the human senses the system input or output will be perceived by.

Monofilament
A long man-made fiber of a single material, such as fishing line.

Multihead
A computerized embroidery machine for efficient mass manufacture, with 6, 12, or 18 heads. Modular versions can embroider different designs at the same time.

Nonwoven
Fabrics made by entangling long fibers through heat or mechanical techniques, often using polymers.

Ohm's law
The relationship between voltage, current and resistance, expressed through a series of equations: V (voltage) = I (current) × R (resistance).

Orthogonal
An arrangement of components following straight lines and right angles.

Output
The result of a process of a system. May include the results of a mathematical problem, a sound, light, or text, for example.

Packet
A unit of transmitted digital information.

Patination
The coloration of metals through the use of chemicals.

PCB board
Refers to the printed circuit board on which components are soldered.

Perfboard
In electronics, a board with regular holes for the prototyping of circuits using solder.

Photonics
The transmission of photons (light) through materials, such as in fiberoptics.

Phronesis
An ancient Greek term for "practical wisdom," found in philosophy.

Plate (in yarns)
The use of more than one type of yarn, worked at the same time, often resulting in fabric with one type of yarn on one face.

Ply
A composite yarn constructed from a number of existing yarns twisted together, such as two-ply and four-ply.

Quantified self
The use of data about an individual's daily behavior and body functions to improve health and well-being.

Resistance
The restriction of the flow of electrons in a circuit.

Scenario
A descriptive account of the use of a product or system, involving relevant stakeholders and their experience with the system over time.

Semiconductor
A material that conducts electricity under certain conditions or to a certain degree.

Sensing
Responsiveness to an external stimulus, such as temperature change, or the presence of given chemicals.

Shape memory alloy (SMA)
A combination of metals that can be "trained" to recover their original form when exposed to certain external conditions, such as heat.

Shed
The space between warp threads when weaving, through which the weft yarn is passed.

Shibori
A Japanese knotted dye-resist technique used to create patterned and often textural fabrics.

Short circuit
When a current finds a shorter route through a circuit, bypassing resistors and diodes, meaning there will be no intended output. May burn out the battery or other components.

Stakeholder
Any person or organization with a vested interest in a design project; includes cleaners and maintenance staff, town councils, and funding bodies as well as end users.

Stripboard
A circuit prototyping board with parallel conductive connections between perforations.

Substrate
A supporting material, usually in sheet or planar form.

Switch
An opening in a circuit that can be closed to allow current to flow. Switches have only two states, on or off.

Tacit Knowledge
Knowledge gained through experience that is hard to articulate or share.

Tangible
In computing, this refers to functionality embedded in objects that can be touched and handled.

Tensile
Stretched; strength characteristics of a material when stretched. Tensile architecture makes use of these characteristics to create thin-shell structures.

Thermal mapping
The use of temperature information to visualize the energy of a person, material or object. Uses infrared imaging techniques.

Threshold
An assigned input value that will trigger a process or program to run.

Trace
A conductive connection between two points in a circuit.

Variable resistor
A resistor in a circuit that can have different impedence values, which will allow different levels of current to flow. A typical example is a volume control on a radio. Many conductive textile structures act as variable resistors when they are touched or moved.

Voltage
The potential power of a circuit, measured in volts, and symbolized by V.

Voltage divider
A circuit that changes a large voltage input into a small voltage output using two series resistors.

Wale
The vertical structure of a knitted fabric; refers to the number of stitches in a row or course.

Warp
The threads fixed to a loom and held in tension in weaving (vertical).

Weft
The yarn continuously passed over and under other yarns in the weaving process (horizontal).

XBEE
See Arduino XBEE.

Key academic conferences and journals

CHI—Computer Human Interaction conferences
(and associated events such as NordiCHI and OzCHI)
http://chi2015.acm.org/

The Design Journal
http://www.tandfonline.com/loi/rfdj20#.Vr5OUVJW4wI

Digital Creativity—Multidisciplinary journal
http://www.tandfonline.com/action
/aboutThisJournal?journalCode=ndcr20#.VMP666h_hHI

ISWC—International Symposium on Wearable Computing
http://www.iswc.net/iswc15/

The Journal of the Textile Institute
http://www.texi.org/publicationsjti.asp

TEI—International Tangible, Embedded and Embodied Interaction Conference
http://www.tei-conf.org/14/

Textile—The Journal of Cloth and Culture
http://www.tandfonline.com/loi/rftx20#.Vr5OsFJW4wI

Textile Research Journal
http://trj.sagepub.com/

Ubicomp
Large multidisciplinary conference on pervasive computing.
http://ubicomp.org/ubicomp2015/

Trade fairs, organizations and residencies

ANAT—Australian Network for Art and Technology
http://www.anat.org.au/

Arcintex—Architecture, Interaction Design & Smart Textiles Research Network
http://arcintex.hb.se/

CES
Annual Consumer Electronics Show, Las Vegas.
http://www.cesweb.org/

e-Textiles Summer Camp
Annual practitioner camp.
http://etextile-summercamp.org/swatch-exchange/

MIT Media Lab, Massachusetts Institute of Technology
http://www.media.mit.edu/

Premier Vision
Global fashion and textiles trade show.
http://www.premierevision.com/

Smart Fabrics and Wearable Technology
Trade conference.
http://www.innovationintextiles.com/events-calendar/
smart-fabrics-wearable-technology-conference/

Steim—Studio for Electro-Instrumental Music, Amsterdam
http://steim.org/

TechTextil—International Trade Fair for Textiles, Frankfurt
http://techtextil.messefrankfurt.com/frankfurt/en
/besucher/willkommen.html

TIO3—Ronse, Belgium
http://www.tio3.be/startpage.aspx

Tiree TechWave
Annual practitioner camp, Scotland.
http://tireetechwave.org/

V2—Institute for Unstable Media, Rotterdam
http://v2.nl/

Waag Society—Amsterdam
http://waag.org/en

Skills resources

Adafruit
http://www.adafruit.com/datasheets/hakkotips.pdf
https://learn.adafruit.com/

An Internet of Soft Things
http://aninternetofsoftthings.com/categories/make/

Arduino
http://arduino.cc/en/Tutorial/HomePage

Crafting Material Interfaces
http://courses.media.mit.edu/2011fall/mass62/index
.html%3Fcat=6.html

eTextiles Lounge
http://etextilelounge.com/

Instructables
http://www.instructables.com/

Kobakant—How To Get What You Want
http://www.kobakant.at/DIY/

MIT Open Resources—New Textiles
http://ocw.mit.edu/courses/media-arts-and-sciences
/mas-962-special-topics-new-textiles-spring-2010/

OpenMaterials
http://openmaterials.org/

Plug and Wear (tutorials)
http://www.plugandwear.com/default
.asp?mod=cpages&page_id=16

PLUSEA
http://www.plusea.at/

SparkFun
https://learn.sparkfun.com/tutorials

The Weaveshed
http://www.theweaveshed.org/

Suppliers

AdaFruit
https://www.adafruit.com/products/1204
Electronic components, microprocessors, tools

Arduino
http://store.arduino.cc/
Open source hardware and software platform

Bare Conductive
http://www.bareconductive.com/
Conductive paint, kits

Bekaert
http://www.bekaert.com/en/products-and
-applications
Conductive fibers and yarns

Cookson Precious Metals
http://www.cooksongold.com/
Jewelry tools, findings, materials

Kitronik
https://www.kitronik.co.uk/
Kits, conductive textiles, Arduino

Lamé Lifesaver
http://members.shaw.ca/ubik/thread/order.html
Conductive thread

LessEMF
www.lessemf.com
Conductive fabrics, Velcro, tapes, threads, inks,
paints, epoxies

Margarita Benitez
http://www.margaritabenitez.com/wearables
/resources.html

Mindsets
http://www.mindsetsonline.co.uk/Site/About
Kits for education

MIT OpenCourseWare
http://ocw.mit.edu/courses/media-arts-and-sciences
/mas-962-special-topics-new-textiles-spring-2010
/related-resources/

Oomlout
http://oomlout.co.uk/
Arduino supplies, breadboards, electronic
components, kits

plugandwear
http://www.plugandwear.com/default.asp
Proprietary conductive and interactive fabrics, kits

Rapid Electronics
www.rapidonline.com
Electronic components and tools

SparkFun Electronics
www.sparkfun.com
Kits, sensors, electronic components, conductive thread

Bibliography

Books

Braddock-Clarke, S. and J. Harris (2012), *Digital Visions for Fashion & Textiles: Made in Code*, London: Thames and Hudson.

Briggs-Goode, A. and K. Townsend (2011), *Textile Design: Principles, Advances and Applications*, Woodhead Publishing Series in Textiles, Cambridge, UK: Woodhead Publishing Ltd.

David, C. (2008), *Futurotextiel 08: Surprising Textiles, Design and Art*, Oostkamp: Stichting Kunstboek.

Eng, D. (2009), *Fashion Geek: Clothes and Accessories Tech*, Cincinnati, OH: North Light Books.

Flyvbjerg, B. (2001), *Making Social Science Matter: Why Social Inquiry Fails and How It Can Succeed Again*, Cambridge, UK: Cambridge University Press.

Gale, C. and J. Kaur (2002), *The Textile Book*, Oxford: Berg.

Hartman, K. (2014), *Make: Wearable Electronics*, Sebastopol, CA: Maker Media.

Hughes, R. and M. Rowe (1991), *The Colouring, Bronzing and Patination of Metals: A Manual for Fine Metalworkers, Sculptors and Designers*, London: Thames and Hudson.

Kirstein, T., ed. (2013), *Multidisciplinary Know-How for Smart-Textile Developers* (Woodhead Publishing Series in Textiles), Cambridge, UK: Woodhead Publishing Ltd.

Lewis, A. (2008), *Switch Craft*, New York: Potter Craft.

McCann, J. and D. Bryson (2009), *Smart Clothes and Wearable Technology*, Cambridge, UK: Woodhead Publishing Ltd.

Pakhchyan, S. (2008), *Fashioning Technology*, Sebastopol, CA: O'Reilly.

Platt, C. (2009), *Make: Electronics*, Sebastopol, CA: Maker Media.

Seymour, S. (2008), *Fashionable Technology*, New York: Springer.

Seymour, S. (2010), *Functional Aesthetics: Vision in Fashionable Technology*, New York: Springer.

Smith, W. C. (2010), *Smart Textile Coatings and Laminates*, Cambridge, UK: Woodhead Publishing Ltd.

Till, F., R. Earley and C. Collet (2012), *Material Futures/01*, London: University of the Arts.

Journals/academic papers/doctoral theses

Berzowska, J. and M. Skorobogatiy (2010), "Karma Chameleon: Bragg Fiber Jacquard-Woven Photonic Textiles," *Proc. TEI 2010*. Available online: http://xslabs .net/karma-chameleon/papers/KC-Bragg_Fiber_ Jacquard-Woven_Photonic_Textiles.pdf (accessed 28 Oct. 2015).

Coyle, S., Lau, K.T., Moyna, N., O'Gorman, D., Diamond, D., Di Francesco, F., Costanzo, D., Salvo, P., Trivella, M.G., De Rossi, D.E., Taccini, N., Paradiso, R., Porchet, J.A., Ridolfi, A., Luprano, J., Chuzel, C., Lanier, T., Revol-Cavalier, F., Schoumacker, S., Mourier, V., Chartier, I., Convert, R., De-Moncuit, H., and Bini, C. (2010). "BIOTEX—Biosensing Textiles for Personalised Healthcare Management." *IEEE Transactions on Information Technology in Biomedicine*. 14: 2, 364–70.

Patel, S., H. Park, P. Bonato, L. Chan and M. Rodgers (2012), "A Review of Wearable Sensors and Systems with Application in Rehabilitation," *Journal of NeuroEngineering and Rehabilitation*, 9: 21. Available online: http://www.jneuroengrehab.com/content /pdf/1743-0003-9-21.pdf (accessed 27 May 2014).

Persson, A. (2013), *Exploring Textiles as Materials for Interaction Design*, PhD thesis, The Swedish School of Textiles, University of Boras.

Shanmugasundaram, O. (2008), "Smart & Intelligent Textiles," *Indian Textile Journal*, February.

Suh, M. (2010), "E-Textiles for Wearability: Review on Electrical and Mechanical Properties." Available online: http://www.textileworld.com/textile-world/ features/2010/04/e-textiles-for-wearability-review-of -integration-technologies/ (accessed 26 May 2014).

University of Borås, Smart Textiles Project. All theses available online: http://smarttextiles.se/en/research -lab/design-lab/publications/dissertations/.

Zeagler, C., S. Audy, S. Gilliland and T. Starner (2013), "Can I Wash It?: The Effect of Washing Conductive Materials Used in Making Textile Based Wearable Electronic Interfaces," *Proc. IEEE & ACM International Symposium on Wearable Computers*, Zurich, Switzerland, New York: ACM.

Reports

Aachen University, "Smart Textiles: Textiles with Enhanced Functionality." Available online: http:// www.ita.rwth-aachen.de/andere_sprachen/englisch /Smart%20Textiles-en.pdf (accessed 28 Oct. 2015).

ASTM Headquarter News (2012), "ASTM Holds Initial Workshop on Smart Textiles Applications." Available online: http://www.astm.org/standardization-news /outreach/smart-textiles-workshop-ma12.html (accessed 28 Oct. 2015).

Berglin, L. (2013), "Smart Textiles and Wearable Technology: A Study of Smart Textiles in Fashion and Clothing," a report within the Baltic Fashion Project, published by the Swedish School of Textiles, University of Borås.

Centexbel (2013), "CEN-ISO Standardization Committees on Textiles." Available online: http://www .centexbel.be/smart-textiles-standardisation (accessed 28 April 2014).

Gartner, "Innovation Insight: Smart Fabric Innovations Weave Efficiency Into the Workforce." Available online: https://www.gartner.com/doc/2282415?ref=ddisp (accessed 11 September 2014).

Purdeyhimi, B. (2006), "Printing Electric Circuits onto Nonwoven Conformal Fabrics Using Conductive Inks and Intelligent Control," NTC Project: F04-NS17.

RWTH Aachen University (n.d.), "Smart Textiles with Enhanced Functionality," Institute for Technical Textiles.

Susta-Smart (2013), "Supporting Standardisation for Smart Textiles (SUSTA-SMART)." Available online: http://www.susta-smart.eu/ (accessed 23 October 2013).

Brochures

Keymeulen, L. (2012), *Bekinox VN: Continuous Stainless Steel Filament for Electro-Conductive Textiles*, Bekaert.

Keymeulen, L. (2012), *Electro-Conductive Textiles: Durable Textile Solutions for Transferring Power and Signals*, Bekaert.

Keymeulen, L. (2013), *Heatable Textiles: Flexible and Durable Solutions for Heatable Textiles*, Bekaert.

Catalogs

Annie Trevillian: Handprint: Design on Fabric and Paper, Selected Work 1983–2006 (2006), ISBN: 0-646-46489-2.

Bresky, E. (n.d.), *Smart Textiles*, University of Boras. Available online: www.smarttextiles.se (accessed 28 Oct. 2015).

Hellstrom, A., H. Landin and L. Worbin (2011), *Ambience '11 Exhibition: Where Art, Technology and Design Meet*, The Swedish School of Textiles, University of Boras, ISBN: 978-91-975576-7-2.

Hill, J. (2005), *Interface: An Exhibition of International Contemporary Art Textiles*, The Scottish Gallery and The Gallery Ruthin Craft Centre.

Vrouwe, A. and R. Smits (2013), *Design Changes Design Exhibition 2013*, Design United.

Other online material

e-Fibre, "Exploring Innovation Around Electronic Textiles," AHRC Network project, http://www.e-fibre.co.uk/.

Igoe, T., Physical Computing resources page, http://www.tigoe.net/pcomp/index.php.

ILP Institute Insider (2013), "Fibers Get Functional," October 3, http://ilp.mit.edu/newsstory.jsp?id=19396.

Mann, S. (2013), "Tree-Shaped Designers," keynote address, e-Leo Symposium, Toronto, Ontario, December 5.

Index

Index

Appendix: further reading and resources

Acknowledgments

The author wishes to thank all the contributing artists and designers who have so generously shared their time, vision and processes to make this book. Thank you also to the fantastic editorial and production team at Bloomsbury. Thank you to the Engineering and Physical Sciences Research Council, UK: the original tutorial materials used in chapter 3 resulted from the EPSRC funded project An Internet of Soft Things (EP/L023601/1). A big thank you to Dr. Martha Glazzard and Sarah Walker for their significant contribution to the book, and of course, a huge thank you to Richard, Ben and Lucie for their immense patience throughout the whole process.

The publishers would like to thank
Tamara Albu, Cindy L. Bainbridge, Georgina Hooper, Jayne Mechan, Toni J. Nordness and Huiju Park.